"Are You in a Hurry, Dear?"

"Are You in a Hurry, Dear?"

A Memoir of Life, Love, and Fabulous Hair

Enjoy my Journey
Best —
Milton 2/2/2017

Milton A. Buras

Some names and locations have been altered to maintain the privacy of some individuals mentioned in the story.
All photos are part of the author's personal collection.

ISBN: 1539515745
ISBN 13: 9781539515746
Library of Congress Control Number: 2016917158
CreateSpace Independent Publishing Platform
North Charleston, South Carolina

To my mother and father,
Henrietta and Milton

Author's Note

I always knew I was different.

I was strongly attracted to men at an early age. As a poor kid growing up in New Orleans in the 1950s, I didn't understand what that meant. I couldn't share my feelings with my family and friends because I barely knew what I was feeling myself. I searched for answers and found them in the French Quarter, where I began to see life from a very different perspective. My first experience with a man, at the age of thirteen, confirmed what I already seemed to know about my identity but could not articulate. It opened me up to a whole new world. Even in the repressive environment of the South, there was a community of men who shared my feelings and desires. I joined this community, survived, and prospered. Once I embraced my true self, I blossomed, and my hopes and dreams took flight.

For as long as I can remember, I had an interest in styling hair. As I grew up, I learned I had a talent for the trade. Trusting my instincts and supported a great deal by my drag-queen friends and professional stylists in the Quarter, I embarked on what became my lifelong career. At nineteen, I followed my dream to move to New York City and become a professional hair stylist. I started at the bottom, and, with hard work and the help of wonderful friends and mentors, I rose to the top of the profession, working in exclusive salons and then on Broadway shows, TV, and film.

I lived through the wildest times and enjoyed (nearly) every minute of it. I traveled the world, worked with many celebrities, and built a successful career. Eventually, I found true love and built a wonderful life with him that I thought would last forever. But, after twenty-five years together, it ended. It took years for me to recover from this devastating breakup, but, like so many times before in my life, with the help of friends and family and a positive outlook, I survived, and now I'm thriving once again.

Writing this book has helped me put my life in perspective. Initially, I thought that writing about the painful experience of breaking up with a lover in middle age would help others cope with a similar loss. As I wrote, I realized that my earlier experiences and life lessons were just as important to share with everyone, young and old.

I wrote this book hoping that my story would help others struggling with their own identity to accept who they are and have patience with those trying to understand them. Here is one of the most important things I have learned: be comfortable with who you are. Remember that anyone who has a problem with that is the one with the problem. Not you.

Milton A. Buras

One

I was born in a trunk in the Princess Theater in Pocatello, Idaho... No, no, no. That was the song Judy Garland sang in the movie *A Star is Born.* I was born in a chest of drawers instead of a crib in the small rural town of Chalmette, Louisiana, Saint Bernard Parish, located outside of New Orleans. I was the third child born to two loving parents, Henrietta and Milton, who came from a humble background. The date was September 10, 1942. My father, after whom I was named, was overseas fighting in World War II and was not around for my birth.

Both my parents had little to no education. My father only completed grammar school. Mother did not even get that far because she had diphtheria as a child, which prevented her from finishing school. Mother was the last of ten children and the first to be born not on the farm. Her father died shortly after she was born, and her mother struggled to raise her and her siblings alone. They were raised as strict Episcopalians.

My parents met at a dance in Saint Bernard Parish, courted for a few years, and married at the age of twenty. I have never known a man to love a woman as devotedly as my father loved my mother.

The first child born was my brother Ronald in 1937, and then my sister Carolyn the following year. The area we lived in was as poor as we were. We rented a run-down, four-room, two-family shotgun house. There was a backyard surrounded by a chain-link fence. Mother had her hands full keeping us fed on what little money my father sent home. Trying to keep track of Ronald and Carolyn was a job in itself. Ronald was always hopping over the fence and running over to the house of my aunt Miette, one of my mom's sisters, a few blocks away. Luckily, Carolyn stayed around the house, but she was still too young to help.

Mother told me stories of when I was still a baby in her arms—of how I cried through the night, and how she tried to console me by singing soft lullabies while walking around the room, rocking me up and down, hoping I would fall asleep. Our next-door neighbor, Heidi, would come over and hold me for a while to give my mother a break. One night, she took me in her arms, looked at me, and said, "Wink for Heidi." I stopped crying and fell asleep. Mother said I did not wink, but I was given the nickname Winkie by the rest of my family.

I was a mama's boy. From the moment I could walk, I always wanted to be near her, following her every footstep. She doted on me, and she became my best companion.

By all accounts, I was a precocious and sensitive child. When I was two years old, I asked my mother, "If the radio falls down and breaks open, will all the people fall out?" She thought my question was so innocent and cute that she wanted to send it to *Smart Talk*, a column in the local newspaper featuring funny things kids said. I don't know if she ever did.

She told me a story of when she was in the backyard, hanging up the wash, with me at her side. She had tears running down her face as she worked the clothespins. I noticed her crying and said, "Don't cry, Mommy. I helps ya." She realized, at that moment, that I thought she was crying because of all the laundry she had to hang up. She reached down and put her arms around me and said, "Thank you, my sweet boy, but Mommy is crying because she misses Daddy."

After the war, my father returned. My mom was overjoyed, as were we children. He resumed his job stocking groceries at the corner store directly across from our house. He made pennies, but it was enough to keep food on the table. Jobs were scarce as all the vets returned from the war. I guess because of his lack of education, he did not seek a better job at the time. He was lucky they took him back. He was a hard worker and never complained. I never heard him raise his voice. My dad was a kind and loving man.

Mother had a remarkable memory. First time meeting anyone, she would ask that person's birthday, and the next year on that date, she would announce, "Today is so-and-so's birthday." She remembered the day and time all five of us kids were born and how many sicknesses we had had, with the dates for each—not only for us, but the rest of our relatives. When Mother passed away, the family record went with her.

In 1947, three years after my dad returned home from the war, my parents were blessed with a fourth child, my sister Bonnie. The house was already full, with Ronald, Carolyn, and me sleeping in the same room. The owner of the grocery store told my father he had to let him go because he could not afford to keep him on.

We moved into the Iberville public housing projects, in one of the poorer sections of New Orleans. Public housing was fairly new at the time. Since we were a family of six, living on next to nothing, we qualified. "The projects," as they were called, consisted of two sections, the white section and "the colored" section. Claiborne Street, a wide, four-lane thoroughfare, separated the two sections.

Segregation seemed normal to me as a white boy growing up in New Orleans after the war. For Whites Only signs were a common sight in restaurants, movie theaters, pools, and any public establishments. Movable signs were put on the tops of seats in the streetcars and buses, separating the seats into two sections—one for white and one for colored. My siblings and I attended all-white Catholic schools. However, my parents taught us all to respect everyone, whatever color they were.

Near the projects, there was a cemetery for whites only with an eight-foot-high brick wall built around it, on which kids would climb and then jump off onto the tops of the graves. Because New Orleans was below sea level, all the graves were above ground. Some graves were elaborately designed like small houses with carvings, and others were very simple and rectangular in shape. Most all of the graves, including the wall around the cemetery, were painted white. In the late afternoon and early evening, kids would play hide-and-seek inside the cemetery.

Each of the project houses had three floors. Each house had three apartments, a ground- or first-floor apartment with its own entrance and two apartments above it with a shared staircase to the second floor. Each of the second-floor apartments were two-floor units with- each with its own a front and back entrance. On the second floor was a balcony in front. There was also a backyard with play spaces. Parking spots were in the rear of each building. It was a huge complex that housed many families.

Two

My father was a Roman Catholic. In those days, my mother had to agree to bring up their children Catholic when they were married. We were baptized in the Catholic faith. When we were old enough, my father wanted us to attend Catholic schools. However, we were too poor to pay the tuition. My father made an arrangement with the local school, St Joseph's, to lower the tuition because he committed to enroll all four of his children. My sister went to the all-girls school next door. Luckily, my father had gotten a job at the Monteleone Hotel cocktail lounge in the French Quarter.

I struggled with school from the beginning. I just couldn't pay attention to the lessons and kept fidgeting. The nuns had little patience with me, and I failed second and third grades and had to repeat each. This made me two years older than the rest of my classmates throughout my schooling. I felt ashamed because my siblings never had as many problems with school as I did. After my failure in third grade, I decided it would never happen again, and I worked hard to keep that promise to myself. My parents couldn't help me, as they had little formal education themselves. My brother and sister did what they could, but I still had trouble passing.

Many people who attended Catholic school at that time remember how mean the nuns could be, cracking the ruler over students' young knuckles or making them kneel on rice in the corner. I never understood why they had to punish us so much for the littlest things. We were afraid of them.

One Saturday morning, a classmate and I were collecting newspapers for the church with my little red wagon. The nuns often had us do errands like that for them. I must have been all of seven years old. I was in the street, alongside of the curb, trying to tie rope around a tall stack of papers so I could load them onto my wagon. Suddenly a pickup truck swerved in and struck me, rolling over my right arm. I was knocked unconscious.

My friend ran to my house and told my parents that a truck had run over me. Apparently, my mother fainted dead away. My father came running. By the time he arrived, I was sitting on the sidewalk, alive but with no feeling in my right arm. I was brought to Charity Hospital, a hospital for the poor, and waited for hours in the corridor to be seen by a doctor. People passing would say out loud, "What's that smell?" It was me. Being hit by the truck had knocked the shit out of me literally, and my pants were soiled.

By the time the doctor got to treat me, my mother had arrived. The break in my arm was severe, and the doctor had a difficult time setting it in a cast. I was screaming in pain as he pulled and yanked at my arm three times. He told me to keep quiet and not act like a spoiled child. Mother did not take that well at all and gave him a piece of her mind. My father tried to calm her down to let the doctor do his work, but I could see he was angry at the doctor as well.

The doctor said he was going to try one more time, and if he couldn't set my arm, he would have to do surgery. My mother, being very religious, started to pray out loud. Finally, the doctor was able to set my arm and placed it in a cast from my shoulder to my wrist. After I was cleaned up and given a room in the hospital, I asked my mother if I could have a Slinky toy. Dad showed up at the hospital the next day with the toy. I had to stay in the hospital two days. I missed three days of school.

When I returned to school, the nuns did not ask me how I was or give me any slack with my studies. I even lost the perfect attendance score I had worked so hard to maintain. Was I bitter? Of course I was. That was the last time I helped the church.

When I was a little older, I became an altar boy, mostly to please my mother. But I did enjoy wearing the long vestments over my clothes. All that turning and swishing around. It was quite dramatic. Of course, being the new boy, I started by assisting the main altar boy for the early-morning Mass. The Mass was all in Latin back then, and I didn't understand a word. Luckily, all I had to do was follow along and not pay too much attention to the ritual.

One morning, I showed up for service and was told I would be serving Mass alone, because the main boy was sick. I, of course, panicked. I had never taken to learn the Latin prayers or the all-important cues necessary to perform the service to the priest.

The principal altar boy's responsibility was to ring the bells at specific points during the service. Ringing the bells was a signal for churchgoers to stand, kneel, or sit down. There were four bells connected to a single handle, not just one little tingly one. Even though the church was huge, the sound echoed throughout the building. The older boy always rang the bells at precisely the right time. I had no idea how to do it and was terrified.

"But Father," I said, "I don't know when to ring the bells."

"Don't worry," said the priest. "I'll give you a sign."

Mass began, and I waited for the first sign. The priest walked over to the right side of the altar, said prayers, and then made the sign of the cross. Eager to do my job, I took this as a signal to ring the bells. The sound filled the church, and the congregation stood. I had jumped the gun. I suppose the priest gave me a look of disapproval, but I was so frightened I must not have noticed. Every time the priest made a sign of the cross, I rang the bells. The priest just kept on with the service, unable to interrupt his prayers to stop me.

After a while, I became so nervous, I just rang and rang those bells. I could hear movement behind me in the congregation; people were confused whether to kneel, stand, or sit. It was like a Lucille Ball or Carol Burnett comedy routine. I thought Mass would never end. Afterward, I wanted desperately to hide in a hole. The priest didn't say a word about it, but that was the last time I served at daily Mass. I remained an altar boy but was put on once a year for the service of the Stations of the Cross during the solemn season of Lent. No bells to ring. I just had to walk in the procession.

Three

Mother was always conscious of her looks, particular her hair. The only place she could afford to have her hair done was a local beauty school called the Marinello System of Beauty Culture of New Orleans. It was a trade school for students studying to be hairdressers, or "hair burners," as they were referred to at the time. The school was for whites only. The school consisted of one large room with a dozen or so chairs and was staffed by mostly female students.

Customers would walk in and were assigned to whatever student was free. You could get a new student who barely knew how to hold the scissors or one who was almost ready to graduate. Their supervisor would decide on the style the student needed to give the customer. Mother had her hair colored, cut, washed, set, and styled—all for fifty cents. She was rather lucky and always left feeling pleased with her new do.

When I was a young child, Mother would take me with her when she had her hair done. I always enjoyed this outing. Ronald and Carolyn were old enough to stay home and take care of Bonnie. Usually, I was the only kid in the room and spent most of my time watching all the people working or getting worked on, looking at the different equipment, and smelling odd smells around the room. There wasn't much chatter. Normally it took a couple of hours.

The one contraption that caught my attention was this giant metal hood on a tall stand with a ton of wires hanging down, each wire having a large clamp on the end. This looked like a device from outer space to me. I found out later that it was the first permanent-wave machine, and it used heat to set the waves. I guess the term "hair burners" came from this device.

I was fascinated by the whole scene and loved watching the stylists work their magic—such as it was—on women like Mother. Looking back on it, I suppose it contributed to my interest in this career.

My first experience as a "hair stylist" involved my sister Bonnie. She had been asked to be the flower girl in our cousin's wedding. Since I had watched my mother have her hair done for years, I decided, at nine years old, that I would do my sister's hair for the wedding. I had no experience or idea what I was doing. Why my mother allowed me to do it, I'll never know. I remembered watching my older sister, Carolyn, make pin curls in her hair, so I decided to do the same with Bonnie's.

Carolyn made it look so easy. But I never bothered to ask for her help, thinking I could do it on my own. I was a very determined young boy. However, I didn't know that there were two types of pin curls, tight ones and loose ones, depending on the length of hair. Also, I didn't know that the ends of the hair had to be tucked into the circle to make the curl and then pinned in place. Bonnie had shoulder-length, wavy hair, which didn't need many pin curls. But in my enthusiasm to do a superb job, I must have made a hundred curls without pinning them inside. It took a couple of hours. Bonnie, being so young, totally trusted me. She slept in pin curls all night.

The morning of the wedding, I took the pins out. Bonnie's hair was a massive mess of tangled curls. The ends of her hair were going in every direction, causing a giant frizzy look, what black folks called "natural" at the time. I tried patting it down, but it was like yeast rising. The hair overpowered her tiny little face. I was shocked and disappointed, but her hair turned out to be the biggest thing at the wedding, and everyone was surprised I had done it. Bonnie didn't mind and loved the attention. My mother was so proud of my work that she had an eight-by-ten photo taken of Bonnie and had it framed and displayed on my sister's hope chest for all to see. That picture remained in the very same spot for years. It became part of our family history.

Bonnie and I were very close as children. We went to school together every day, and I took care of her. When we had a few pennies, we stopped and bought something to eat while waiting for the bus to take us home. One day it was popcorn, and we were a bit late. When I saw the bus coming, I grabbed her hand and told her to run. We just made it. I jumped in first, and she followed but tripped on the top step, causing her bag of popcorn to fly everywhere, including on the bus driver and everyone sitting in the front seats. Seeing everyone covered in popcorn seemed so funny that we both laughed. The bus driver and the other passengers didn't find it quite as funny as we did. That was the last time we were allowed on the bus with anything in our hands.

Bonnie and I attended dance class together at school a couple of times a week. Despite the wedding-do disaster, she let me do her hair. I always fixed her hair either in a ponytail or a bun decorated with flowers or barrettes for dance class. We always ran late, so I had to do it in the car as Dad drove us. She sat in the front passenger seat next to Dad, with me in the backseat styling away. By the time we reached class, her hair was done and beautiful.

Four

When we lived in the projects, we occupied the second and third floors of the unit. As children, we all had chores to do. Mine were to sweep the front and back staircases, weed the little garden out back, and cut the grass. Of course, none of us got an allowance. We were too poor. When I started making money cutting other people's grass, I had to give a portion of my earnings to the household. At the time I thought this unfair, but I'm grateful to my parents for this training. I was the only one of us children to earn money back then.

We all pitched in to clean the house for Mother. But Mother was very particular about cleaning. If our cleaning did not meet her standards, she would have a fit and start yelling about it. Bonnie was a sensitive child. If she heard Mother yelling, she would get very nervous and throw up. When that happened, Mother would stop. We all caught on to that quickly. We always made sure Bonnie was around when Mother inspected our work.

In 1950, after my younger brother, Glenn, was born, Mother had a nervous breakdown. We didn't know why it happened, but looking back on it, it was most likely postpartum depression. My father tried to bring her out of her funk, but even he couldn't help. She had to be institutionalized in a division of Charity Hospital and had several shock treatments. At the time, shock treatments were one of the newer therapies for dealing with personality disorders. We all were worried, but Dad assured us that she'd be fine. All we were told was that Mother was sick and needed rest. I think my older siblings Ronald and sister Carolyn understood more than we younger ones did.

My father's job at the hotel had him working nights and weekends. He couldn't care for all us children by himself and continue to work. He had to rely on our extended family for help. My aunt Ilya moved in to take care of baby Glenn. The rest of us were sent to live with different relatives scattered throughout the area for a year. We were not told the reason why, nor would I have understood at my age.

I went to the home of my mother's niece, Mercedes, and her husband, Tony. They were much older than we were, so we called them aunt and uncle. They took me in with open arms. They had two daughters, Dee, who was my age, and Beverly, a bit older.

My aunt and uncle made me feel at home from the moment I walked in. They lived in a five-room shotgun house in Chalmette, a small town in St. Bernard's Parish, just east of New Orleans. The girls doubled up and gave me my own room to sleep in. It was heaven after having to share a room back home with my brother. My aunt enrolled me into a local public school during that time.

I got along very well with her two girls, playing dress-up and having make-believe tea in the afternoon. The girls shared their costumes and even their princess crowns with me. I had great fun with them. I guess that was the first sign that I was different from the other boys my age. Aunt Mercedes just thought it was cute.

Every now and then, Uncle Tony would take me home to visit Dad. Mother was still in the hospital, and he visited her often. But he did not think it was a good idea for me to visit her in her condition, for fear I would get upset. The year seemed to go by quickly. We all got together for holidays during that time, and we exchanged stories.

When Mother was well enough to return home, so did we. We were happy to be home. But Mother was not the same. Formerly an active and efficient homemaker, she had become much slower, less organized, and even more exacting. Before Dad left for work at four in the afternoon, he did all the work around the house, cooked dinner, and washed the clothes until we kids learned how to fend for ourselves. He taught us all how to cook, sew, and clean. When he returned at one in the morning, we were all asleep.

Mother had become so slow at doing things; we would just take over to get the chores done. "Go lie down, Mom," we urged her. "We'll take care of things." We did not realize that not enabling Mother would create a bigger problem later.

My dad was a gentle man who loved my mother unconditionally. When we asked Mother for a glass of milk, she would take a clean glass out of the cabinet and start to wash it over and over before remembering to fill it with milk. It would take forever. Instead of Dad getting angry with her, he would say, "Henrietta, you are washing the flower off the glass." We learned not to ask her anything, but just to get it ourselves.

Dad was an excellent cook and prepared most of the meals. At times, Mother did cook with Dad, and they were good together. He had so much patience with her. When she would say to him, "Milton, you are not doing that right," he would either hand it over to her or just continue what he was doing without comment. I never heard them argue.

What amazes me to this day was how he brought up five children and a wife on sixty dollars a month plus tips, working in a hotel cocktail lounge. We were poor, but we always had food on the table and a roof over our heads. He did all of this out of care and love. Besides being named after my dad, I am fortunate to have inherited some of his qualities, especially patience, thriftiness, and dedication to hard work. He was and will always be the best man I have ever known.

Since Dad wasn't around in the late afternoon and evening because of his work hours, Mother enforced discipline and order in the house. She was particularly harsh on the girls, sometimes whipping them for even the most minor reasons. After her stay in the hospital, she had little to no patience. Whenever she felt we were misbehaving, Mother would say, "I am going to knock you down, and the floor is going to give you another one." She had a habit of pinching you under the table or in church if you made a noise during the service. That pinch came with a twist that made you want to yell out, but that didn't stop her. Yet when company came over, she was friendly, warm, and talkative. We loved when friends or relatives came to visit because we got a little relief from her harsh rules.

Five

In the early 1950s, we moved from the projects to a house in the 2400 block of Royal Street, close to the French Quarter. Dad moved us because the projects were becoming unsafe, and the rent for the new house was not much more than what we were already paying. It was a five-room, two-family house. A common wall separated us from the other family living there. It was similar to our shotgun-style house in Saint Bernard Parish. These houses were designed for one to enter from the living or front room and walk through several rooms, arriving at the last room, usually the kitchen, with no hallway or privacy for any of the bedrooms. Off of the kitchen was a one-step-down bathroom, most likely an add-on, which was for the whole family.

There was a door leading out of the kitchen into a backyard with an open shed toward the back for a washing machine. The yard was cemented over and bordered by narrow flower beds on each side, with clotheslines hung overhead. We had one large window fan in the kitchen, our only source of cooling. The windows were always open for whatever breeze we could catch. Air conditioning was only in rich homes, department stores, and movie houses. We had one phone in the house, which was in the room I shared with my younger brother, Glenn, next to the kitchen.

I was eleven years old when I started school at Holy Trinity, the local Catholic school. It was four blocks from the street we lived on. I made friends quickly but struggled with my schoolwork. Whenever I didn't understand the assignments, I would seek help from friends or classmates. My grades were improving. I did not give up.

Mother's condition improved slowly. I believe that it was mainly because of her strong faith in God. Since we all went to Catholic schools, my older sister, Carolyn, wanted Mother to be a Catholic like Dad and the rest of us, and she agreed. Mother always had a deep religious faith, but it intensified when she converted from the Episcopal faith to Catholicism. Mother was so devout that every day, she would make us all kneel in front of the radio on the hard linoleum floor and say the rosary with the priest on the broadcast.

After the rosary, still kneeling, Mother would say, "Let us pray for the dead." *They're dead. Why don't we pray for the living?* I thought. Not only did we have to pray for the dead, but Mother named them, one by one. Of course, I never mentioned my doubts to Mother. I would have been knocked to the floor, and the floor would have given me another one, as Mother always said.

Holy pictures of Jesus, Mary, and Joseph were mounted up on the mantel. One of my chores was to dust each and every one. It was a lengthy procedure, but Mother insisted that the "holy family" be dust free. Whenever we drove in the car, Mother would announce every church we'd pass. She would say out loud, "Church," and we in the backseat would have to make the sign of the cross with her. Sometimes, sister Bonnie and I would see the church before Mother and yell, "Church!" She would be pleased.

Six

When I was around ten years old, my mother asked my older brother, Ronald, to take me fishing. I supposed she wanted me to learn more about the hobbies that most Southern boys enjoyed. Ronald loved fishing from the time he was old enough to hold a pole or cast a net. It was all he ever thought about—besides girls and sports, of course. He went out several times a week and always brought home fish. The last thing he wanted was to have his wimpy little brother on the lake with him, especially since he knew I had no interest in fishing. But fearing the wrath of our mother, he obeyed.

According to him, the best time to catch shrimp was at night. One of the best places was the lakefront seawall steps just outside the city. There were around nine cement steps leading down to the edge of the water; the bottom step was used to cast out nets. The water was about eight to ten feet deep. We had to wear thick boots because the seawall steps were covered with sharp barnacles. They would cut up your bare feet in no time.

All we had was a little kerosene lamp to cast light in the area. First, Ronald would drop some kind of smelly bait into the water. I watched him throw the net out, very artfully. He waited a minute and then pulled it up and dumped what seemed like hundreds of shrimp on the steps of the seawall. The shrimp were all over the place, snapping their tails and jumping around.

"Pick them up!" he yelled. "We'll lose 'em!"

The shrimp had the smell of a stagnant lake and were very slimy. Every time I tried to pick one up, it pricked my finger with its spear-like head.

"Ow!" I howled.

"Pick up the goddamn shrimp, Milton!"

I picked up one at a time while he picked up four or five and threw them into our bucket. We lost most of them, and he had to cast his net several times to fill up the bucket. Needless to say, he was not happy with me as a shrimping partner.

But, urged on by Mother, he continued to take me along on his fishing adventures. This time it was crawfishing. A Louisiana specialty, crawfish live in the mud and swamps outside the city. We drove to a swampy area and parked the car on the side of the highway. There was nothing in sight except for dead-looking trees growing out of the muddy waters, with Spanish moss hanging from their leafless branches. We put on high boots, grabbed round nets with bait tied in the middle, and buckets, and then we proceeded to enter the swamp.

I followed my brother into the muck as he placed nets down. It was early evening, and the mosquitoes were all around us, which got to me but not my brother. He was in his element. I would have been happier sitting on the porch listening to music, sipping lemonade, and watching people go by. We went deeper into the swamps and set our nets down. All I could think of was getting back to solid ground because I was tired of fighting against the thick mud as I trudged on. It was exhausting.

Suddenly, I felt something wiggle under my foot.

"It's a snake!" I yelled, and then I fell forward directly into the mud. My brother thought this was hilarious. He laughed and laughed but did not help me up. I struggled back to my feet. I was a muddy mess.

"Damn, ain't no reason to be scared of snakes. Swamp's where they live."

"Yeah, but I don't."

We gathered up the nets, which were filled with the slimy little creatures, and headed back to the car and solid ground. Seeing me covered in mud, Mother relented. That was the last time I went fishing. Amen.

Seven

When I was twelve, I started wanting things like records, stylish clothes, and pocket money to spend. But we were too poor for luxuries like these. Dad's rule was, if you wanted something, you had to work to pay for it. Since we had moved from the projects, most of the yards in our neighborhood were cemented over or just too small for making extra money by cutting grass. The only option for a kid my age was delivering newspapers on weekends. I saw an ad for it in the classified section of the local newspaper. It was something I could do, and I discussed it with my dad.

First, I needed a work permit. Since I was under the legal working age of fifteen, Dad had to sign for me. He was more than willing to take me down to the Transit Authority office to do so. Next, I needed a heavy-duty bike with a basket deep enough for delivering newspapers. Dad took me to the local bicycle store, where he agreed to buy a brand-new Schwinn on credit. He signed for it, but I had to make the payments.

My dad drove me to the newspaper pickup to apply for the job. The pickup station was located about twelve blocks away from our house, on the other side of the Claiborne Street overpass. The station was nothing more than a small shed. I got it on the spot. I guess there was a real need for newsboys. None of my friends delivered papers at the time, so I had to learn the ropes on my own. My assigned delivery route was on the opposite side of the station, on St. Rock Street.

Pickup time was 5:00 a.m. on Saturday morning. I had to get up an hour before and ride my bike over the underpass to pick up the papers.

Getting there was easy enough. But what I hadn't thought about was how heavy the basketful of papers would be. After picking up the load, I had to go back up the overpass to my route. The papers were so heavy that I couldn't peddle up the steep hill, so I walked the bike to the top. It was all I could do to keep the bike steady. Once I reached the top, I thought it would be smooth sailing. Sailing was the word. I jumped on the bike and took off down the overpass. I picked up speed so fast that I couldn't control it, and I fell off. I watched as the bike caromed down the hill, newspapers flying every which way, until it hit bottom. Luckily, the bike was in good shape, and I managed to collect the papers and get back on the route.

Delivery was a bit late that morning.

After my third weekend working out of this pickup station, they transferred to me a different station and route closer to my house so I wouldn't have to ride up and down that overpass. I guess they got tired of my delivering the papers late and crashing into the station door when I returned. My new route suited me perfectly, and I never missed a delivery. I was proud that I had a job making regular money along with tips. After contributing some to the household expenses and paying off the bike each week, I still had enough to buy some of the things I wanted. I've always been a saver, especially when I had a particular goal in mind. When I saw something I liked, I saved enough money to buy it outright. Soon, I had enough for my first Motorola record player. I already had a collection of forty-fives, which I played at a friend's house. Now I could play them in my room at home.

Eight

It was around this time that I started hanging around girls like the other boys did and going to dances on the weekends. In those days, they were called sock hops. I don't know why, because everyone wore shoes. I enjoyed dancing, and the girls were fun to dance with. I was rather cute at that age and looked a bit older, so I had no problem finding partners. There was one girl I seemed to favor and hang around with. Her name was Gwen. She was a little older than I was. She had long, beautiful red hair and a fair complexion. We lived a few blocks from each other. In the afternoons, I would visit with her and other kids our age on her front porch.

One day, Gwen was visiting with me and my mother at our house. Completely out of the blue, she said to Mother, "I am going to marry your son." Of course, Mother did not take this seriously because of our young age, but she was very happy at the thought that this girl liked me so. I felt uncomfortable about it, as I didn't feel as strongly as Gwen did. But we kept company for about a year, mostly at her insistence.

One late-summer evening, Gwen and I double dated with Ronald, the fisherman, and his girlfriend Diane. We drove to the lakefront. It was humid and damp. There was a chill in the air. We had the car windows rolled up. My brother and his girl got out of the car and disappeared, leaving Gwen and me sitting in the front seat together. We talked for a few moments, and then she slid over toward me. I inched away, but she kept getting closer until she was almost on top of me. I was flustered. Then she started kissing me. I had never kissed a girl before. I tried to turn my face away, but she kept at it. Then she started putting my hands on her breasts and unbuttoning my shirt. In a matter of seconds, the windows in the car were fogged up and I was half undressed.

This was not a turn-on for me. It felt more like an attack. I struggled to get free and hit the horn by mistake. We both jumped. Sweating and out of breath, I said this was not working out. She looked annoyed and moved away, toward the passenger door.

It seemed like forever until my brother and his girl returned. Gwen asked to be taken home. It was obvious that she was upset. She told my brother's girl that I had come on to her. I didn't know what to say to that. But Mother always told me to be a gentleman, so I didn't say anything, not wanting to embarrass us further. Later, I told my brother the truth. He just laughed. He could not understand how I could turn a willing female away. Most guys would have run with it, he said. I guess I just wasn't like "most guys." I didn't see much of Gwen after that.

Soon after my "romantic" encounter with Gwen, I started to feel something was missing from my life. While I had friends, I always felt out of sync with the other boys at school. I didn't much care for sports or fishing. Girls were fun to dance with, but I didn't find them attractive the way the other boys did. I was more interested in music, movies, and fashion. My hormones were raging, like any other teenage boy, but I began to realize that the objects of my fantasies were different from my friends. I found myself noticing men. How they dressed and walked. What kind of physique they had, if their legs were slightly bowed or straight. How handsome they were. I started to feel attracted to them.

Tab Hunter was my first movie-star crush. These feelings were new to me, and I was not sure what they meant. I didn't know the word "gay." I did not mention any of my feelings to my classmates for fear they would think I was queer. I wasn't even sure I knew what to think about them myself. All I knew was that they were real.

Nine

The French Quarter of New Orleans was only eight blocks wide and thirteen blocks long. But it was huge in its position in the history of the city. Since its beginning, it had been famous for its unique entertainments and grand if infamous lifestyle. It was a magical place. The whole place turned into a glamorous world of glitter and fantasy for a week once a year. As a child, I remember watching the parades during Mardi Gras with my sister as the colorful floats passed us on Royal Street, with gaily dressed men and women throwing coins and colored beads at the onlookers.

At thirteen, I began to explore the French Quarter for myself. Roaming in the Quarter on my own during the rest of the year was very different. Gone were the crowds of tourists, the lavish floats, the noise, and the crazy party atmosphere. It was like entering into a new land for me, full of subtle mysteries. I noticed the closeness and the colors of the buildings, the elegant wrought-iron balconies, and the lush courtyards with running fountains hidden from public view behind beautiful iron gates. The streets were narrow and quaint, as were the sidewalks, with old-fashioned lampposts on every corner. This was totally unlike the working-class world I lived in; it seemed so grand and rich. I wanted to become part of it.

There were two main streets in the Quarter: Royal Street and Bourbon Street. While they ran parallel to each other, the difference between the two was like night and day. In many ways, these two streets represented the two aspects of New Orleans. Royal sported elegant hotels and antique shops. The Hotel Monteleone, where my father worked, was on Royal. Bourbon had a trashier reputation and was known for its strip joints and jazz bars. We never visited Bourbon Street during Mardi Gras with my family. It was just not suitable for us, according to Mother. Of course, as a teenager, I was drawn to Bourbon because it was taboo. By its very nature, it was exciting.

When weekends came around, I went to the Quarter, telling my parents I was going to a friend's house or to the movies. I'd wander along Bourbon alone. I didn't know what I was hoping to find there, but somehow I knew it was a place I needed to explore. As I moved on down the street, past all the girlie places with barkers outside and the touristy bars, I found myself in a quiet section at the corner of Saint Peter and Bourbon. I leaned against the lamppost there and just watched people. I noticed that mostly men went in and out of the nondescript bars there. While this was true of the more raucous part of the street, here it was different somehow. The men in this section seemed more furtive, less overtly wild. There was a bar called the Driftwood to my left; Dixie's Bar was directly across from me, and the Bourbon House Coffee Shop in back of me.

Why I picked that spot remains a mystery to me. Maybe it was instinct. Maybe it was because I just felt comfortable there. Whatever the reason, I had no idea that it was the most notorious gay corner in the Quarter. In fact, I had no idea that anything like a gay scene even existed in New Orleans or anywhere else. I had no idea what "being gay" even meant. At the time, everyone referred to homosexuals as "queer." I was still naïve about these things, but somehow, I felt I had landed in the area where I belonged. I was looking for my identity, and this place seemed a likely place to start.

As I leaned against the lamppost, I noticed that I was the only young guy around. Most of the other men going in and out of the bars were older. Cars circled the block; the men behind the wheels would slow down to look at me and then move on, nearly crashing as they turned the corner. At the time, I had no idea why they did this, but I certainly enjoyed the attention.

Occasionally, young, effeminate-looking guys would offer comments on my standing there as they walked by. I heard them say things like "What a cute hustler" or "Honey, this section is too busy for hustling." I didn't understand what they meant, so I didn't say anything and just tried to look cool.

I always dressed the same: button-fly jeans, bottom button undone, white T-shirt with sleeves rolled up, and high-top tennis shoes. It was a look made popular by James Dean, and nearly all my friends wore some version of it. I had medium-brown wavy hair, flattop with sides combed up and falling down in the center. I was tall and thin and looked older than my thirteen years.

Of course, I was not aware of my image at that time, but looking back at old photos of me, I can see how easily people mistook me for a hustler. It was not my intention. I didn't even know what a hustler was; I just wanted to look cool.

One weekend night, I was standing on my favorite corner, poised against the lamppost, watching the action around me, just waiting for something, anything, to happen. Having something to lean on made it easy for me to be there hours at a time. It also helped me to pretend I was waiting for someone.

I noticed this great-looking guy walking toward me from the Driftwood bar. He seemed to be in his late twenties or early thirties. He was extremely handsome and tall, and he had blond, wavy hair. I tried not to let him know I had noticed him. As he drew near, I turned away. Chills started running through my body, and I wondered, "Will he speak to me? And if he does, what will I *say*?" I was getting more nervous with every second.

Finally, he approached me and said, "Hi."

"Hi," I said, doing my best to seem nonchalant.

"Would you like your oil changed?" he said, smiling.

Even though I had never heard that expression used other than for cars, which I knew he wasn't referring to, I took it for something sexual. His direct approach caught me by surprise. I became nervous and frightened.

"No," I replied a little quickly. Deep down inside, I wanted to find out what he meant, but was afraid. As he walked away, I wanted to yell, "I changed my mind," but didn't have the guts.

I never saw him again, but I felt that I had missed an important experience. I desperately wanted to belong to this new world. I was still confused about my attraction to men but felt compelled to find out more.

One block down from St. Peter Street, there was another corner I liked. It was quieter, more residential. I would switch corners depending on the flow of people or if I was getting bored. The guys in cars always seemed to find me, though. Some would stop and call me over to chat. I became good at talking to these strange men. I guess I was learning to flirt with them; nothing ever came of it. I just loved all the compliments and attention.

Ten

Holiday weekends were as bad as Mardi Gras because hordes of party people filled Bourbon Street. I had to move off my favorite corner and retreat to a corner farther down on Bourbon and Orleans Streets.

Not long after my encounter with the handsome blond man, something finally happened. I was standing on the corner, dressed in my usual jeans and T-shirt, feeling as if I owned that spot, when a tall guy in his early to midtwenties walked up to me. He was well dressed, and he had medium-brown hair parted on the side, a slender build, and a warm smile.

"Hello," he said, smiling. "You live around here?"

"No, just enjoying the sights," I said, trying not to look too nervous.

His approach was slow and gentle, not like my first encounter. Even though I was inexperienced and young, I could see the kindness in his eyes, which made me feel comfortable and safe.

"My name is Steve. What's yours?"

"Milton."

We stood there awhile, chatting about all the tourists and the noise. Then he asked if I would like to visit his picture-framing shop a few blocks away.

I thought for a moment. Framing shop? No harm in that. Besides, he seemed nice, and I was curious.

"Okay."

We talked a bit while walking. He didn't ask my age. I could only assume he took me for sixteen or seventeen, because I looked and acted older. In any case, my age did not seem to matter to him.

We arrived at his shop. It was on Decatur Street, well outside the tourist area. He unlocked the door. The room was large, with a worktable toward the back. There were dozens of frames of all sizes mounted on the walls. I followed him to the rear of his shop to a dark spot not visible from the street. He drew near, put his arms around me, and kissed me on the mouth. I responded naturally, as if I had done this before. My first kiss from a man. I was not a bit nervous. It seemed normal to me, not like the time with Gwen.

He proceeded to unbutton my jeans. By the time my jeans hit the floor, I had a full erection. My insides started to swell with his gentle touch. He went down on his knees and put my penis in his warm mouth. I watched as he slowly went up and down on me, over and over. I felt my blood racing through my veins. Suddenly, I felt light headed and weak at the knees. I wanted this pleasure to last and last, but the buildup became so strong, I could no longer hold back, and I exploded with a climax that seemed to go on forever.

By that age, I had started masturbating and experienced orgasms, but I hadn't felt anything like this. It left me with a new high and wanting more. This was my first blow job *and* my first experience with a man. I knew now what my feelings for men meant.

I pulled up my jeans. Neither of us said a word. Steve handed me a slip of paper with his telephone number. "Call me anytime," he said quietly, smiling. I just nodded, too overwhelmed to say anything. I left him in the shop and went home. My whole world changed that night. My first experience with a guy had been satisfying beyond my wildest fantasies. And I wanted more.

During the following week, I couldn't get what had happened with Steve off my mind. The whole feeling came back every time I jerked off. I had a new thirst to satisfy, my desire to be with men. I got up enough courage to call Steve from a pay phone and arranged to meet him again that weekend. It was even more exciting than the first time.

Soon after that, I started seeing Steve regularly at his apartment on Burgundy Street in the Quarter each weekend. Sometimes, after a dance or party, feeling the urge, I would call him and see if I could come over. He was always happy to see me. I never revealed my true age, and he never asked. I was used to hanging around some of the older kids and didn't think much about it. I was naïve. I didn't realize the possible consequences. I was thirteen years old, a minor. Serious jailbait for any adult who had sex with me. If we were caught, Steve could go to jail, but that issue never entered my mind. The sensation was worth the gamble. I was fortunate not to have anything serious happen.

Steve taught me a lot about having sex. Instead of my simply standing while he went down on me, we explored other positions, in and out of bed. As I got more experienced, I realized that sex came natural to me. I was one horny little bastard.

Time passed, and my visits lasted longer and longer. I enjoyed Steve's company. He taught about more than just sex. He loved to tell me stories about the men he'd met. He never revealed where he was from or how he got into the framing business. He gave me my first exposure to classical music. Of course, sex was the main reason for my visits with Steve, but the time spent afterward with him became exciting to me as well.

One time, while listening to the *1812 Overture* at his place, he was going down on me. As the music heightened to its crescendo, so did I. My buildup seemed to be in perfect sync with the overture. When that first boom from the cannon went off, so did I, followed by several more booms. Now, whenever I hear a cannon go off in the *1812 Overture*, I can still feel the excitement of that time.

Eleven

Even though I felt increasingly comfortable with myself and my relationship with Steve, I was not ready to reveal my secret to my family or friends. It was the 1950s in the South, after all. My friends always made jokes about "queers" or "faggots." I continued to lead a double life of sorts. I was a mature thirteen years old. I certainly had been taught right from wrong by the nuns. I knew having sex outside of marriage was a sin. Having sex willingly with another man under any circumstances was even worse. I would learn later that it was against the law. But none of this stopped me. I realized I had entered into the secret world of men loving men. My world. I would just have to be careful what I did and said.

I enjoyed hanging around my classmates doing what sixth-graders did, but only during school days. I was two years older than my classmates, and only my teachers knew my real age. But aside from schoolwork and dances, I found I had little in common with them. If I didn't have anything to do with the family or school parties on a Saturday night, I would make up some story to get out of the house to go the Quarter. My parents never questioned me. Since my father worked late most weekends and my mother went to sleep early, it wasn't that difficult to get away.

After arriving in the Quarter, I would go directly to Steve's apartment, ring his bell, and see if he was in. If he wasn't home, I would walk around the Quarter, which was one of my favorite things to do, always ending on one of my corners. Just being there was exciting, but I didn't dare pick up any other men. It was so risky.

Time passed, and I started seventh grade. In addition to schoolwork and social activities, I requested to expand my newspaper delivery to include weekday afternoons as well as weekends to make extra money. My life was very busy, but no matter what, I always made time for trysts with Steve. It was a struggle keeping up with my class work, but I managed to pass. Sometimes my older sister or a classmate helped me.

One weekend after I turned fourteen, I attended my cousin's wedding as one of the groomsmen. I was dressed in a white tuxedo dinner jacket, looking very grown up. The wedding ceremony was at noon in Our Lady of Guadalupe church near the French Quarter, followed by a reception in a Catholic school auditorium in the Quarter on Decatur Street. After several hours of dancing, I decided to sneak away and try to see Steve, whose apartment was several blocks away. I found him sitting in the courtyard of his building with some friends having drinks. I stood at the entrance and waved at him.

He looked surprised to see me. At first I thought it was my tux. He was used to seeing me in jeans and a T-shirt or nothing at all. But judging from the reactions of the other men, I realized it was because he had not told them about me. Nevertheless, he introduced me to his friends. They greeted me with friendly handshakes and asked me to join them. Who can resist a young man in a tuxedo? I sat with them for a while, had a drink, and then went home. I can imagine what was said after I left, but from the looks on their faces, I'm sure I made a good impression.

After that introduction, I started meeting more guys through Steve. I made friends quickly. One introduction led to another. Steve even told me where the best bars were. At first, I was afraid to go into a gay bar. I was underage and didn't want to get caught. But since the whole scene was somewhat underground, no one seemed to care. Steve was kind enough to come with me the first couple of times. After a few times with no problem, I became a regular. My days on the corner were over. Instead of observing the scene, I was part of it.

Dixie's Bar was my favorite place to hang out. Dixie was the owner. She was a small-framed woman in her late forties who wore little to no makeup; her brown hair was short and curly, and she always dressed in a ladylike fashion. I didn't know she was a lesbian until a friend told me much later. Not that it made any difference, but I was surprised because the few lesbians I had met were so butch. I avoided speaking with her because of my age. I was frightened she'd kick me out for being under the legal drinking age. Later, I found out Dixie was the first person to bail out any of her customers if they were caught in a police raid in her bar and put in jail. There were times when the vice squad or police would come into the bar to check IDs. None of my friends knew my real age, but they all knew I was underage. They would either stand around me or hide me under a table until the police left.

Now that I had started going into the bars and being more social, I had to give up my jeans and T-shirt look, at least in the evening, for slacks and a dress shirt. I became quite a stylish dresser, mimicking the style of older guys. I used nearly all my newspaper route earnings for my new wardrobe.

The Bourbon House Coffee Shop was another big meeting place for me. There were two sides to the Bourbon House. One side was a full bar, mostly straight, and the other a coffee house and pub with mixed gay and straight. It was a popular place to hang out and be seen.

One time when I was in the Bourbon House sitting with a friend, a huge fight broke out between a six-foot-one, 250-pound butch lesbian and a straight guy. Her name was Lois. She had bleached-blond hair cut short and combed straight back into a DA, one of the most popular hairstyles in the fifties for men. Apparently, this guy had hit on her girlfriend, Charlene, who was beautiful, young, and very feminine. The guy didn't see the tornado heading toward him until he felt it. Lois picked up a chair, cracked it over his back, and came after him with a broken beer bottle. She had to be subdued by several people. I never saw the man in there again. Everyone knew never to mess with Lois's woman. Lois and her Charlene were regulars in the Bourbon House, and eventually we became good friends.

The legal drinking age in New Orleans was eighteen. While I had been going into the bars regularly and avoiding the issue with the help of my friends, I thought it would be prudent to get some form of fake ID, just in case the issue came up. Steve, who had become just a friend at this point, told me where I could obtain a forged draft card. It was more expensive than I expected, but I got it anyway and kept it on me. It made me feel safe.

I was so comfortable in the bar scene, I started to play the field. Lois introduced me to this great-looking guy who took a fancy to me. He was in his late thirties, tall, and very masculine, with dark hair combed to the side in a pompadour wave. Looking at him, one would never know he was gay. Everyone called him Tiger, and he certainly lived up to his name in bed.

One day, we all decided to double-date and go to the drive-in movies. Lois drove a big, flashy car—of course, to fit her size. In those days, cars were long and heavy with huge trunks, about the size of some small New York kitchens. Just before arriving at the drive-in, Lois stopped the car and told her girlfriend and me to get into the trunk to save on the admission. No argument there, and besides, there was lots of room. Getting in for free in those days was big. After passing the collection booth and parking, we got out of the trunk. Lois and her girlfriend sat up front, Tiger and I in back. I don't remember the movie, but I do remember Tiger and I crawling all over each other in that huge backseat.

As I became more familiar with the scene, I hung out with all kinds of people. I met this one guy in the Bourbon House named Dick, who preferred to be called Magnolia—a real Southern belle. He was around thirty-one years old and handsome, with neatly cropped dark hair and a great sense of humor. He was sort of the gay den mother of all the young boys like me. Magnolia had studied to be a priest at Notre Dame Seminary in New Orleans since he was sixteen, but he dropped out sometime before ordination. He had many stories of the wild goings-on in the seminary. Since I was the youngest in the crowd, he called me his baby.

I learned quickly that all the gay guys I knew gave one another campy names. I always had a problem remembering people's names when introduced, so I came up with my own nickname and called everyone Winnie. Eventually, everyone started to call me Winnie.

There were even names for the police, such as Lola or Tillie-Law. I became familiar with the numbers on license plates of unmarked police cars, for fear of being picked up walking through the Quarter late at night. When I recognized one of the cars, I would duck into a doorway or turn my face until they passed.

As magical and flamboyant as New Orleans was in the fifties, homosexuals had to lead a closeted life. There was no "Don't ask, don't tell" or tolerance in any way. Homosexuality was illegal, plain and simple. The gay bars in the French Quarter were subject to police raids constantly by police.

Since New Orleans was deeply segregated, gay bars for blacks were located outside the Quarter. A male dancing with another male was not allowed. Dressing in drag was permitted only on Mardi Gras day within the city limits. There was a famous drag club called the Club My O My located at the lakefront. It became famous in the sixties, drawing tourists gay and straight. But in the fifties, it was still underground.

Another drag bar I frequented was Tony Bacino's. All the waiters were drag queens. But since drag wasn't allowed, they wore black pants with a white waiter's jacket. Each queen wore a full face of makeup and a chiffon scarf tied artfully around his neck. Some of them wore their hair long, tucked under a smart knitted cap. I thought the waiters looked beautiful. They were all so glamorous to me. Of course, I was at a very impressionable age.

There was one drag queen at Tony Bacino's with whom I became very friendly. Everyone called him Pepper. I never knew his real name. Pepper was handsome as a male and gorgeous as a female. He was tall and lean with delicate features. Painted up, he looked more female than most real women. Pepper had had polio as a child and was disabled. He just sat around looking beautiful and holding court. Since drag was illegal, all the drag queens I met never went out during the day. I called them "night people."

But Mardi Gras was their big day. They planned their outfits for months in advance. Each year, we couldn't wait to just see what Pepper would be wearing. Pepper always wore high heels, but because of his polio, he was escorted, arm in arm, by two tall, handsome guys in tuxedos. Each year, he walked through the French Quarter looking like a movie star, turning the heads of everyone in the crowd.

Tony Bacino's had two black female singers, Myrtle and Angel. Angel was the feisty one, with bright-red hair and light skin. On weekends, both of them would sing the most delicious risqué songs, such as Lil Johnson's "Get 'Em from the Peanut Man (Hot Nuts)." The bartender—or should I say "barmaid"—at Tony Bacino's, Candy Lee, was a five-foot-one outrageous queen who would insult everyone who came in. There was a six-inch platform behind the bar for him to walk on so he would appear taller. Everyone enjoyed her banter, and she packed them in, gay and straight alike.

In New Orleans, Mardi Gras balls, or krewes, were and still are popular in both the straight and the gay worlds. The term comes from the traditional name of the organizations that were licensed by the city to put on parade floats or balls. The Mardi Gras balls were always held a month or two before Mardi Gras day. Attendance was by invitation only, and the attire was strictly formal at both gay and straight affairs. Each ball had a theme and was presided over by a king, a queen, and their court. In the gay world, both the king and queen and their entire court were men, all dressed in the most elaborate female costumes. Their court followed suit.

The Krewe of Yuga—KY for short—put on one of the earliest gay balls. The organization had chosen a private children's-school auditorium outside the city limits in Jefferson Parish to avoid any problems with the police. The bars were abuzz with anticipation for the event. It was all new to me, and I got caught up in all the excitement.

Bill, better known as Bette Davis at the bars, was a friend who was attending the ball, and he asked me to style his wig. I had been practicing on my sisters for years and had gotten rather good at doing hair. I told him I had never done a wig. "That's all right, honey," he said. "I have a huge headdress going over it." The wig turned out glorious.

I didn't attend the ball and was glad I didn't. The next day it was all over the news. Despite its venue outside city limits, the police raided the ball. Taken by surprise, the queens, dressed in their finest, ran for their lives, chased by the police. Many queens were caught and put in jail. It was a huge scandal. What was supposed to be a happy event turned ugly.

My friend Bill was one of the lucky ones and escaped without being arrested. He described the scene to me the next night at the bar as pandemonium. As soon as the police arrived, the queens scattered into the surrounding countryside. Wigs fell off, and dresses ripped on tree branches as they ran through the woods and jumped fences. High heels were scattered everywhere. Those in tight gowns who couldn't hike them up enough to clear a fence were caught and arrested.

Bill and his date, a bodybuilder dressed in a jockstrap and long cape, also fled through the forest in terror. Luckily, they came upon a house off the main road with lights on. Bill, still looking very much like a real woman, if a bit disheveled, motioned to his date to stay out of sight while he approached the house. He knocked on the door, and an older woman answered. Bill immediately started crying in his best woman-in-distress impression. He sobbed that "her" boyfriend had thrown her out of his car and left her stranded. The older woman listened with great sympathy and invited Bill into the foyer while she called a cab to take her home. When the car arrived, Bill thanked the woman, got into the car, and picked up his boyfriend farther along down the road.

Not all my friends were as lucky as Bill. One of our friends, Carlos, dressed in a costume with more than a thousand rhinestones hand sewn into the dress, fled and climbed a tree to hide. However, the bright reflection of police's flashlights on the rhinestones of his costume gave him away, and he was arrested.

Fortunately, that raid did not stop the organization from giving Mardi Gras balls. The following year, my dear friend Robert was queen of the ball. He was dressed as Marie Antoinette. His gown was gorgeous, all white with silver appliqués and a skirt so full, a family of four could fit under it. The wig was snow white, with wave after wave starting at the forehead going to the very top, about two feet high, with silver pins running through it. They used to say in those days of beehive fashion, "The higher the hair, the closer to God."

Over the years, other gay organizations started their own krewes. Eventually, the gay balls became huge extravaganzas with costumes and headdresses so large the men needed escorts to help them maintain their balance when they were presented in the "march." In the late 1960s, the laws concerning drag loosened up, and the gay krewes began to be held in the city proper.

Twelve

I was an active fourteen-year-old and having a gay old time (pun intended). In those days, nobody discussed safe sex or venereal disease. Sex was rather free; condom use was not as widespread in the gay culture as it is today. Even among my friends in the Quarter, the subject rarely came up. Nobody mentioned condoms. I thought condoms were only used to protect a girl from getting pregnant, something I didn't have to worry about with guys. I was a complete ingénue about the entire subject of venereal disease.

One day, while getting ready to take a bath, I felt this burning sensation when I urinated. I did not know what this burning meant. When I looked down at my penis, I noticed a discharge coming from the tip. I was scared. I could hear my dad's voice in the kitchen. I called out for him to come in. It was very embarrassing to ask my dad to look at my penis. One look at the discharge, and he knew immediately I had a venereal disease.

As I said before, my father was a quiet, patient man. He did not ask where or how I had gotten it. I am sure he thought I had gotten it from a girl. He just sent me to the doctor to get it taken care of and told me to be more careful in the future.

Poor as we were, we didn't visit doctors much. So it was even more embarrassing for me to expose myself in the examining room to a strange man, even though he was a doctor. I dropped my pants and shorts and stood there buck naked. The doctor examined me and then asked me to squeeze my penis so he could take a sample of the discharge.

"Son," he said, "you've got something called gonorrhea. It's a serious disease you get from sexual relations."

I swallowed hard, afraid he'd ask me for details. I just nodded.

"We'll fix you up this time, but you've got to be more careful. You're awful young to be having this problem. You need to tell the young lady about it and tell her to see a doctor. You hear?"

I nodded, relieved he didn't ask me any more questions. "Yes, sir. I will. Thank you."

He gave me a shot of penicillin and pills to take and sent me on my way. The doctor did not explain about condoms, nor did he give me any. I wish he had.

I did inform the guy whom I was sure I had caught it from to see a doctor and avoided seeing him thereafter. My dad never asked me how I had made out at the doctor's office or spoke of it again. As soon as I was well, I was back out there, but I became more aware of the character of the men I had sex with.

Thirteen

Every day after school I rushed home and changed from my school uniform into my paperboy-cum–James Dean outfit and set off on my bike to pick up my load of papers to deliver. Normally, I raced by every house on my bicycle, throwing each paper on the porch or steps in a mad dash to finish on time. I rarely took the time to speak with my customers except to collect my weekly fee on Saturdays.

One afternoon, I was stopped by a customer I hadn't seen before. He was sitting on his porch when I rode up to drop off his paper. He was in his late twenties, tall with blond hair and blue eyes.

"Hey, paperboy," he said, smiling. "What's your name?"

"Milton, sir." My mother always taught us to be polite.

"Well, Milton, I want to thank you for your hard work and always delivering my paper on time."

"You're welcome, sir."

He stood and eyed me up and down. "Would you like to come in for something cold to drink? You look hot."

As young as I was, I knew where this was going, but I decided to play it coy.

"Thank you, but I really need to get going."

"Aw, you've got a few minutes to spare, don't you?"

"I guess," I said, leaning my bike against the house.

I went inside and had that drink plus an afternoon blow job. I didn't stay long because I had to finish the rest of my delivery. I walked out with a big smile on my face and thanked him for the drink. My deliveries were a bit late that day. The next day as I peddled down his block delivering the news, I noticed him sitting on his porch as if he were waiting for me. I was hoping for a repeat of yesterday's event. He smiled as I handed him his paper and asked me to come in. I was eager and horny but asked if I could come back after I finished my delivery.

"I'll be waiting," he said. I took off in a flash.

Thirty minutes later, I was knocking on his door. This time not only did I get a blow job but ended up in bed. We carried on for some time. As I was getting ready to leave, he told me to stop as often as I wanted, but only during the week. *Why not on weekends?* I thought but didn't ask.

Kent didn't even tell me his name until after my third visit. As I got to know him better, I asked if he lived alone. He said he was married, and his wife worked during the day. I was shocked at this news. He was so comfortable in bed with me on top, which made the sex even hotter. Another life lesson for me. I had had no idea that you could be married but still enjoy sex with men. We saw each other regularly until they changed my delivery route. I never did meet his wife.

Fourteen

Trying to balance school, a secret social life, and this job was rather challenging but worth the effort. Unless I had a school party or family gathering, my weekend routine began on Friday night. Usually telling my mother I was meeting friends from school, I was out of the house by seven o'clock and headed for the Quarter. I started with the Bourbon House hoping to run into friends, and then we'd all go bar hopping.

Seven o'clock was on the early side in terms of nightlife, so when I arrived at the Bourbon House, it was mostly empty. Usually I was hungry, so I would get a table and order a burger. While I waited, I loved to read the wooden tabletop. It was covered with carvings of names, designs, and shapes of all kinds from customers decades before my time. The owners had preserved them with a heavy coat of shellac. I realized that this place had history. Hundreds of people had sat at its tables and left their marks over the years.

My weekend delivery pickup time was still 5:00 a.m., which left little time for me to enjoy weekend nights out. Like Cinderella, I had to be back home by midnight. While it put a limit on my time in the bars, it helped make my reasons for my time out more credible with my mother. But I often spent my weekend mornings with a hangover as I inserted extra sections into each paper before loading up the basket. Weekend deliveries took two loads as opposed to one on weekdays.

My only reward for getting up early and finishing Saturday- and Sunday-morning delivery was stopping at the doughnut shop. I arrived at 6:10 each morning, exactly when the first batch of glazed doughnuts came out of the oven. I always ordered the same thing: three twist doughnuts for fifteen cents. The guy behind the glass had them ready as soon as I arrived. If I close my eyes, I can still recall the smell of those doughnuts, how warm and fresh and delicious they were.

One weekend, I was at the Bourbon, waiting on the hamburger I'd ordered, when two straight-looking guys walked in. They sat at the table next to me and ordered beers. The one opposite me said hello after sitting down. Everybody was friendly in the Quarter, so I didn't think anything of it. I said hello. My hamburger arrived, and I started eating.

The same guy reached over, extended his hand, and said, "The name is Eddie."

"Milton," I said, wiping off the hamburger juice before I shook his hand.

Eddie continued talking as I tried to size up the situation. Eddie was about six foot two, in his middle twenties, built like a football player, wore tinted glasses, and spoke in a heavy Texas drawl. Not your typical gay guy who frequented the Bourbon. Then again, there were a fair number of straight guys who drank there.

"May we join you?" he asked.

"Sure thing," I said, making room.

They shifted their seats to my table. "This is Joe," Eddie said. "We just got into town from Texas. We're looking for an apartment in the Quarter." Joe shook my hand but didn't say much.

Eddie did most of the talking, saying little about himself but wanting to know about me. He spoke to me directly in a rather soft, playful tone. He asked me a bunch of questions. Did I live nearby? Did I go to school? Did I have job? I answered honestly. Joe just sat there sipping his beer.

I sat talking with them for nearly an hour and half. I started to get it. Eddie was coming on to me. He ordered another round and asked me if I wanted one, but I declined. During the entire time, not one of my friends came in. Eddie asked me if I knew of any good bars.

"Well, there's Dixie's across the street."

"What do you say we all have a beer there?"

Why not, I thought. This guy seems like fun. "Okay."

Eddie paid the bill, including my meal, and left a generous tip, something I wasn't used to doing. I wasn't sure where all this was going, but I certainly was enjoying all the attention. We walked across to Dixie's. I steered him away from the bar and quickly suggested we sit at a table. I didn't want to draw too much attention to myself. The gossip was fierce there. We continued to chat, checking out the crowd. It was getting busy. After a couple of beers, I said we should check out Tony Bacino's.

We arrived just in time to catch Angel's latest sultry number. Eddie and Joe loved it. Eddie flirted with all the queens. I introduced them to Pepper, who was sitting at the bar looking as gorgeous as ever. One of the queens whispered in my ear, "Where did you pick up those two butch numbers?" I just winked. I was getting a little tipsy.

It was almost midnight, my witching hour. I said I had to leave because of an early work call. Eddie offered to drive me home, saying his car was close by. I was beginning to like this guy.

"Thanks. I appreciate it."

We left Joe in the bar, walked a few blocks, and stopped at a new white Cadillac convertible.

"Hop in."

Trying to act as if I rode in Cadillacs all the time, I just got in without a word. But inside, I was all smiles. I asked him to drop me off a block from my house, for fear anyone would see me coming out of a car like that. After he stopped the car, he put his arm around me and gave me a gentle kiss. He asked if I could meet him tomorrow night at the Bourbon.

"Sure, I'll be there."

As I walked down the street to my house, I was elated. It had been a while since I had met someone who wanted more than a quickie. It was exciting to look forward to a "date."

The following night I met Eddie at the Bourbon House. He was sitting alone. A big smile appeared on his face as I walked in. I was happy to see him too. I had hardly sat down in my chair before he said, "Hungry? Let's order something."

He wanted to know how my day had gone, and I wanted to know more about him. When the food arrived, I asked him if he had found a place yet. He said they had found a place in the Quarter, and Joe was taking care of the final arrangements. It made me wonder a bit about how Joe fit into the picture. Were they together, or just friends? I still found it hard to believe that this big, masculine-looking guy was gay and interested in me. I figured out why he wore tinted glasses, though. His right eye drifted toward the corner, which I knew was called a lazy eye. I had had one as a child but grew out of it.

After we finished eating, Eddie paid the bill, and we went to a quiet place for drinks called the Old Absinthe House, one of the oldest straight bars in the Quarter. I became curious, wondering what kind of work this guy did because he had money and drove an expensive car. I tried to ask him, but he demurred. I figured he was just rich from his family. We talked and laughed a lot. He had some great stories to tell.

It was getting kind of late, and the bar was getting noisy.

"It's a nice night," Eddie said. "How about going for a ride?"

I would be crazy to turn down an offer like that, in a shiny Cadillac convertible. "Sure," I said eagerly. I was hoping for more than a ride.

We drove along the lakefront in the balmy breeze. Eddie made me feel special. I thought I could get used to this. We circled back to the Quarter and stopped in front of a small building on St. Ann Street.

"Here's my new place. Want to come up for spell?"

I spent a couple of hours with him. For a big, rough-looking guy, he treated me as if I were made of china. I was so caught up in pleasure that I didn't notice the time. It was nearly one in the morning. I told him I was sorry I had to leave, because I had to be at work before five.

He was sympathetic. "I'll take you home." All the houses on my street were dark. He dropped me off in front the house with a kiss.

It was just before five that Sunday morning and still dark as I started to leave my house on my bike. I noticed Eddie on the corner, standing in front of his car.

"Need a lift?" he said, smiling.

"What are you doing here at this time in the morning?"

"Waiting for you to come out." He said he didn't want to miss me, so he had just stayed all night. This guy was full of surprises.

Boy, I felt as if I had hit the jackpot. I turned the bike around and put it in the alley next to my house and jumped into his car.

We drove to the station and picked up my papers. *This is going to be a first—a paper boy delivering papers from a white Cadillac convertible,* I thought. I made quite a hit at the station, and, for the first time, I was able to fit the entire Sunday load in one pickup. Eddie even helped me stuff in the extra sections. He had the top down, so I was able to sit in the backseat with the papers and throw them from the car. I finished delivery in record time.

Forgoing my usual doughnut snack, I suggested we go to Café Du Monde, the bistro in the Quarter famous for their beignets and café au lait. Beignets were a favorite of mine, but Eddie had never had them. It was early, and we were among the few customers in the place. Eddie loved the warm dough treats. I started to pick up the check to thank him for his help, but he grabbed it.

The city was starting to wake up. I yawned and said we both needed some shut-eye. I thanked him for the most exciting delivery ever. He asked about seeing me again. I told him to meet me at the Bourbon on Friday, as I was busy with school all week.

Fifteen

Despite my busy schedule, the rest of that week seemed endless. When Friday night came around, I was ready for Eddie. I told Mother I was going to a movie with a friend. Eddie was waiting for me in the same place. When I arrived, he stood. I looked surprised.

"Don't sit. We're heading to a restaurant nearby called Tujague on Chartres Street for dinner."

I was so excited. I knew of the place. It was a real fancy restaurant. One of the oldest places in the Quarter. I'd never been to a place like that. Eddie sure knew how to impress a date.

We stepped out of the Bourbon House and bumped into Ruthie. Ruthie was a character in the Quarter everyone knew and loved. Picture Little Bo Peep, five foot two, about seventy-five pounds, around twenty-one years old. She had shoulder-length, natural-blond wavy hair, with protruding teeth and lots of gums showing when she smiled. Her demeanor was very childlike. She wore a flowery dress down to her ankles and Mary Jane shoes. She had a pet duck at her side that followed her everywhere. She stopped at every store and bar front, bringing cheer to everyone and collecting a few tips along the way from tourists.

"Hi, this is my duck," she said. She was very proud of her pet.

"Hi, Ruthie," I said. "This is Eddie."

"Nice to meet you both," he said politely.

She smiled, and off she walked with her duck waddling behind her, quack, quacking away.

We continued to the restaurant and went inside. Eddie gave his name to the maître d', and we were escorted to our table. It was a small place with ten tables, each covered with a white tablecloth and decorated with a lit candle in a wine bottle. The waiters wore white jackets. It was elegant. Like something out of a movie.

The menu was in French. I tried to act nonchalant about it, but I didn't know what any of the dishes were. Eddie could see I was struggling, so he ordered for us both. I guess he knew French. Another piece to the mystery about him.

Eddie seemed pleased just watching how I enjoyed the food and the ambiance. When he looked at me, I felt so appreciated. We talked during the entire meal. He loved to tell stories, and I was an avid listener.

After eating, Eddie asked me what I was having for dessert.

I looked directly into his eyes. "What I want is not on the menu." I had never been quite that bold before.

He just smiled and signaled for the check.

After he paid the bill, I was expecting to go to his place. But once again, he surprised me. We left the restaurant and walked to a small, dimly lit place playing soft jazz.

"Is this okay with you?"

I nodded. I'd never been to one of the jazz places in the Quarter because I was too young and afraid I'd get kicked out. Nobody even blinked. We got a table and had a beer. The music was soft and jazzy, ideal for after dinner, and we enjoyed it. After about an hour, I leaned over and said, "Is it time for dessert?"

"Come on. Let's get some."

We drove to his place and enjoyed a perfect ending to an exceptional evening. Afterward he dropped me off at home. I said thanks for the evening, and he just smiled. I was so excited afterward, I could hardly sleep.

As I stepped outside that morning, I saw Eddie sitting in his car, this time with the top up.

Ready to work?" he said with a smile.

Another day of special delivery. The guys at the paper station asked who this guy was. I told them he was my uncle from out of town. After delivery, we went to Café Du Monde again. He drove me home and said, "How about tonight?" We made plans for me to meet him at his place that night at 7:30. After getting some rest, I set out on my bike for Saturday's collection. Most of my customers paid me weekly; some every other week. I finished my route and headed home wondering what excuse I would drum up to get out of the house that night.

After getting home, I discovered my dad had fixed supper, as he usually did before leaving for work. Dad always left by four o'clock. Carolyn had already gone out with her boyfriend. Mother was lying down because she was not feeling well. I heated the food Dad had prepared and served it to Bonnie and Glenn, with a small portion for myself. By seven, I was dressed and ready. My mother was still in bed, so I left her a note that I was out with some friends from school.

When I arrived at Eddie's place later, there was Joe, the mystery man I hadn't seen since that first night. We chatted a bit, and then he said he had to run to meet a few people. I still couldn't figure out his deal, but it didn't matter. I had Eddie all to myself.

"How about we drive out to the lakefront and have some seafood," Eddie suggested.

"Great. I love seafood."

As we left the Quarter, I was hoping my friends would see me in Eddie's car. I hadn't told anyone about Eddie at this point.

We arrived at a popular local place with dozens of people waiting outside, which was typical in New Orleans for a place serving Cajun and Creole food. It wasn't too long before we were seated. When you go to a place like that, you don't expect to get out in a hurry. The food was fresh and took time to prepare. Eddie had a platter full with everything, and I was happy with crawfish and two dozen oysters. We washed it down with iced tea.

By the time we got to his place, I was more than ready for "dessert."

Being with this man took me to a new high. No one had ever treated me as he did, sexually or otherwise. I was so satisfied and comfortable lying in bed next to him, I never wanted to leave. But after another helping, it was time for me to go.

Sure enough, Sunday morning at five o'clock, there he was, waiting for me. We drove to the station, and this time he even helped me stuff the papers. The other guys were jealous and starting calling me Special Delivery. I didn't care. The boss was happy, as I finished my route in half the time.

I could get used this, I thought after Eddie dropped me off. He was something special.

Sixteen

Eddie had just gotten a phone installed, and he gave me his number. I promised to call him later in the week. When I did, he said he wanted to pick me up at school on Friday and take me to lunch. I thought it was a great idea as long as I could sneak away from the prying eyes of the nuns. I was almost fifteen, and I thought everything was possible and was always looking for adventure. I didn't think of the repercussions. I just wanted to be with Eddie.

That Friday, I left the school yard at lunchtime, pretending I was going home for lunch. Our house was only four blocks from the school, and I often went home for lunch to check on my mother. Eddie was waiting in his car one block away. I jumped in. As we drove uptown, we passed my house, and I saw my dad on the porch fixing something. I quickly slid down in my seat so I wouldn't be noticed because this certainly would have been difficult to explain. Lunch in the Quarter was far superior to the school cafeteria—no contest there—and I even got a quickie "dessert." We made plans to meet that evening at the Bourbon.

I was late getting back to school and had to walk into the classroom after class had already started. There was a hush in the room; all eyes were on me. Sister was sitting at her desk staring at me with cold, stern eyes as I sat down. She continued the lesson. The nuns who taught at our school belonged to the order of Sisters of Charity but were anything but charitable. They dressed in their traditional habits with headdress designed like gigantic white wings. All you could ever see was a small portion of the face and their disturbingly judgmental eyes.

After class, Sister told me to stay behind and approach her desk.

I was afraid to get too close and kept my hands behind my back because I knew one of her favorite punishments was to crack a ruler over your knuckles.

"Why were you late?"

"My mother asked me to help her around the house. Sorry, Sister."

"That's no excuse. Report to the principal's office."

I knew I was in trouble. Our nickname for the principal was Cruella de Vil. She was meaner than all the other sisters put together.

When I got there, I knocked tentatively on the door.

"Come," the principal said sternly.

I entered and stood in front of her desk.

"Well?"

"Sister sent me because I was late to class after lunch."

She glared at me. "Why were you late?"

"I had to help my mother. She's sick and—"

I could see right away she wasn't buying it.

"Detention after school until further notice. Dismissed."

I just stood there.

"Well?"

"Sister, I'm sorry if I was late, but I have a job delivering newspapers after school to help my family. I will lose my job if I don't show up."

She just stared at me for a few seconds. "Very well. You will write 'I am sorry that I was late to class' two hundred times on the blackboard before class begins tomorrow."

"Thank you, Sister. I promise not to be late again."

She just waved at me to leave. I was lucky she didn't call my parents.

Seventeen

I got to the Bourbon a little early and found my friends sitting around a table. They greeted me with sly comments about where I'd been and with whom. I coyly mentioned my new beau, and then he walked in. Eddie's strong masculine appearance caused a couple of jaws to drop.

Eddie came over, smiling as usual. I introduced him to all my friends. We all sat and talked for a while. Eddie really turned on the Texas charm, and all my friends ate it up.

After a while, Eddie stood up. "Good to meet y'all. But Milton and I have plans to be somewhere."

I knew that was my cue to get up and leave. I said my good-byes with promises to see them all soon.

We walked through Jackson Square and went into a popular restaurant called Court of Two Sisters. I had heard about this place but never dreamed I'd ever go there. How did Eddie know about all the best places to eat in the city? Another bit of the mystery about him. We ate on the patio in the open air. We shared a mountain of seafood served on an open newspaper. Real down home.

While we were eating, Eddie looked at me and asked, "Would you do something for me?"

"Like what?" I said a bit hesitantly.

"Would you pose for a professional photo for me?"

It was a strange request. I never had a professional photo of me taken before. I felt a bit awkward doing this, but after all Eddie had done for me, I felt it was the least I could do. "I guess so, if you want me to."

He smiled broadly. "Thanks. Meet me at the photographer's studio on Royal Street after you're finished collecting for your paper route on Saturday." He gave me the address.

We finished eating and went back to his place. Later, he drove me home as usual and said he's see me in the morning. Next morning at five o'clock, there he was, right on time. What more could a paper boy ask? We skipped the beignets so I could get a little more sleep. I wanted to look my best for the photos.

After getting some rest, doing chores around the house, and finishing my paper collection, I took a bath and got dressed in one of my favorite outfits. I told my mother that I was going to an afternoon party at one of my classmates'. By the time I got to the studio, they were set up and ready to shoot. All I had to do was pose. There were lots of pictures taken, mostly portrait style. I had no idea of the cost, but I knew it had to be expensive. The photographer said all pictures would be ready in a few days. After the photo session, Eddie took me to lunch and a quickie at his place.

Later on we took a drive to the lakefront and sat on the beach. I asked Eddie why he wanted so many pictures of me. He said he just wanted them for him to remember me. I thought that was a strange answer, but it was romantic. No one had ever done that before. After spending most of the day with him, I thought it best to go home early and not push my luck with the family. Eddie said he would be in his usual place Sunday morning. I walked into the house, and Mother asked about the party. I said it was fun and there had been good music to dance to.

While I was getting used to this treatment—going to fancy restaurants, driving in a Cadillac, and not paying for anything—I still wondered where Eddie's money came from. He never spoke of his family or a job. I was a kid and just shrugged it off. Eddie was fun to be with, and I left it at that.

Next morning, there he was in that big white car waiting for me to come out. I would have been disappointed if he wasn't. We finished my route and headed for those delicious hot beignets. I told Eddie I had to spend the rest of Sunday with the family and I would talk with him on Wednesday. He gave me a squeeze and drove off.

I tried him Wednesday. No answer. He must be out, I said to myself. Then again on Thursday. Still no answer. By Friday, I was really worried. I rushed through my paper delivery and made some excuse to get out of the house and headed into the Quarter to his apartment. There was no sign of Eddie or Joe. This was not like him, and I started to think something terrible had happened. I decided to check out the Bourbon House. Looking in, I saw a friend sitting alone who motioned for me to come in. Before I could sit down, he said, "Did you hear what happened to Eddie?"

I must have turned white. "No. Is he okay?"

"He was picked up and put into prison."

"For what?" I replied.

"For cashing bad checks."

Well, that explained the mystery of where his money came from. Eddie was a con artist. He had seemed so genuine, a person of good character, but what did I know at such a young age?

The next morning, when I left for work at five o'clock, there was no Eddie, no Caddy. It was back to peddling that heavy-duty bike. The guys at the station ribbed me a bit about it, but I just said my uncle had to go back home.

Eddie was my first real crush, and I missed him. I knew what Eddie did was wrong, but I had to admit, I enjoyed being showered with attention. He showed me a lifestyle I hadn't known before, and I was grateful for the experience. I never heard from him again.

Eighteen

I went back to my usual routine and started hanging out with my friends again. While I had missed our group and enjoyed being with them again, I missed the feeling of being part of a couple that I had had with Eddie. And, of course, the more glamorous lifestyle he had shown me. New Orleans was an elegant place, but as a poor kid, I could only experience a small portion of its allure. Eddie had given me a taste for some of the nicer things the city had to offer.

One evening that following November, Magnolia made one of his appearances at the Bourbon House and announced that he was taking a trip to New York to visit relatives for the Christmas holidays. Dick was born in Louisiana but had spent many years living in New York as a young boy. None of us had ever been to New York, and we listened to Magnolia talk about all the amazing sights there were in the city. I hung on his every word.

"I wish I could visit New York," I said to Magnolia. "I know I'd love it there."

"Why don't you come visit me? I'll show you around."

"Thanks, but my parents would never let me go."

He shrugged. "If you find a way, you know you're welcome."

That night, I could hardly sleep. New York, the greatest city in the world. I had to find a way to get there. It was a once-in-a-lifetime opportunity. When would I ever get another chance? I had a good amount of money saved from my paper route, so I thought I could afford it. But how could I get my folks to give me permission to go? It wasn't the kind of thing that my parents would agree to, especially because it was so expensive. Except for my father's military service, neither of them had ever been out of New Orleans, let alone the state.

Slowly, a plan emerged in my mind about how I could make that happen. Both my parents were devout Catholics, particularly my mother. She nearly worshipped our parish priest and respected the sisters at my school. My idea was to tell Sister Cruella that my friend Richard, who was at the seminary and tutored me after school, was going to visit his relatives in New York over the Christmas holidays and had asked me to spend the time with them. He promised to take me to Midnight Mass at the grand St. Patrick's Cathedral there. I knew that if the nuns approved of my trip, my parents would surely allow me to go.

I dug up the courage to discuss my trip with Sister Cruella. At first she was skeptical, but when she heard I'd be staying with this young seminarian's family and would attend Mass at St. Patrick's, she relented.

"If your parents approve, I see no reason not to allow it. I'll need a note from them. Just be back in time for classes after the holidays," she said and dismissed me.

I told my parents about the trip and said that Sister approved if they did. My mother was sad because it would be the first time one of her children wouldn't be home for Christmas but happy for me, the first child in the family to travel. My dad, always practical, asked about the cost of the trip and my paper route. I told him I had enough money to cover the trip and that I would arrange for someone to cover my paper route during my absence. It was all set. They gave me the note of approval.

Magnolia was thrilled with the news, and we started making plans. First, I had to take an airplane to save traveling time. I had never been on an airplane before but was looking forward to the experience. I was a little nervous all the same. Dick calmed me down and said it was no different from taking the bus, only it was in the air. I was willing to do whatever I had to do to get to New York. He said there were two airports in New York City because it was so huge. He said to make sure I arranged to fly into the airport named LaGuardia.

Instead of staying with him and his relatives in their small apartment in someplace called the Bronx, he suggested I stay in Manhattan at the YMCA because it would make sightseeing much easier. It was cheap and full of good-looking guys. We'd visit all the attractions, including the bars in Greenwich Village, Mass at St. Patrick's Cathedral, the Empire State Building, Macy's Department Store, the works. I couldn't wait.

The first challenge was the airline flight. I didn't know the first thing about air travel. I went to Dick's travel agent and had him book the flight on Capitol Airlines. I nearly fainted when I had to hand over the $111.98 for the round-trip flight. It was the most money I'd ever spent in one place in my life. My departure date was December 23. I gave Magnolia all the information. He was leaving a few days earlier and said he's meet me at the airport. I was so excited, I could hardly contain myself.

Not having one of my own, I had to borrow a suitcase from one of my friends. I started to plan the clothes I would need for colder weather. I already had some good-looking slacks and sweaters and a sport jacket, but I also decided to bring a medium-weight jacket. I went to Gauchos', a men's store on Canal Street and Saint Charles at the time, and bought a beautiful long tweed topcoat on sale. I decided to pack my blue jeans and white T-shirts to run around the YMCA.

On December 23, Dad drove me and the rest of the family to New Orleans Moisant International Airport (now Louis Armstrong International Airport). Dad parked the car while the rest of us waited for him in front of the huge terminal building. We entered the terminal, which was bustling with people walking and running in every direction. Looking all around like tourists, we walked to the Capitol Airlines counter. After checking in with my ticket and luggage, the family and I headed for the departure gate. In the 1950s, family and friends were allowed to accompany you to the gate—not like today, with all the security.

My flight was scheduled to leave at 7:30 p.m. We had no sooner arrived when boarding was called. Just before passing the doorway, I looked back and smiled, and everyone waved back. Mother had a big grin on her face as she held back her tears. In those days, all passengers entered the plane on the airfield. As I climbed the steps to the plane, I could see the whole family waving vigorously. I was sad to be leaving them for the first time but excited for this new adventure.

The inside of the plane was smaller than I had expected. My seat was on the aisle toward the front. The engines were beginning to rev up. I could still see my family waving as I looked out the window over the passenger next to me. I was too excited to be nervous, and I did not want anyone to think I was a novice. I had become an expert at hiding my emotions, after all. The takeoff was smooth, but I became scared when the plane tilted to the far left while climbing. I tried to act cool, as if I had done this before, but I was dying inside.

It was a long flight, and I dozed off. I was awakened by an announcement: "We will be landing in New York's LaGuardia Airport in twenty minutes." I looked out the window and saw what looked like millions of lights below.

As I stepped out of the plane into the cold, wintery New York night, I could see Magnolia behind the glass window of the terminal. It was a wonderful sight to behold. He greeted me with open arms.

"Welcome to New York City!"

All I could do was smile.

We walked what seemed like miles to reach the luggage area. LaGuardia airport was nothing like the small airport in New Orleans. It was a good thing Magnolia knew his way around because I was lost with all the hundreds of people waiting for their luggage.

Once I got my suitcase, we had to stand in line to board the Greyhound shuttle bus into the city. The bus ride was thrilling. I had a window seat and a great view of Manhattan as we crossed a huge bridge over what Magnolia said was the East River into Manhattan. The vastness of it all was overwhelming. I had never seen so many tall buildings so close together. The bus terminal where we got off was just a short walk to the YMCA on Thirty-Fourth Street.

Despite the late hour, the streets were bustling with crowds of people, which made it difficult to walk carrying my heavy suitcase. I had never seen so many people in one place before, all walking as fast as they could. The storefronts were beautifully decorated with Christmas cheer. I felt as if I had walked into a winter wonderland.

We arrived at the YMCA well after midnight. Magnolia told me to get settled in, and he would pick me up around nine thirty in the morning. Then he took off to go back to the Bronx.

I walked into the lobby on the ground floor. The room was huge, with brick walls, tall ceilings, and cement floors. Sound echoed through the room. There were loads of tables and chairs, and a few benches in the center. I walked to the far side toward what looked like the check-in desk. Fortunately, Magnolia had made a reservation for me. I checked in and was given a large key with a heavy weight attached to it. I was told the gym was on the other side of the room behind the large doors, and the pool was located in the basement. At that point, I'd never even been to a hotel before, let alone one with these amenities.

I was rather intimidated with it all but preceded to the third floor to find my room. It was the size of a large closet with a single bed, a small table, one chair, and no window. A clean towel and a small bar of soap were on the bed. The bathroom was down the hall. The room was so small I had to leave my suitcase on the floor. There wasn't even a closet to hang anything up, just a few hooks on the wall.

I checked out the bathroom. There was a wall of urinals and a few stalls without doors. Opposite the stalls was a row of sinks with mirrors above. Everyone could watch you take a dump as they shaved. That was a little too public for my taste. The communal shower room was to the right. The shower area was one big room with multiple showers heads placed around the walls. Another first for me.

I returned to my room and tried to get some sleep.

Nineteen

Morning arrived, and I headed to the bathroom to clean up. The room was bustling with guys, eighteen to twenty-one years old, some nude and others with just a towel around them. I had my pajama bottom on and carried my soap and towel. I felt overdressed. I couldn't tell if they were gay or straight. Everyone seemed busy doing their thing—shaving, brushing teeth, combing their hair. Very little socializing. While I waited for a sink to be free, I watched the guys taking a shower. *What a treat,* I thought. I felt my pecker start to stir at the sight of all those wet, naked bodies. Good thing I still had my pajamas on.

Brushing my teeth with a bunch of guys I didn't know was one thing, but showering was another. And given my reaction to watching the men shower, I was worried I'd embarrass myself. I waited until the shower room was nearly empty before taking mine.

As I was soaping up, two other guys entered the stall. There I was, all soaped up, naked as a jaybird. They each turned on a shower and started to wet down. I could feel them checking me out. It made me feel uncomfortable. Cruising on the corner or at the bars with all my clothes on was one thing. Having naked men check me out while I was naked as well was quite another. All I could do about it was to finish my shower as quickly as I could, grab my towel and pajamas, and get back to my room.

I returned to my room and discovered the door was locked. I didn't realize I had to take my key with me. There I was in the hall, locked out with only my pajamas on. I had no choice but to go down to the front desk and get another key. I felt embarrassed but was told it happened often.

I got dressed and went out looking for something to eat. It was around eight thirty in the morning. The YMCA served a complimentary hot breakfast, but the cafeteria was packed, so I decided to look for a place outside. Salvation Santas were already out ringing their bells. I was amazed at the masses of people outside on the street that early on Christmas Eve morning, moving at a fast pace. Everything looked so big and foreign, so different from the relaxed lifestyle of New Orleans.

I decided not to veer too far from the Y for fear of getting lost. Just around the corner, I found a big restaurant called the Horn & Hardart Automat and went in. I'd never seen anything like it before. It was a huge room. Half the walls had dozens of little window boxes with different food items ready for the taking. There were stations sporting shiny spigots from which you could serve yourself coffee. A middle-aged woman, noticing me looking around confused, helped me figure out how the system worked. After we got our food, we sat together. She was very friendly, and we chatted over our coffee, scrambled eggs, and toast, all for the grand sum of fifty cents.

I wished her a merry Christmas and then wandered back to the Y and waited in the lobby for Magnolia. He finally arrived, and we started a tour around this magnificent city. Our first stop was Macy's, a couple of blocks from the Y. The store was massive, with ceilings as high as the sky, all decorated to an inch of its life. It was so crowded with last-minute shoppers that we could hardly move.

Next, we walked over to Fifth Avenue and saw all the expensive storefront windows with animated figures moving around. I had never seen such glamorous and festive displays. We stopped in Saint Patrick's Cathedral, and I was overwhelmed with its grandeur.

From there, we walked to the Empire State Building. It was too crowded to go to the observation deck. Just looking up at it made me dizzy. We stopped for one of the famous hot dogs from the street vendors and then walked over to see the huge Christmas tree at Rockefeller Center. Then we made our way to Times Square and the Broadway marquee. Magnolia really had me on the move. I was not used to this fast pace, but I did not want to miss anything.

Next we headed downtown to Greenwich Village by subway. It was noisy and more crowded than a streetcar at Mardi Gras, but fun. I was amazed at how fast the trains went. The tiny streets of the Village reminded me of New Orleans. Magnolia was quick to point out a couple of gay bars on Christopher Street. By that time, it was getting late, and he had to get back to his family in the Bronx. He dropped me off at the Y and told me he'd pick me up the next day so I could spend Christmas with his family. I was exhausted. After a quick dinner at the Automat, I collapsed on my tiny bed.

I called my parents Christmas Day using the public telephone to wish them a merry Christmas and tell them I was having a great time. I told Mother all about St. Patrick's. Magnolia took me to the Bronx to meet his Aunt Teresa and Uncle Joe and share a typical Italian Christmas dinner full of pasta dishes, all kinds of meats, and delicious desserts. Afterward, Magnolia put me on the subway, instructing me to get off at Thirty-Fourth Street. He said he'd pick me up the next day for more sightseeing.

True to his word, he was waiting in the lobby that next morning. He showed me Central Park, with its horse-drawn carriages; ice skaters; and historic restaurant, Tavern on the Green, all lit up for the holiday. We visited the Cloisters, the only serene stop in my whirlwind tour, and listened to a choir singing in the courtyard. Magnolia said it also had the best view of the Hudson River.

Over the next few days, Magnolia took me to some holiday parties and introduced me to his circle of longtime gay friends on the Upper East Side. Most of the guys were in their twenties or early thirties. I wore my dark dress slacks, white shirt, fancy narrow tie, and snappy sport jacket. Everyone at the parties wanted to meet me, a cute, young Southern boy from New Orleans. I became the center of attention.

I took a fancy to one guy I met at the first party. His name was Jerry. He was about thirty and tall, and he had dark, wavy hair and blue eyes. He told me he was an interpreter at the United Nations. After talking for a while, he gave me his telephone number and made me promise to call him. I was so excited for a date with a sexy New York guy.

I called Jerry and set up a date to meet him at his apartment the next evening. He gave me his address on someplace called East End Avenue and told me to take a cab. I had never taken a cab before. New Orleans was so small that I walked everywhere or rode my bike. But I had no idea it would be so scary. The gruff drive took off like a shot, and I had to hold on to my seat. The driver was darting in and out of traffic like a maniac but got me to Jerry's in record time.

His apartment was spacious and lovely. We had a drink, and then he took me to a fancy restaurant in his neighborhood. We finished the evening in bed at his place. He was some sexy guy. I took a cab back to the Y, reeling from the experience.

Magnolia was pleased that I had met someone. I spent most of my days with Magnolia as he continued to show me around New York. We saw Little Italy, Chinatown, Wall Street, and even took a ride on the Staten Island Ferry. I managed to see Jerry in the evenings. He had a car and drove me all around Manhattan, covering the East River, Battery Park, and up the Hudson River. It was fantastic seeing New York at night lit up as we drove along the river. He always invited me to his apartment at the end and drove me back to the Y afterward.

My four days in the New York City were coming to an end, and I had to return home. Sadly, I had to say good-bye to Jerry, but he said he would keep in touch. I gave him my name and address. Magnolia accompanied me to the airport. He was spending another week before returning to New Orleans. I gave Magnolia the tightest hug and thanked him for the most incredible opportunity of seeing New York, an experience I would remember for the rest of my life.

I was excited and relieved when the plane landed at Moisant Airport. I could see my parents waving as I stepped out of the plane. I put my arms around Mother, and she said, "I prayed to God for your safe return." Dad gave me a hug as well. I told them how big and fast-moving New York was and about the millions of tall buildings stacked together. I raved about how wonderful my friend Richard's aunt and uncle were to me. They were pleased I had had a nice family to spend the holidays with and that my friend was so nice to show me around the city. I just smiled. I couldn't wait to share all the juicy details with my friends in the Quarter that weekend.

Twenty

I was in Dixie's Bar one Friday night with some friends when I saw this young, handsome guy checking me out from across the room. He had dark hair, dark-brown eyes, and fair skin, and he was about five foot eleven. He was dressed very stylishly in dark slacks and a white-and-black sport shirt. When we locked eyes, I felt an instant attraction. He walked toward our group, never taking his eyes off me. His smile was warm and friendly.

As he approached, he held out his hand and said, "My name is Andy." It seemed as though the group I was with disappeared as I took his hand.

"Milton," I responded, holding on to his hand a bit longer than I needed to. I introduced him to my friends, and he was polite.

"Want to join us?" I asked.

"Thanks, but I'd rather find a table for you and me."

I looked at my friends. They nodded and shooed me away to spend time with my new hunk.

I showed him to a quiet table in the corner. We ordered beers and settled down to talk. He told me he had just moved down to New Orleans from Los Angeles and was working as a hairdresser in a small upscale salon in the Quarter. We talked for a long time. I don't remember exactly what we talked about. I just remember being transfixed by his friendly manner and handsome face. I must have told him a little about myself and my recent trip to New York. I remember that we laughed a lot.

"How about we take a walk to my place?"

All of a sudden, I snapped out of it. I probably came off a bit too eager, not my usual cool self. There was something about Andy that was different from the other hookups I'd had. I agreed.

We arrived at his place on Ursuline and Burgundy Streets, four blocks from Dixie's bar. He had a one-room apartment in one of the large old houses in the Quarter. We entered through the courtyard. As soon as the door closed, he gave me a kiss. His touch was gentle, his voice soft. We made our way to the couch and kissed and embraced for what seemed like hours. It was not just some hot, quick sex. We took it slow, as if we were making love. The first time I'd felt this was with Eddie, and it had sent chills down my spine. I loved it.

Afterward, we lay in bed together, both out of breath and sweaty. He started rubbing his fingers along my body. "How old are you?" he asked in a casual way.

For some reason, I had a feeling that was coming. It was the first time anyone had ever asked me my age. "Fifteen," I replied. He didn't flinch.

"How old are you?" I asked in return.

"Eighteen."

He was the youngest guy I had been with and the best looking. He was as mature as the older guys I knew and just as experienced in bed. We made love again before I had to leave. He gave me his number at the salon.

"Call me," he said, and we kissed again before I left.

That first encounter with Andy started a long, beautiful relationship.

I saw Andy often, but not as much as I wanted. I was still in grammar school and juggling a paper route in the afternoon. He worked crazy hours at the salon.

At first, we met only on weekends, hanging out with friends in the Bourbon House or Dixie's for a while and then going off to his place. Occasionally, I managed a couple of nights during the week when I did not have too much homework. Andy had a great personality, and I loved being with him. I told him about my interest in doing hair. He was excited about it. I told him about my first disastrous experience with my sister

Bonnie and how I had gotten better since then, with the instruction of my sister Carolyn and some of the drag queens I knew.

"Why don't you come visit me at the salon some Saturday and watch me work," he said. "You'd get to see how a salon works."

One Saturday after my paper route, I met him there. It was nothing like that beauty school I had visited with my mother as a child. This place was first rate. I watched how he cut and colored hair and set the hair in rollers and put each customer under the hair dryer. It was very amusing watching these women in a row under the dryers talking to one another in a loud tone, not realizing the whole salon could hear everything they were saying. I really got a charge watching him create beautiful hairdos for these women. He was a talented stylist.

I visited Andy at the salon every chance I got, enamored with him and the whole scene. The more I watched, the more committed I was to becoming a hair stylist just like him.

My bond with Andy became stronger and stronger. He was my first real love. We'd been together for several months, and I thought it was time I introduced Andy to my family. It was the first time I had brought home any of my friends from the Quarter, and I was a bit nervous. There wasn't a big gap in our ages, and the fact he was new in town and didn't know many people would make Mother want him to feel at home. My mother loved people, and she was quite a talker. I knew she would adore Andy because he was handsome, very friendly, and a professional hairdresser. One way to get on the good side of my mother was to offer to do her hair for free.

It was love at first sight. Andy charmed her, and when he offered to fix her hair, she was delighted. After that, he was at the house several times a week for supper. He even did my sisters' hair on occasion as well. They all adored him. Since my father worked nights, he got to see Andy only on Sunday afternoons. I'm not sure what he thought of my relationship with Andy. Working at the hotel, he must have seen his fair share of relationships of all kinds. But being the kind and nonjudgmental man he was, he never said a word and treated Andy as one of the family.

Since Andy had Mother's approval, it was easy to get out of the house and say we were meeting up with some friends, going to the movies, or just hanging around. Sometimes we did go to the movies and then joined some friends in one of the bars. We always finished off the evening at his one-room apartment in each other's arms making love.

Twenty-One

Things were going well. I was passing my classes. Andy and I were enjoying each other more than ever. Thanks to Andy, Mother and my sisters were looking stylish. Life was grand.

Carolyn decided to throw a fifteenth birthday party for me. She invited all my classmates and asked if I'd like to invite Andy also. I thought about it and decided it would be for the best not to invite him. I told her that he didn't know any of my school friends and wouldn't feel comfortable. She was surprised and disappointed, but she understood. So did Andy.

It was the early part of September, and the weather switched from beastly hot to pleasantly cool. Carolyn thought the backyard was a perfect place for the party because it was all cement and good for dancing. She decorated the clotheslines with colorful streamers and put the record player in the outside shed for music. She also baked my birthday cake. The party was a big success, and I made points with my classmates, both boys and girls.

Halloween was fast approaching. It was the biggest holiday after Mardi Gras in New Orleans, and all the queens started making plans about what they would wear. I hadn't participated in the past and had just helped the drag queens get ready for the many costume parties around town. This year was different. I wanted to join in the fun.

I became friends with my next-door neighbor. His name was Freddie, and he lived there with his mother. We talked over the wooden fence that separated our yards while he groomed his chow dogs. Freddie was in his early thirties, and his gestures and looks were very effeminate. I could see he was "as gay as a goose," as they used to say. I'm sure he knew about me also. Gay people tend to recognize their own, even if the person does not know it himself. Freddie's mother knew he was gay and loved and accepted him wholeheartedly. But Freddie never hung out at any of the bars in the Quarter. He had a whole set of friends outside the city.

Freddie invited me to a Halloween party at one of the camp houses (excuse the pun) on Lake Ponchartrain. I knew all about these houses. My aunt rented one every summer. They were houses built on stilts over water. In order to get to them, you had to cross railroad tracks and walk along a narrow wooden walkway above water. It was ideal for fishing and shrimping over the side, but not for walking in spike heels in fancy dresses.

It was the first time I'd been to a party there, and I was grateful for the invitation. I asked him if I could bring Andy.

"Of course," he said. He'd met Andy on several occasions at the house.

He gave me directions, and we chatted a bit more about it. It sounded like quite an elaborate event.

"What are you going to wear?" I asked.

He had it all planned out. "I'll be in a long black satin dress with a cape lined in bright emerald green and a black feather coming from my hat."

"Sounds very elegant."

"What about you?" he asked.

"I don't know. I'll have to think about it."

"Let me know if you need any help," he trilled.

The idea of dressing as a woman had always intrigued me. I had spent so much time around all the drag queens, it seemed like the natural choice for my costume. I thought it would be fun, and I certainly could get tips from all the drag queens I knew.

I told Andy about the party and my idea to go dressed as a woman. He was excited. "I'll do your hair and makeup and be your date."

I started putting an outfit together. I called Bill (Bette Davis) and asked for a little help, which he was happy to give. My idea was to look elegant, not over the top. I found this black velvet top with a sweetheart bustline and narrow straps. I ran over to Bette's place and showed him what I had to work with.

"My dear, I just happen to have some black velvet fabric hanging around, and it would make a gorgeous long skirt."

After putting it together, he said it needed a little punch, and he had just the right thing. He took some white fabric and draped it around my waist, using the rest to make a wide panel down the back, which was secured under the bottom of the skirt. I found the perfect spike heels in a metallic gunmetal color. Bill showed me how to walk in heels, one foot in front of the other. My first walk across the room was a little shaky; by the time I turned around, I was walking like a pro. I was all set.

I told my mother about the Halloween costume party, and she was delighted. She asked me what I intended to wear as a costume, but I demurred, saying I hadn't decided yet. I knew that my mother might not be supportive of my dressing like an elegant woman instead of pirate or some other kind of Halloween character. While no one in my family ever mentioned anything about my being gay, it probably was naïve to think they didn't sense it.

Andy bought a short, dark, curly-haired wig and combed it into the most fashionable style of the day. When he finished, the hairstyle looked like Gina Lollobrigida's, one of most popular European actresses at the time. I added light streaks in the wig, hoping for the look worn by Audrey Hepburn in *Breakfast at Tiffany's.*

The party night arrived. As I was getting dressed in my room, Mother peeked in.

"Is that your Halloween costume, Milton?"

"Yes, Mother. Andy is coming over to help me."

She shook her head and walked away into the kitchen. She gave me the silent treatment for the rest of the evening and didn't even say goodbye. I did not know what I was thinking when I decided to dress at home, but the damage was done. The only saving grace for the situation was that my family adored Andy.

Andy arrived and started my makeup in the front room, four rooms away from the kitchen. He blocked out my own heavy eyebrows with wax and makeup and then drew new ones with a high arch farther up on my forehead. Sometimes, brows like that are referred to as "surprise brows." He managed to draw my lips fuller than I had ever seen them. I got the full picture when the wig, dress, and string of pearls went on. The outfit was complete with long black opera-length gloves. In no time at all, he had transformed me from a cute fifteen-year-old boy into a very attractive woman.

I was quite surprised when I looked into the mirror. I looked fabulous! It's amazing what a little powder and paint can do. Andy got dressed in his suit and tie, looking very handsome. We made quite an elegant couple as we left for the party.

Andy and I met with Freddie and another friend outside his house, all dressed up and ready to party. We exchanged compliments—how gorgeous we all looked. Freddie was particularly surprised how beautiful I looked. I returned the compliment, saying he looked great, but I thought, he looks like Freddie with a dress on and a hat with feathers. He had made no attempt at applying any makeup except lipstick and rouge. I thought some makeup would help to soften his male features, but he was happy with his look, and who was I to disagree? It was my first time in drag.

Freddie drove us to the lakefront and parked the car on the side of the road. After getting out of the car, Freddie said, "Come on, girls, pick up your skirts. We have to cross the tracks." That was easier said than done. I wasn't quite ready for this. It was dark, and I could barely walk in my long, tight dress and high heels.

There were *two* sets of tracks to cross surrounded by loose rocks. I tried hiking my dress up, but it was cut so slim, I couldn't get it past my calves, and lifting a leg up and over each track was almost impossible. My heels got stuck in the rocks with each step. All I could think about was getting trapped on the tracks in front of an oncoming train. I could see the headline:

GIRL/BOY IN COCKTAIL DRESS HIT BY TRAIN!

Even with Andy's help, I couldn't clear the tracks. Finally, he picked me up and carried me across. Chivalry wasn't dead, and he was my knight. The next challenge was the long narrow walkway over the water that led to the camp house. Who in his right mind would give a drag party in such a remote, difficult area? I suppose smart queens with sensible, short cocktail clothes. The only good thing about the location was that it was so far out of the way, it wouldn't be raided by the police. Holding on to Andy's arm, I gingerly made my way, careful not to get my heels stuck in the spaces between the planks.

At last we arrived. The party in full swing. Despite the treacherous path, everyone looked as fresh as if they had just walked down the red carpet. There were around twenty-five queens scattered around the room. A few were dancing to music, and the rest were standing in small groups around the room. Every head turned as we walked in. I recognized a few of them from Tony Bacino's, but they didn't recognize me until I told them who I was. Andy got us bourbon and 7UPs. There were all sorts of outfits, some seriously glamorous like mine and others rather tragic like Freddie's, but everyone was having fun. Only Andy was dressed as a man. He was so handsome, all those bitches were after him. They didn't have a chance.

I noticed a couple of older queens on the far side of the room checking me out. I could tell it wasn't a look of approval. Before I could say "girl," they were in my face, asking all kinds of questions in a bitchy tone.

"Honey, you look fabulous, and your skin is flawless. Who did your makeup?"

I just pointed to Andy, my makeup artist.

"He's a magician and sooo handsome. What is your secret?"

"Youth."

They turned and walked away.

Judging from their backhanded compliments, my first drag outfit was a success. We stayed until midnight. Freddie left with us and drove us back to Andy's apartment before going home. I took off the dress, washed my face, and jumped into bed with Andy for some hot sex. When I got home, everyone was asleep.

The day after the party, my mother acted as if it had never happened. I'm sure she told my father about my costume, but I didn't hear another word about the whole affair. Andy continued coming to the house several nights a week and did everyone's hair. My family even let me experiment with them—under Andy's watchful eye, of course. I loved it. From then on, I knew that I wanted to be hair stylist.

Twenty-Two

The Christmas holidays were near, and Andy said he would spend them with his mother in Los Angeles. I knew I would miss him but didn't realize just how much until he was gone. We were in love and committed to staying faithful while apart. By the time he returned, I was bursting with sexual energy. So was he. We just couldn't get enough of each other.

As the dull winter months progressed, everyone looked forward to Mardi Gras. This was to be Andy's first. Since my first attempt at drag had been so successful, I decided to try it again. Andy and I went shopping and found not one but two outfits for me, one for daytime and one for evening. The day outfit looked like a sexy French maid. It was a very short halter-neck dress in pink satin with an overlay of black toile. I wore black fishnet stockings.

For evening, I used the same black top I had worn for Halloween, with a gigantic pink taffeta skirt with several layers of crinolines, a scarf twisted with pearls around my neck, and the long opera gloves from the Halloween party. I topped it off with a large-brimmed pink hat trimmed in black netting. Andy decided to dress as a sailor, and I must say he made a very cute one.

The big surprise was that Andy's mother was coming to New Orleans that year for Mardi Gras with her boyfriend. His father had died years before. I was looking forward to meeting her but was concerned she'd see me in drag for most of the visit. Andy said not to worry. His mother knew he was gay and loved and accepted him for who he was. He said she would probably even help me dress. Not wanting a repeat of my mother's reaction to my costume, I planned to get ready at Andy's place.

Andy's mom and her boyfriend arrived the night before Mardi Gras day arrived and stayed at one of the hotels in the Quarter. Her name was Alicia. She was a very attractive woman in her early forties, with stylish hair dyed a copper red and a fair amount of makeup. Her boyfriend's name was Philip. He was tall, dark, and fairly handsome. He dressed in sporty clothes and was friendly but quiet.

I was fully dressed in the French maid outfit when his mother walked in with her boyfriend. Andy hugged her and turned to introduce me. "Mother, I would like you to meet my boyfriend, Milton."

I felt rather awkward dressed like that, meeting his mother for the first time, and I didn't know what to say. But she broke the ice and put me at ease. "Nice to meet you, Milton. You look great." Then Andy stood next to me in his sailor costume. She smiled knowingly and said, "Looks like my sailor boy got lucky. Let's go out and have a good time!"

His mother and her boyfriend turned out to be fun, real party people.

Around eleven thirty in the morning, the four of us started walking into the Quarter on Bourbon Street, where all the best costumes appeared. All of a sudden his mother stopped and said to me that I could walk better in heals than she. We laughed. I felt so comfortable with her. It was such a relief not to worry about hiding my true self, as I did with my own mother.

Mardi Gras day is a twenty-four-hour party with thousands and thousands of people filling the streets, especially Bourbon Street. In order to stay together, we held hands and snaked our way through the crowds. Every now and then, we would stop, get a beer, and watch the passersby. They were overwhelmed with the spectacle and gaiety of Mardi Gras. People were so friendly and generous, throwing beads from the balconies above. Just standing still watching the parade of people pass was a party in itself.

We spent the rest of the day milling around in the crowds. I showed them all the sights, including Canal Street, which led to one of the main shopping areas. After several hours of fun, we searched for a restaurant for some badly needed food and rest. All the local places were packed, so I suggested the Roosevelt Hotel, a posh, expensive hotel off Canal Street. There, after an hour wait, we had a delicious lunch, away from the madness. If it had been any other day, I would not have been allowed in the hotel dressed in drag. But it was Mardi Gras, and even the somewhat snooty manager had the party spirit. Philip picked up the tab.

Around five thirty, Andy and I went back to his apartment to change into my evening outfit. Alicia and Philip went to their hotel to rest and freshen up. They said they would meet us at Andy's in a few hours or so. I took off my outfit, kicked off the heels, and lay down before getting ready with the evening dress. Andy touched up my makeup and helped me get dressed. By the time his mother arrived, I was completely ready. Andy's mother thought I looked like a Southern belle.

We hit the streets and paraded through the Quarter. My skirt was so big and wonderful that the crowds parted for us as we walked. We even walked into some of the big hotels on Canal Street. The only hotel I avoided was the Monteleone Hotel, where my father worked. He'd be on duty by this time, and although he probably would not have recognized me, he'd know Andy, so I didn't want to take the chance. By ten thirty that evening, I had had enough partying and went back to Andy's apartment and got out of drag and went home, exhausted. Andy rejoined his mom and Philip and stayed out until they closed the streets at midnight.

Andy's mother stayed on for a few more days after her boyfriend returned to Los Angeles, so he got to spend some quality time with her. She even visited the salon and had her hair done.

When I mentioned to Mother that Andy's mom was in town for Mardi Gras, she insisted I invite her over. Andy briefed his mother not to mention that we were gay.

I was more than a little nervous about their meeting. The two women couldn't be more different. Picture my mother as Melanie from *Gone with the Wind* and Andy's mom as Belle, who ran the whorehouse. My mother was deeply religious and simply dressed with brown, mousy hair and no makeup to speak of. Andy's mom had dyed red hair, a full face of makeup, and a bright dress. But despite the difference in their appearances, both had big hearts and loved their children. They chatted for hours over tea. Mother even repaired Alicia's dress, which she had torn on the way over. It was a lovely visit.

Before leaving town, Andy's mother said how happy she was for the both of us and what a wonderful time she had had during her visit. She loved the French Quarter and thanked me for showing her around. She invited me to visit them in Los Angeles anytime.

Twenty-Three

Andy and I had been together almost a year. It was the longest relationship I had ever had at that point. We started having several friends in common outside my gay group at the bars. One girl in particular was named Tina. She had a one-room furnished apartment in the same building as Andy. She was seventeen and very beautiful, with long dark hair and fine features. She never wore makeup; she didn't need it. Her eyes were big and expressive; her lips were full and naturally deep rose. Tina was very warm and friendly and full of life.

We didn't know much about her past or her family life. I could tell she wasn't from Louisiana from the way she spoke, but that was about it. She didn't have a boyfriend, nor did she mention anyone special. She picked up odd jobs waitressing in the Quarter. We often hung out together in the Bourbon House or one or the other's apartment, having a bite, telling stories, listening to music, or laughing over silly things. Andy and Tina became inseparable.

As time went on and I got to know her better, I noticed a certain sadness beneath her happy-go-lucky persona. She often got into black moods, and Andy was the only one who could coax her out of them. One night, Andy called and asked me to meet him at Tina's place as soon as possible. He didn't give me a clue as to what it was about. I'd never heard Andy so upset, so I rushed over.

I arrived within a half hour and knocked on her door. Andy answered with a scared look on his face. Looking in, I had the shock of my life. There, huddled up in the corner, was Tina in her underwear, head shaved and clumps of her rich, dark hair covering the floor around her. She looked so tiny, so very sad. She wasn't talking. We finally got her to sit in a chair. She was frightened, shaking, with tears running down her cheeks.

Andy put his arm around her. "Tina, honey, what's wrong? Why did you shave off your beautiful hair?"

She looked down at the floor and didn't respond. I tried to take the lighter side and said, "I guess you were tired of all that long hair." She just stared at me. Then I thought it best not to pursue it any further.

Andy and I looked at each other as if to say, "What should we do?" This beautiful creature, our friend, had deep problems. We had never seen her like this before. We suggested going out for a drink and talking it over, but she wasn't up for it. Seeing that there wasn't anything I could do, I returned home, but Andy stayed with her through the night.

The next day, I called Andy. He said Tina was feeling better. He said it had taken several hours for her to calm down, but with a little encouragement, she had opened up and revealed her feelings. She said she was confused as to where she belonged, what she was doing, why she was even alive. She was seventeen, living alone in a one-room apartment, barely surviving. Her life was a mess. I felt so sad for her.

I waited another day before seeing Tina. She seemed better but still sad. Even with her shaved head, she was beautiful. When we went out, people stared, but it did not bother her. She didn't care what people thought. Andy and I kept an eye on her for any further signs of depression.

A few weeks passed. Tina seemed to be her full-of-life self again. She let her hair grow out a little and started dressing for her short-haired look, even wearing earrings. Tina, Andy, and I started going out dancing again on the weekends, usually ending the evening in the Bourbon House having a late snack. Tina never spoke about that night again, nor did we. But I sensed that beneath Tina's laughter and playfulness, there were more troubles ahead for her.

One weekend, I was just about to leave to meet Andy and Tina at the Bourbon House when I got a hysterical call from Andy. He was crying.

"Andy, calm down. What happened?"

He paused, trying to catch his breath. "It's Tina. She's...gone."

Between sobs, he told me that he had just returned home from work and decided to check in on Tina. He knocked on her door, but there was no answer. He went to his room and called her on the phone. Still no answer. He knew her routine and found it odd she wouldn't be in at that hour, especially since we had plans to get together that evening. He waited for an hour and called. Still no answer. He became concerned and went to the building super to open her apartment. He found Tina lying on the bed with her eyes closed. Andy touched her body to wake her up, but she was cold and lifeless. There was a glass of water and an empty pill bottle near her bed. She had committed suicide.

I gasped. "I'm coming right over!"

Andy ran to me when I arrived, and we embraced. Crying, he kept repeating, "It's all my fault. It's all my fault. I should have seen the signs."

I put my arm around him. "It's not your fault. You are her best friend. You tried to help. We both did. She was fighting her own demons, and this time they won."

Neither one of us knew where she had gotten the pills. She had been more troubled than we had thought. All I could think about was that now she had found peace. We called the police. They asked us all kinds of questions, especially about Tina's background. We couldn't answer them because we just didn't know anything about her family or where she originally came from. Later, we found out they did an autopsy, and it confirmed she had died of a drug overdose. With no family to claim the body, she was turned over to the state and buried in a common cemetery for the poor outside of the city.

Andy took Tina's death very hard, blaming himself for not being aware of how fragile she really was. She had been my friend, and I missed her. But mostly I was worried about Andy. It was the first time that we'd experienced this kind of tragedy, the loss of a friend our age. After a couple of weeks, Andy and I got together with other people who knew Tina to celebrate her life. We toasted her and reminisced about the good times. It helped us both heal.

Andy hadn't spent any time with my family since Tina's death, so I encouraged him to visit us as often as he could. I knew my family missed him, and it would help cheer him up to spend time with them.

My mother was particularly happy, as he started to do her hair again. Usually, the hair session started after supper. I would shampoo Mom's hair in the kitchen sink. I watched carefully how Andy put the rollers in and made pin curls. I think the style was called "the Italian boy" at the time. Mother was in her glory and talked through the whole process.

At that time we didn't have a hair dryer to dry Mother's hair. Sleeping on the hair to set it and then combing it out the next day was one option. But she didn't want to wait that long, so she would hold her head near the exhaust end of the vacuum cleaner, letting the warm air dry her hair. It was a bit uncomfortable, but anything for beauty, right? When it was dry, Andy would comb it out. He always made it look beautiful, which always put a big smile on Mom's face.

These times with my family helped Andy heal after Tina's death and brought us closer.

Twenty-Four

Andy made friends easily and often because of his dynamic personality and good looks. I was proud of Andy's gregarious nature and loved to meet his friends. Except for one. His name was Almo. He was an older gay man, probably in his seventies, which, of course, seemed ancient to me. He and his lover of many years owned an exclusive antique shop on Royal Street in the French Quarter. I didn't know how they met, but Almo had taken a liking to Andy.

Every now and then, Andy stopped and visited with Almo at his shop. He always told me of his visits, how charming and generous Almo was. He even showed me some gifts he had given him. I had to admit that it was the first time I was truly jealous. One night, Almo invited him to dine at the Columns, a posh restaurant in the Garden District. I was busy studying or something, so Andy accepted. The next day, Andy told me that nothing had happened. I trusted Andy, but I didn't trust that old queen.

Andy could tell I was not happy about it, so he took me to meet Almo at his shop. I was a bit surprised to see how unattractive he was. He had a huge potbelly and was losing what little hair he had. I felt silly to feel jealous of him. I apologized to Andy afterward.

We met so many talented people in the Quarter. Joey and Herbie were a longtime couple who owned a florist shop in the French Quarter. We met at one of the many parties Andy and I attended, and we became good friends. They made exquisite floral arrangements.

In the Catholic religion, May was the month dedicated to Mary, the mother of Jesus. My mother, being very devout, offered special prayers every day to the Virgin Mary. Mother had a large statue of Mary prominently placed in our backyard, facing the alleyway for all passersby to see. My mother always wanted to participate in the tradition of placing a wreath of fresh flowers on the head of the statue, but we were too poor to afford one. Instead, she had bought a tacky wreath of fake flowers and used it each year.

I loved my mother and always tried to find little ways to make her happy. Besides, I couldn't stand that old dusty wreath she used on her beloved statue. So I contacted Joey and Herbie to arrange to have a fresh wreath of flowers delivered to my mother each day during the month of May.

On May Day, the lovely flowers arrived, and Mother was overjoyed. We all had to attend a special prayer ceremony to lay the wreath on the head of the statue. Then, every afternoon that month before my father went to work, Mother had a ceremony and proudly placed a fresh wreath of flowers on the statue of Mary. Of course, all the family had to attend. Mother was pleased and felt proud to honor the Virgin Mary in such a way.

She wanted to go to my friends' florist shop to thank them for the beautiful gift personally, but I talked her out of it and said a phone call would suffice. I didn't want Mother to meet my florist friends because they were screaming queens. Mother probably would not have noticed how effeminate they were, but I didn't want to take any chances.

Twenty-Five

I thought that day would never come, but at long last, it was graduation day. I had worked so hard to pass all my classes and was relieved to be finished with grammar school. The graduation ceremonies took place in the school auditorium. My whole family was there, along with Andy. Everyone in class received a diploma plus a piece of paper in the shape of a scroll with a short saying about his or her character. I don't know who was responsible for writing these little sayings, but whoever it was didn't mark in my case. It read, "A movie hero to make all the girls swoon. He's Milton, if only he could croon." If only they knew the truth. But I didn't care. I was just happy to graduate at last to escape those horrible nuns.

Andy celebrated my graduation with me and my family back home with a huge cake. Later on we continued celebrating in the Quarter with friends.

I applied to Saint Aloysius, a strict, all-male Catholic high school, located near home on Rampart Street and Esplanade Avenue. It was run by the Brothers of the Sacred Heart. It had a great reputation. I visited there once for some kind of class function. The thing that impressed me most was the brothers' clothes. They wore long black vestments over their pants and white shirts. They looked like priests without the white collar. I loved the way their robes swished when they walked, and they still looked masculine—except for one brother who gave it quite a turn.

While I knew I wasn't academically prepared for this school, I promised to do everything I could to succeed if I was accepted. I wanted to make my parents proud of me. I didn't think I had much of a chance of getting in, given my grades. However, several weeks later, I received news that I had been accepted. My family was so happy to hear the news, but I was terribly frightened by the sheer prospect of the amount of work it would be. But I decided to deal with it in the fall and just enjoy the summer and start saving for tuition.

One weeknight after his usual visit with the family, I told Andy I was going to sneak out of the house and meet him at his place after one in the morning. We hadn't had sex for a few days, and I just couldn't wait until the weekend. At first he was not in favor of the idea. He didn't want me to get in trouble with my folks. The police picked up kids roaming the streets at night and reported them to their families. But I convinced him I had a plan.

I knew my father returned home from work regularly at one in the morning. The kitchen light was left on until he got in. My bedroom was next to the kitchen, so I often heard him rummaging around before he turned off the light and went to bed. All I had to do was to wake myself up and leave from the back door a few minutes after he had closed his bedroom door. I shared a room with my brother Glenn, but he slept like a rock, and nothing ever woke him up. I'd be back before everyone in the house woke up around seven o'clock. Andy thought I was crazy, but he knew he couldn't convince me against it. I said I'd see him later.

That very same night, I put my plan into action. I was so excited that I didn't sleep. At one o'clock, I heard my father get in. After a few minutes, he turned off the light and went to bed. My brother always slept on the other side of the bed with his back to me. I got dressed quietly in the dark, unlocked the back door, and proceeded up the alleyway toward the street. I was careful not to make any noise while passing my family's bedrooms. The night was so still, I could hear my own breathing. I lifted the latch very slowly on our chain link gate, trying not to make a sound. So far, so good, I thought.

Andy's apartment was nearby in a quiet section of the Quarter, only a ten-minute walk. The streets were quiet except for an occasional car.

No cops in sight. I arrived at his place out of breath and very excited. He couldn't believe his eyes, that I was actually there and had done such a crazy thing. I undressed and jumped into bed with him for some late-night loving. As he wrapped his arms around me, I told him to wake me at dawn so I could be home before the house woke up. He set his alarm clock.

It was barely light outside when Andy's alarm clock went off. He nudged me to wake up, saying it was time for me to leave. The feeling of waking up and seeing his beautiful smile sent chills through my body. After some more quick love, I was out the door and on my way home. As I walked, I felt the early-morning mist on my face, the stillness in the air, and that beautiful calmness that falls before the rising sun.

In no time I was home, tiptoeing down the alley. I listened for any noise but only heard the early-morning crickets and a loud racket coming from our large window fan. I opened the back door. All was quiet. Everyone seemed to be asleep. I tiptoed to my room, slipped out of my clothes and into my pajamas, and rolled into bed without waking my brother. Before drifting off to sleep, I relived the whole night; it put a big smile on my face.

It was around seven when I heard my dad in the kitchen getting the morning started. Of course, I was curious if he knew I had been out during the night. Part of me wanted to know immediately, but then the other part thought, "What the hell; I'll face the music later." By the time I got out of bed, the rest of the house was up and having breakfast. Everyone acted normal, and there wasn't any mention of my having been out. Success! I had pulled it off.

When I saw Andy that Friday night, the first thing he said was how wonderful it had been to have me next to him while we slept, even if it was only for a few hours, but he was concerned for my safety. I told him that being with him was worth the risk.

That night of sneaking out became the first of many that summer. It was wild and exciting. Sometimes I would meet him in one of the bars, but mostly at his apartment. As long as I was with him, it didn't matter.

So far, no one in the house seemed to suspect or notice my leaving or returning. Of course, this lack of sleep started to get to me every so often, so after my paper route, I took naps. At sixteen, I bounced back quickly.

Before one of our late-night trysts, Andy reminded me to bring an alarm clock, as his was broken. I agreed. But that night, as I tiptoed down the alleyway, the clock fell out of my hands onto the pavement directly below my parents' bedroom window, making a loud noise. My heart stood still. I listened for several minutes for any sound but heard none. The rumble of the window fan had masked the noise, I thought. I lifted the gate latch ever so slowly and walked out.

At Andy's apartment, just before we fell asleep, I tried to wind the clock. It wouldn't work. I discovered it had broken when it fell. I was concerned about waking up without an alarm clock, but Andy assured me that he'd make sure I'd wake up in time.

Fortunately, I did wake up in time, but when I arrived home, the back door was locked. I knew I was in trouble. I knocked gently on my sister Bonnie's bedroom window, trying to get her attention. She opened the window and said that Mom and Dad knew I was out. She said the whole house had awoken around three in the morning because Glenn had a bad dream and started yelling. When they went into our room, they saw my side of the bed was empty. My parents locked the back door. I would have to ring the front door bell to get in, and they would confront me. Their plan didn't work. I scrambled through her window and went to bed.

Later that morning, while fast asleep, I felt my mother shaking me and yelling at the top of her voice for me to wake up. I was still half asleep and struggling to sit up when she shouted, "Where were you last night, Milton?"

Mother must really be angry, I thought in my sleepy stupor. It normally took her twenty to thirty minutes to say her morning prayers in front of a mantel filled with twenty-five statues of Jesus, Mary, and Joseph before she had breakfast. She had interrupted her ritual to yell at me.

"I was at a slumber party...with my friends," I mumbled, not yet thinking clearly.

She glared at me. "What friends?"

I didn't respond.

"Don't you lie to me, son. Boys don't have slumber parties!"

At that very moment, I realized she knew I was gay. I was speechless, not knowing what to say. She just continued to glare down at me, and then, without saying another word, she stormed out of my room. I was crushed. I don't remember what happened next. I just got dressed and left the house in tears. I passed my dad, who was busy in the kitchen, but he didn't say anything.

I got on my bike and rode to Andy's place, crying all the way. I had known that someday I would have to tell my parents about my sexuality, but I had certainly hoped it would be when I was older, and not under these circumstances. When I got to Andy's, I fell into his arms sobbing and told him what had happened. I said that my secret was no longer a secret, that my parents knew I was gay, and that I was afraid of what might happen next.

He comforted me and told me not to worry. "I'll go to their house and have a talk with them. It'll be fine."

"What are you going to say?"

"Trust me," he said, smiling in that cute, confident way he had. "I'll do your mother's hair, and we'll chat. We'll see what happens."

I delivered papers that afternoon and then went back to Andy's. When he got back, I could see from his expression that his conversation with my parents had not gone well. He said he didn't want to come out and say we were gay. Instead he explained that I had been out with him in the Quarter, and, because of the hour, I stayed at his place and then returned home at first light. Mother was in shock and remained silent. My father didn't say a word. Andy offered to stay and do Mother's hair, but she didn't accept his offer. A first for her. At that point, he said, he felt rather awkward and left.

I told him that he was very brave to face my parents because legally they could have him prosecuted for corrupting a minor. Knowing my parents, I was sure they would never do such a thing. Besides, I think they seriously liked him and wouldn't do anything to cause him problems. They just felt betrayed. Andy decided that it was best he didn't come to the house unless he was invited, and I agreed.

I didn't return home until after dinner that evening. I took a deep breath and walked into the house. Mother was sitting in the kitchen. She looked at me and then away, giving me the silent treatment. I decided to lie down in my room and collect my thoughts.

After a couple of hours, I got up and had a bath and dressed, all the while thinking of what to say, how to act with my mother. Her silence was deafening. I knew she was hurting, but so was I. I thought the best thing for me was to go out for a while, and besides, I was anxious to see Andy. Once I was with Andy, I started to feel better, although I didn't stay out late.

My parents weren't the kind of people to confront an issue head on. If there was a problem, they would just not talk about it—at least not in front of the children—and hope it would simply go away. I think that deep down, my mother had known I was gay for years, but it took this event for her to face the fact.

I found out years later that my father had known I was gay well before this episode but had not shared it with Mother. He told me about opening a letter from New York City intended for me. He didn't say, but I was sure it was from Jerry, the hot guy I had met while visiting New York. When I gave him my address to keep in touch, I didn't think about the fact that my father and I shared the same name. Seeing a letter addressed to Milton Buras, my father had opened it thinking it was for him. When he read the contents, which probably were rather steamy, he threw it away without mentioning it to me or to my mother.

My life at home became strained after that. My mother gave me her usual silent treatment. My dad made small talk, but nothing more. I tried to get them to talk, but they refused to sit down and discuss the matter. I didn't know what to do. I hoped they would understand in time.

Andy and I didn't see each other for a while. I was an emotional mess, and I missed him desperately.

Twenty-Six

After a few weeks, my parents informed me that they had spoken to our family doctor, and he suggested that they take me to a psychiatrist for help.

Help? With what? I thought. I wasn't crazy. I just liked men. I wondered what kind of help they could give me with my sexual desires. After all, it was not like fixing a broken leg or something. It was just their way of avoiding the issue and hoping the doctor would "fix it." Since I was a minor, I had no choice but to accept the situation. If all that came out of it was a better understanding between my parents and me, I was for it. Of course, my parents, feeling the shame and embarrassment brought upon the family, kept my doctor visits secret.

Not knowing who else to turn to, I told Andy about it. Andy consoled me. "You're doing the right thing. Maybe when it's over, your parents will accept you." I hoped he was right.

My first appointment with the psychiatrist was boring—except for the fact that he was an older man and I found him attractive. All I did was lie down on a couch and talk while he took notes. *Does he really get paid for this?* I said to myself. I thought it would be more interesting if he were lying *next* to me on the couch, but I guessed that would defeat the purpose.

Before I knew it, my time was up, and the doctor said, "See you next week."

"That's funny," I responded. "That's how Loretta Young ends her show every week."

Loretta Young was a very beautiful actress who had a weekly TV show in the fifties. At the beginning of each show, she would enter through a door in a way no other star could, each time in a fabulous dress, and greet the audience. At the end of the show, she would show her gorgeous smile and say, "See you next week." I loved that show.

The doctor was not amused.

I met up with Andy at the Bourbon shortly after my first appointment.

"Well, how'd it go?"

"It was a boring ton of bullshit. All that happened was, I talked, he listened, and then he said my time was up." I told him about the Loretta Young comment, and he laughed.

"I just don't get it. I'm telling stories and answering questions. I'm doing all the work, and he's getting paid to listen."

My next visit turned out to be a little different. The questions got to the point right away. He asked me, "How do you feel about girls?"

"I like girls. I have several girlfriends, and we have fun together."

"No. How do you really feel about girls?"

"What do you mean? Do I get excited when they look great in an outfit? Yes, I love fashion."

"That's not exactly what I meant."

"Oh, do you mean 'Does my dick get hard and I want to bang them?'"

"Something like that." He wrote something on his pad.

"I only get hard when I see a hot-looking guy and want to bang him."

More notes.

"Have you ever had a sexual experience with a girl?"

"No. I came close, though, when I was thirteen." I told him about Gwen and how she had scared the shit out of me and then accused me of getting fresh with her.

More notes.

"In fact," I continued, "it was right after that when I had my first experience with a man."

More notes. Then he said, "Time's up. See you next week."

My third visit was my last. I had become increasingly annoyed with the whole process and was anxious to get to the heart of the matter. After settling down on the couch, I said, "What kind of help do you think I need?"

He was rather surprised at the bluntness of my question and stumbled with an answer, saying, "I think you reached the age of puberty very young and became confused with your sexual orientation."

"Ever since I was a young boy, I've been attracted to men, not women. I just didn't know what that meant until I had my first sexual experience with a man."

Notes.

"Your parents are worried that you lead a normal life."

"I know, and I love them for it. But I know who I am. I like men. It feels normal to me."

The doctor seemed surprised at that but made no comment; he just wrote more notes on his pad. "What do you mean by 'normal'? Most young men are attracted to women, not men."

I tried to answer the best I could, but he wasn't having any of it.

Then he looked at his watch and announced, "Time's up. See you next week."

"I don't think so. But thanks anyway."

I was done. I hoped that the doctor would convey to my parents that I was comfortable with who I was and that there was no need for further visits.

My parents never asked or spoke about my visits with the psychiatrist. Regardless of what the doctor told them, I truly felt that they would accept me, but it would take time.

Twenty-Seven

My relationship with Andy came to a standstill. He no longer came to the house, and our time together became more and more limited. It had been so much easier when I was in the closet with my family and he was welcome in our home. It was a sad situation because we loved each other, but the obstacles seemed insurmountable. Now that my family knew my sexuality, my being a minor put Andy in a dangerous legal position. I didn't want him to get into trouble. We talked it over for a long time. Eventually, Andy decided it would be best for him to leave New Orleans and move back home to Los Angeles. The mere thought of his leaving broke my heart, but he assured me that we would stay in touch and that we would continue to see each other.

In August, I helped him pack for his trip back. It was a tearful time for us both. As he got into his car and was about to leave, he gave me a letter. "Open this after I'm gone." We hugged; he got into his car and drove away.

I opened the letter and read it.

Our love is closing now and no more our hearts will meet.
For the time is hear when we must say goodby.
We have shared a love no others have shared.
Dont look back my love for all you see is crystal
tears and a broken heart.
Look on to the future for life is full and our
hearts are young. The time will come when we'll
meet again and then your heart will feel no pain.
Your eyes will gleam and sparkle like stars at
night.
So once again I'll say goodby, be sweet my love
and have no tears no sighs no cry's, but just
a heart of beautiful memories. For love
is eternal and our love is eternal, forever & ever & ever.

Andy

I stood there in the Quarter like Humphrey Bogart at the Paris train station in *Casablanca* after reading Ingrid Bergman's farewell letter. Only my tears of sadness didn't make me bitter. His words, so beautifully written, gave me the strength and encouragement to continue on.

Over the next year, every now and then we contacted each other, mostly by mail, and we caught up on what we were doing and how much we missed each other. He also wanted to know how my parents were dealing with the fact that I was gay, to which I was happy to reply that they were more understanding. He was my first love, and I'll always remember our times together fondly.

Twenty-Eight

On my first day at Saint Aloysius high, I was nervous about starting high school. The school itself was intimidating, a tall, three-story red brick building with a large front yard and a four-and-a-half-foot brick wall around it. Thank God there were no nuns to deal with. The brothers seemed much nicer, at least at first.

The only person I knew was Guy, a classmate from grammar school who was accepted by Saint Aloysius as well. We lived a block from each other, which would make it easy for us to study together. I was terrified that first day as I stood in the yard with a few hundred other students, but I dared not show it. At least I had Guy to hang with. The bell rang. We were told to line up into our assigned groups, and then we were ushered into our classes.

As I had expected, the challenges of the new classes weighed on me heavily. With school and my paper route, I had no time to go out on weeknights in the Quarter. Without Andy, I really didn't want to anyway. But I went to the Quarter, only on weekends, and hooked up with some of my friends and the occasional trick. My mother didn't question me too closely anymore about my nights out. I'm sure she just didn't want to know.

For the past few years, I had been hearing about this gay guy, in his midthirties, named Herman. He gave the most fabulous invitation-only parties at his house on Esplanade Avenue. The Esplanade was one of the most elegant streets in town, lined with big, historic homes. Tom, a friend of mine at Dixie's, invited me to go to one of Herman's famous parties as his date. There was nothing sexual between us. Tom was in his early twenties and good looking, a tall, slender guy. He worked as an assistant manager at the Orleans Inn in the Quarter. Tom did not know Herman personally, but the circle of friends he traveled in did, and they were able to arrange an invitation. Tom told me that Herman, not very attractive himself, had a reputation of surrounding himself with attractive men. I had no idea what kind of party it was—only that it was the in place to be.

The party started at seven on Saturday night, and to cover myself, I told my mother I was going to a dance with a schoolmate and would probably be out late and most likely stay at his house afterward. I had used this excuse before, and she didn't question me about it. She just nodded and told me to be careful.

I met up with Tom so we could arrive at the party together. I wore light-brown dress slacks and a brand-new pale-pink long-sleeve shirt. I was going to wear a tie and jacket, but Tom said that might be too formal. The house was set back from the street with a wrought-iron fence around it. It was painted white with a wraparound porch and tall French windows.

The party looked as if it was in full swing as we passed through the gates. Most of the party was in the parlor. There were dozens of gorgeous men drinking, smoking, and dancing.

As soon as we walked into the parlor, Herman came running over and greeted us. "Hi, I'm Herman. Welcome to the party." He was rather short, balding, and a bit heavy around the middle. His white linen shirt strained at each of its pearl buttons. The colorful bow tie he wore looked to be silk. From the way he looked me up and down, I could tell I was his type, but he was definitely not mine. "Get a drink, and we'll talk later." And off he flitted to play host.

"Wait here," Tom said. "I'll get us a drink." By the time he returned, I was happily flirting with two guys I didn't know. Tom arrived and handed me the drink. "Looks like you're doing fine. I'll catch up with you later." He disappeared into the crowd.

I wasn't much of a drinker, but that night I always seemed to have a fresh drink in my hand brought to me by someone who wanted to spend time with me. Before long, I had been introduced to practically everyone at the party and was quite drunk.

I remember dancing, not with one guy but several at one time. Every now and then, I would stop, have another drink, and continue dancing. I don't remember how long this went on, but I recall that at some point I was sitting on a sofa with a couple of guys. We started making out. Each direction I turned, I bumped into another set of hot lips. The last thing I remember was my shirt coming off.

I woke up several hours later lying on the sofa with one of the guys next to me passed out. Neither one of us had clothes on. In fact, the whole room was piled with naked bodies. It was nearly dawn, and I had no idea what had happened. I looked around for Tom but couldn't find him among the passed-out bodies.

I looked at the time and became frantic I'd miss my Sunday paper pickup. I searched for my clothes and got the hell out of there before anyone woke up. From the looks of it, these people wouldn't stir for hours. Now I knew what made Herman's parties so popular.

I rushed home, changed, got my bike, and just made it to the station in time.

Later that day, as I was walking through the Quarter, I ran into a couple of friends. "We heard you went to Herman's party," one of them said.

"Yes, it was a great party."

"We heard you *were* the party!"

I blushed. Gossip traveled fast in gay circles.

It took a long time for me to live down my experience at Herman's party. The way people talked about it, I was the belle of the ball—or "balls," as the case may be. I wished I could have remembered what really happened. From all the accounts, it must have been fun. But since I couldn't remember, I decided just to accept the stories and even embellish them a little.

Twenty-Nine

As my social circle expanded, I met a wide variety of people. I was a young, hot kid looking for new experiences, so I just went along, perhaps a bit recklessly at times. Sam was a nineteen-year-old I met in Tony Bacino's through some of the drag queens. All I knew about him was that he had sandy-blond hair and a nice build, and he chain-smoked cigarettes. We had a few beers and laughed a lot in the bar. We didn't hook up sexually. One night he told me he was going to Baton Rouge the next day and asked if I wanted to tag along. It was a short ride from New Orleans; he said we'd do it the same day, so I agreed. He told me to meet him later that day on the corner of Burgundy and St. Ann.

When I arrived, Sam was waiting for me in a Ford sedan. Another guy, named Don, was sitting next to him.

"Nice car," I said. "Is it yours?" I asked Sam.

"I just got it today."

I slid into the backseat, and we headed for the highway. No sooner were we out of the city limits when we were stopped by a state trooper.

"Why are they stopping us?"

"I don't know," he replied nonchalantly.

I was nervous. I told Sam I had a forged draft card in my wallet, and if I was searched and it was found, I would be in a lot of trouble.

"They probably won't check, but just in case, you'd better hide it."

I quickly took the card out of my wallet and hid it in my sock, thinking it would be a safe place.

The state trooper walked up to Sam's window and asked for his driver's license and registration. Sam hesitated and then said he had forgotten it at home. The three of us were then told to get out of the car and line up on the side of the road with our hands above our heads. Sam was first in line, and Don, and then me. I felt like a criminal, lined up in full view on the highway, but had no idea the worst was yet to come.

A second trooper appeared with a piece of paper in his hand and said something to his partner. The first trooper stood in front of us and said, "This car was reported stolen. Looks like you boys got caught."

When I heard this, my heart sank. What a dumb shit Sam was to have done such a stupid thing. I was even dumber for trusting him.

Then the troopers started to pat down Sam and Don from top to bottom and checking their IDs. After seeing that, I started to tremble for fear they would find my fake card in my sock. I reached down, pretending to scratch my ankle, to retrieve my card and throw it under the car, but one of troopers saw me do it. He walked over and bent under the car to retrieve the card.

"And what do we have here?"

"My ID, sir."

"What's your age?"

"Eighteen, sir."

He looked at the card, then at me, and then at the card again. I knew he suspected something by the way he looked at me. He walked over to his partner and showed him the card. The two of them came back to me.

"Now, son, why don't you tell us your real age," one of the troopers said. "This card here is a fake."

I felt trapped. I didn't know what do and just mumbled, "I'm sixteen, sir."

"Boy, you're in a lot of trouble. Forging a draft card is a federal crime." He told me to turn around and keep my hands up as he patted me down. Then he handcuffed me while Sam and Don just stood there watching.

Instead of Sam getting handcuffed for stealing the car, which initially was the reason for our being stopped, he and Don were told to wait in the backseat of the stolen car until the New Orleans police arrived. I was escorted to the police car.

"What about him?" I said a little too forcefully. "He stole the car."

"Shut up and get in the car!"

I waited in the patrol car until the New Orleans police arrived to pick up the stolen car and the two other guys. As I sat with hands behind my back, facing the metal partition, a thousand things ran through my head, the first being *How will I explain this to my parents?* I became frightened as I stared hopelessly through the metal grill, wondering what was going to happen. After the police left, the state troopers returned to the patrol car and drove me back to New Orleans.

When we arrived in New Orleans, I was taken to the local police station at Rampart and Conti Streets, directly across from the Quarter. This station was familiar to me because I would often pass it on the way to church on Sundays. I had never imagined I would be taken there under arrest. The inside of the station was drab, with walls and molding painted a pale, putrid green. It was one large room with two small desks with chairs to the left of the entrance. To the right was one long desk three feet above the floor and two benches across from it. There were policemen and other characters milling about.

I was told to sit down on a bench and wait until I was called. One of the state troopers walked over to an officer sitting behind a desk and started chatting. The wait seemed interminable, but finally I was called to the front desk, accompanied by another officer. I was told to state my name, age, address, and phone number.

I complied.

"Where did you get that draft card, son?"

I looked down at my shoes and said, "I don't remember, sir."

I hoped this was going to be fast, like getting a slap on the wrist and a notice of when to appear again, but I was dead wrong. It was the complete opposite.

"Son, you are under arrest for possession of a forged federal document. You'll be held in jail until the federal investigators arrive."

"What happens when they arrive?" I said, trembling.

"That depends on your answers."

The officer grabbed me by the arm and led me to a back room, where I was released from my handcuffs. He told me to empty my pockets and put the contents on the beat-up table next to me. Then he proceeded to pat me down. The officer gathered my personal things and put them in an envelope and gave me a dirty heavy wool blanket that smelled of urine. I almost gagged at the thought of using it. I was too afraid to ask if there were any in cotton. The officer walked me though a couple of hallways, passing occupied jail cells, and stopped at the very last one, which was empty, and unlocked the metal door.

It was small and rather bleak, with two cots, one on top of the other, a toilet without a seat, and no windows.

"Get in."

After the cell door closed and locked, the officer walked away. I stood in total silence, only a brick wall to look at. I felt so alone. I wondered if they had notified my parents.

After several hours, I heard footsteps coming down the hall. I got excited and hoped I was getting out. But instead, it was the same officer with a young guy in a sailor suit. The officer opened the cell door and said, "Here's your roommate!"

In walked this cute guy. He was a five-foot-ten, blond, blue-eyed beauty. I thought, "Things are looking up." If I had to share a cell, this guy didn't seem so bad. At least I wouldn't be alone.

At first, he just sat down and didn't say much. But I decided to make the best of it and asked him his name.

"Peter."

"Where you from?"

"Mississippi. I was hitchhiking, trying to get back home, when I was stopped by the police."

"Is hitchhiking against the law?" I asked.

"No, but after they checked my ID, they discovered I hadn't reported back to the base for duty, and they arrested me."

"Does that mean you're AWOL?"

He nodded. "I'm being held in this jail until the MPs come get me. What about you?"

"My friend stole a car. They stopped us on the road, and they found my fake draft card ID."

He looked surprised. "You ain't eighteen? You look it."

"Nope. I'm really sixteen."

He shook his head. "It looks like we're both in a shitload of trouble."

We talked for a while. I couldn't help staring into his big blue eyes. And he didn't seem to mind it.

We heard noise coming from the hall. It turned out to be a guard bringing sandwiches and water to all the jail cells. I figured it must be around six in the evening but couldn't tell for sure because there was no clock. The guard dropped off our food. Some kind of cheese on stale white bread. Neither of us could eat it.

Not long afterward, the guard came to collect the trays, and then someone down the hall yelled, "Lights out!" Just before the lights went out, a guard came around checking the cells. I took the bottom bunk. Peter got the top one. When the lights finally went out, it was so dark all I could see was a dim glow coming from down the hall.

I waited until I didn't hear any noise and then whispered to Peter, "If you're not comfortable up there, come down and bunk with me."

No sooner was the invitation out of my mouth than he was climbing down just in his shorts. By the time he hit the bed, he had a full erection and my full attention. I took off my clothes. We carried on for hours, trying to make as little noise as possible. I got carried away a couple of times and hit my head on the top bunk. Finally, we both climaxed and fell on each other, all sweaty.

"So, is this what jail is like?" I whispered.

"I don't know. It's my first time."

"Why'd you go AWOL?"

"I got drafted when I was eighteen. I hate the navy. All the guys would make fun of me because I didn't fuck women. And some of them tried to fuck me. I had to get out." We lay together for a while. Finally, Peter climbed up to his bunk, and I fell asleep.

I was awakened with a flash of lights and a guard yelling, "Everybody up!" A guard came along, checking each cell. He stopped at our cell and ordered Peter to get dressed. "The MPs are waiting on you," he said.

I couldn't help notice how hot he looked in his uniform. As he left, I wished him luck. He gave me a look full of worry and said, "You too."

Then the entire row of cell doors opened, and we were told to fall in line. They herded us into one large cell room called "the bull ring." There were all sorts of characters, some mean looking and others not so. Of course, I was the youngest. I walked around the room, keeping to myself, afraid to talk to anyone. I hoped it would be over soon. For breakfast, we were given doughnuts and coffee or a small carton of milk.

After a couple of hours, I was pulled out and brought to a dimly lit room with three chairs, one facing the other two. There was a bright light shining directly on the single chair. I was told to sit in that chair. Then two men dressed in dark suits carrying pads and pens came in and sat down without saying hello. At that point I started to tremble.

"Do you know why you're here, son?"

"Yes, sir."

"Do you know you can go to jail for forging a federal document?"

"No, sir."

"Did you forge the card?"

"No, sir. I did not."

"Where did you get it, then?"

"It was a while ago. I really can't remember."

This started a whole line of questions. I tried to remain calm, but these guys were getting tougher and tougher. They kept drilling me over and over, asking the same questions. The light shining on me became hot, making me even more nervous.

Finally, I couldn't take it anymore and starting crying.

"Just tell us where you got the card, son. It'll be all over."

"I told you. I can't remember. It was some guy I heard about."

"How'd you hear about it?"

I paused. I felt trapped and didn't know what to do. I rubbed my eyes.

"Some guy named Steve told me. I don't know his last name. I met him in the Quarter."

"Where's Steve live?"

"I think he lives somewhere on Burgundy Street."

I regret to this day that I gave Steve's address because I involved him in something he had nothing to do with. Steve was the first guy I had had sex with. He was a nice, caring guy. I hadn't seen him for years.

"That's all for now."

I was taken back to my cell. I was so angry with myself for getting Steve involved. I wanted desperately to take it all back, but it was too late. I could only hope, if they contacted him, he would just have to answer a few questions and be done with it.

The hours seemed to pass slowly, and it looked as though I would be spending another night in that shit hole. As I lay on that smelly cot thinking of all that had happened, Peter popped into my head, and I wondered about his situation. It made me think about last night and how we had comforted each other.

All of a sudden I heard "Lights out." The guard checked the cells. Then the darkness brought on more loneliness and despair. Eventually I fell asleep.

It wasn't long after breakfast, which consisted this time of a dry roll and cold cup of coffee in the bull ring, that I was taken to that same interrogation room. The same federal agents were already sitting when I entered. They told me that because of my age, I was being released on a five-year probation. If I stayed out of trouble, I'd stay out of jail. I would be appointed a time and day each month to report to a probation officer. If I violated that order, I could be sent to jail. I was told my parents had been called and were on the way.

After an hour or so, I was brought out front to sign release papers and retrieve my belongings. Then I saw my dad. Even though I was relieved to leave that place, I couldn't help feeling that I was jumping out of the frying pan into the fire when I got home. I walked up to my dad and said, "Thanks for coming for me. I'm sorry."

He just nodded and led me out to the car. The whole way home, he didn't say a word. Once we got home, I explained the whole story about the stolen car, the forged draft card, and how frightening it was to be in jail. I told him how sorry I was for the shame I had brought upon our family and myself and that I had learned my lesson. No more fake IDs. I had to learn to choose my friends more carefully also.

After we talked, the whole incident was dropped and never mentioned again, which was the norm in my family. My father wrote a note to the school principal stating that I had been absent three days because of sickness. I was grateful for that. When the notice came about my probation appointments, I was diligent and never missed one.

For weeks after getting out of jail, I remained close to home, concentrated on school, and worked my paper route. It took all that time after getting home for me to build up enough courage to call Steve to explain. When I did, his roommate, Jim, answered and said, "Steve isn't here. He was picked up by federal agents. Something about a fake ID."

I was dumbfounded and just hung up. The tears rushed down my cheeks, and a feeling of tremendous guilt came over me. It was unbearable for me to think I was the person responsible for sending a friend to jail. To this day, I feel the only crime committed was putting an innocent man into prison. Many underage people had fake ID's; it was my misfortune to have gotten caught and pressured to drag him into it.

Months later, I found out through another friend that Steve was tried, convicted, and sent to a prison out of state. He had no idea of where or for how long he would be in prison. I never did see Steve again.

Thirty

In New Orleans, any excuse to dress up in drag became a party, and I got invited to my fair share of them through the drag queens I knew. One party was in Metairie, outside the city limits. It was primarily a drag ball, but I heard that not all the guests were going in drag, which made it more interesting. Through friends, I found a fabulous gown with a skirt so full I couldn't enter a bathroom without help. A friend gave me the name and number of someone who lived in the Quarter who would help with my makeup, since Andy was no longer around. I called and set up a time to meet at his place on Barracks Street a few hours before the party. His name was Earl.

When I arrived, a slim, six-foot sexy guy in his twenties opened the door, and I melted. I kind of got the feeling it was mutual, but he didn't let on.

"Come on in. Good to meet you," he said with a warm smile.

"Nice of you to help me out," I said as I followed him to the kitchen.

He proceeded to do my makeup, but the sparks were flying with every stroke of the eye pencil. It was hard for me to keep still. Earl's roommate, Joey, suddenly appeared. I recognized him immediately. He was part owner of the flower shop that had arranged for the May flowers for my mother. The Quarter was such a small world. I greeted him warmly. We chatted as Earl worked to transform me from a cute boy into a beautiful woman. I thanked Earl and told him I'd call to tell him how I was received at the party, and then I left.

I went to a friend's house to get dressed. Once I was put together and looking fabulous, all I needed was to get through the doorway and into my chariot, which I had arranged ahead of time—a brand-new Cadillac, courtesy of Howard, an older man who had the hots for me. He worked as a top salesman for the largest mortuary in New Orleans. Unfortunately, the only thing flashy about Howard was the brand-new Cadillac he drove. When I showed up in drag, Howard seemed disappointed. I guess he had expected a cute boy, not a glamorous woman. The party was fabulous, and I made quite a splash with all the queens. But I didn't see much of Howard after that.

The next day I called Earl to tell him what a hit I had been at the party, thanks to his wonderful makeover. He was happy to hear that I had been a success and told me to visit anytime, which was exactly what I wanted to hear. I took advantage of his offer and said, "How about this Saturday?"

"That works for me," he said. "See you then."

Saturday couldn't come fast enough.

When I arrived at Earl's house Saturday evening at eight o'clock, wearing jeans and a tight pullover sport shirt, he was alone. After he offered me a drink, we sat down and talked. I found out he was a hairdresser. He worked under the name Damon in the Royal Orleans Hotel Beauty Salon, which catered to the elite. One of his favorite clients was an older woman who was related to the Rothschild family. I told him I was in high school, had a paper route, and wanted to be a hairdresser when I graduated. He was impressed.

"Do you like to dress in drag a lot?"

"Not really," I said. "It's just a fun thing to do at parties."

He looked relieved. "Good. I don't date drag queens."

I stared at him and smiled.

He got up, put his arms around me, and planted a big wet kiss on my lips. Then he started pulling my clothes off, licking and kissing my neck and working his way down. He picked me up and carried me to bed, and we made love. His slim body was firm, with the most beautiful, shapely ass—fit for a Greek statue—and well endowed.

That night started a three-year relationship. Any chance I could, mostly on weekends, I would go to his house, a typical shotgun house in the Quarter with a living room, two bedrooms, and a kitchen in the back. I came directly from my paper route, still in jeans, white T-shirt, and tennis shoes, on my Schwinn bicycle. He liked my James Dean look. I always parked my bike below his front porch while visiting. Friends and neighbors noticed the frequency of this heavy-duty bike with the big basket in front of his house and nicknamed Earl Helen of Schwinn, the Face That Launched a Thousand Bicycles.

Thirty-One

Earl introduced me to two of his friends, Van and Richard. Van worked in television, and Richard was a photography student. They'd been together quite a while and lived in one of the first apartment buildings built in the Quarter, on Dauphine and Esplanade. The building was built of red brick, a new style for New Orleans at the time. It was only three stories high and had its own pool in the patio area. One of the most famous Bourbon Street striptease dancers of the fifties, Blaze Starr, lived across the hall from Van and Richard. She was the mistress of Governor Earl Long. Everyone in the building was friendly. I loved it there.

One Sunday afternoon while Earl and I were sitting with Van and Richard by their pool, Blaze came down and proudly paraded around in the new white terry-cloth bikini bathing suit she had made herself. She looked great until she stepped into the pool and her bikini became so heavy with water, it fell off. She was not embarrassed. After all, she *was* a stripper, and she just laughed it off. We gave her a towel, and she sat with us for hours chatting. A couple of times on my way to visit Van and Richard, I nearly tripped over Governor Long as he waited on the steps for Blaze to come home late at night.

Van, Richard, Earl, and I became close friends.

Tiring of the apartment living, Van and Richard asked Earl to join them and rent a recently restored pre–Civil War house in the Quarter.

The house was all brick, including the floors, with floor-to-ceiling windows and solid shutters. Since the house was built street level, the shutters were kept shut at all times for safety. The entrance to the house was through an alleyway that led into a lush slate patio with a running-water fountain and beautiful vines growing up the adjacent building. There was a twelve-foot wall on each side of the patio.

The main house consisted of one bedroom and bath, which Van and Richard occupied; a large living room; and a kitchen overlooking the patio. Earl's bedroom and bath were in the back of the patio, in what had been "the slave quarters," which was perfect for privacy and close enough to use the main house as his living room and kitchen. I was able to park my bike in the alleyway.

I spent many happy days there.

We'd been together for two years when Earl changed jobs, from the Royal Orleans Beauty Salon to a small salon or "shop" on Bourbon Street catering to the strippers and call girls. I was shocked when Earl decided to leave the chic salon. But he said he was bored with the rich old ladies and wanted to do more varied hairstyles. The strippers and hookers were more fun and certainly kept him busy. He made a lot more money there in tips alone.

His day didn't start until afternoon, which was when all the girls woke up. Miss Rothschild, his elite client from the chic salon, loved his work so much she followed him to this tacky shop. Earl always scheduled her appointment in late morning to make sure her hair was done and she out of there before the strippers arrived. One day, Earl was caught still doing her hair when one of the girls flung open the door and yelled, "Morning, motherfuckers!" Earl immediately put his hands over Miss Rothschild's ears and hurried her through.

All the girls loved Earl. When they did well, he did well. Earl was the only hairdresser around who could put a fake ponytail in their hair and make it stay in place all night. He used wire to attach the ponytail to their hair, making it impossible for it to fall off while they were dancing.

I loved to watch him work at the new shop. I had visited him at the Royal several times, but this place was different. It had a more relaxed yet exciting atmosphere that suited Earl's personality. His technique was unusual. He was incredibly charming and creative. I learned a lot from him.

On weekends, Earl had several of the working girls pop over to his house for a re-comb after they had turned a trick and wanted to start fresh for another. Van and Richard didn't mind the girls being there; in fact, at times it turned into a party. Those girls had some funny stories about their johns and loved to share. I ate it up.

Samantha was a favorite of ours. We all called her Sam. She was a natural blond-haired girl with deep blue eyes, but she dyed her hair jet black. The contrast made her fair skin look flawless and her eyes pop. She loved to shock me with her stories, such as the time she took on an entire professional football team. Ouch. She explained how she manicured her pubic hair into different shapes such as a heart or diamond and made "my batch match my snatch." I asked what that meant. "Honey, you dye the bottom to match the top." That was one of my first lessons in hair coloring.

Thirty-Two

Earl, Van, Richard, and I were in Dixie's bar celebrating my eighteenth birthday when the owner, Dixie, came over. I'd been dodging her ever since I had starting coming to the bar because I was a minor. But tonight was different. I told her I was celebrating my eighteenth birthday. She looked a bit surprised, as she'd been seeing me there with my friends for the past four years.

"Well then, happy birthday, hon," she said with what looked like relief that I was now a legal patron.

We made the rounds of all the bars that night. It was a great feeling to be able to drink without always worrying about being found out.

Right after my eighteenth birthday, I decided not to continue with the fourth year of high school. School had always been a struggle for me, and I didn't see much point in having a high school degree. My parents were not pleased with my decision. However, when I told them my plan to become a hairdresser, they seemed to take it in stride. Hair styling was a trade they understood and one I could make money doing. Besides, they had seen me work on the women in the family for years and knew how much I enjoyed it. I assured them I would finish up my high school education by taking GED night courses at the public high school.

I had saved nearly all my money from the paper route and could afford to pay for beauty school. I registered at a local cosmetology school called Marinello System of Beauty Culture of New Orleans to become a hairdresser. It was the same beauty school where my mother had gone to have her hair done when I was a child. Since I had spent so many hours there, it seemed like the most logical place for me to go.

Marinello was located on Canal and Magazine Streets, a fifteen-minute bus ride from our house. The school was on the second floor. As soon as you walked in, you could smell the chemicals. Each student had to punch in at the time clock near the door. In order to receive your license, you had to complete a thousand hours, which was approximately one year. The room was large, with a two-station setup every ten feet, totaling twenty stations. There was a long line of chairs with hair dryers and shampoo basins at the back. All the students were white girls. I was the only male.

The teacher was some old fuddy-duddy matron type with a hairdo from the forties named Miss Ruby. She might have been old-fashioned, but she was expert at teaching us the basics and kept a keen eye on our progress. After the first two months of schooling, we were allow to do customers with her strict supervision.

My first day was a little tense. As I was the only male student, the girls seemed a bit nervous around me. Most of them probably hadn't met many gay men and didn't know what to think. But having grown up close to my sisters, I was comfortable around girls and was very friendly. After a while, they got used to me.

I was given a station next to a girl named Pat. She had already completed two weeks of the course. Pat and I became good friends, but we mostly kept to ourselves. Pat wore her hair in a beehive, the chic look at the time. Between customers, I often did her hair.

Unlike high school, beauty school was exciting because at last I was fulfilling my dream to learn about hair and how to create hairstyles. Having had the good fortune of having boyfriends who were expert stylists, I already knew how to set and comb out hair, but the basics, such as finger waves and pin curls, were a challenge. I hated doing them, thinking they were for old ladies. But, as I had learned from both Andy and Earl, matrons could be a big part of the customers I'd need to serve, so it was important to master them.

There was a great deal to learn, such as cutting, perms, hair coloring, and how to adjust styles to the shape of the face. But because of my interest and natural talent and the years of watching professionals such as Andy and Earl, I soon became the best student in the class. After the second month, I got to work on my first customer. She was a sweet old lady. I gave her a blue rinse; trimmed her already-permed hair; set her hair in small magnetic pink plastic rollers, new at the time; and placed her under the dryer. After thirty minutes I combed her hair into a beautiful blue bubble, just like all the old ladies were wearing. She was thrilled and gave me a twenty-five cent tip. Miss Ruby came over and gave me an A.

I attended the night class three times a week, as I had promised my parents. It was boring but necessary for me to graduate with a high school diploma. I had never been in a public school and was surprised at how lax it was. No nuns or brothers to crack the academic whip. The room was usually three-quarters full, and the students were not the most motivated. I kept to myself, not feeling the need to meet anyone. My strong background of three years at St. Aloysius gave me the knowledge to finish my test papers before anyone else. I was usually out of there in forty-five minutes. I just wanted to finish and meet up with Earl afterward.

I had almost finished my course at beauty school when the owners of the Royal Orleans Hotel Beauty Salon contacted me. Doug and LaMont were both gay and had been together for over twenty years. They had remained friends with Earl even though he had left their salon. Earl told them that I was nearly finished with beauty school. Of course, they remembered me from the time I had spent watching Earl at the Royal. As it happened, they needed another hairdresser to work in the salon, and Earl recommended me. I went to meet them, and they offered me the job on the spot. They said I could start just as soon as I got my license. I was over the moon at the job offer. Best of all, I could finally quit the paper route.

When I informed Miss Ruby, the school was impressed that I had been offered a position at such a prestigious salon. Since I was their top student and scored mostly As with the customers, they awarded me my diploma and license well ahead of my class so I could start as soon as possible. Pat was happy for me, but the other girls were green with envy.

The Royal Orleans Hotel Beauty Salon was small, with only four styling chairs. Doug and LaMont took three. They had a steady clientele and needed a third hairdresser to take care of walk-ins from the hotel. The salon was very elegant. I had to wear a jacket and tie to work each day. They supplied the tools I needed to work. It seemed like a dream come true.

But the dream soon turned into a nightmare. The customers at the hotel were demanding and in a hurry. From almost the first day, I was in over my head. I didn't have the experience to handle this kind of clientele. I was used to less fussy women who got their cuts almost for free and were grateful for it. Doug and LaMont had to bail me out on more than one occasion.

After working there for a couple of weeks, the owners realized that while I had great potential, I needed more experience before I was ready to continue at the hotel salon. They owned another, less upscale salon in a large residential building outside the Quarter called the Claiborne Towers Beauty Salon. They suggested I transfer there to get a little more experience. Of course I was disappointed but thankful to them for the opportunity. I discussed it with Earl, and he thought it was the right move.

The salon was small, with two chairs, one hairdresser, and one colorist. The hairdresser was a gay man named Thurman. The colorist was a woman named Marge, nice but quiet. It was more of a working-class clientele. They both were very welcoming and generous with their advice and customers. I felt more comfortable there and started to develop my own customers. I was making more money than I had ever made before.

After working at Claiborne Towers for over six months, I had saved enough money to buy a car. I had been driving the family car since I had been fifteen and was tired of that old Schwinn. My first car was a shiny, black, British-made 1958 MG convertible sports car with red leather upholstery and wire wheels. I found the car listed in the newspaper under the section Used Cars. When I saw it, I fell in love with it and knew I had to buy it. My father and brothers thought it was crazy not to buy an American car, but I didn't care. Style was everything to me in those days.

I felt so sophisticated when I drove around in my MG. I was proud of the fact that at eighteen, I had paid for it myself. Van and Richard drove a 1956 two-seater red Thunderbird. Now that I had my weekends free, the four of us would go on outings in our respective sports cars, either to the races or the lake.

Earl and I were nearly inseparable. I shared my experiences at the salon with him, and he gave me advice on how to handle the clients. We went out nearly every night I didn't have my night class and had loads of fun. Now that I was eighteen, I started spending nights at Earl's house.

Every now and then I would stop at Tony's after school, before I went over to Earl's, to see if any of my drag-queen friends were up and around. Earl did not care for drag queens, and I mostly went by myself.

Drag queens told the funniest stories about their experiences. George (a.k.a Rita), a gorgeous drag queen, shared the story of how he had managed to prevent getting arrested by the local police. He was driving his car in full drag on the way to a party. He was in a hurry and driving too fast. A local policeman stopped him. When the hunky cop walked over, George asked him if he had a tail light out in the sweetest voice. The cop said he had been speeding and asked for his license. Knowing that he could be arrested for being in drag if he showed the policeman his license, which had his male name on it, he showed the officer his brother's ID card stating he was a police sergeant. The policeman smiled and started to flirt with "Rita," finally asking him out on a date. George flirted right back, took his number, and said he would call. Needless to say, he didn't get the ticket nor arrested.

The next day his brother, the police sergeant, asked him, "Where were you last night?"

"Why do you want to know?"

"One of my officers came to me and asked if he could get a date with my sister."

George smiled. "What did you tell him?"

"That she just left town."

We all got a good laugh at that story. I admired George's quick thinking.

Thirty-Three

One Saturday night, Earl and I took a couple of our favorite working girls, Sam (Samantha) and Gina, out drinking and dancing. We hit a couple of the straight bars in the Quarter. The dance floors were small, but the music was hot. One would have thought we were two straight guys out with two hot chicks because of the sexy way we were dancing with the girls.

After hours of partying, we stumbled out of the last bar into the early dawn light. Earl invited the girls over to the house for a nightcap. I was looking forward to sex with Earl and hoped they wouldn't stay long. We sat on the patio and had one more drink. It was a delightful sensation to feel the cool drops of the morning dew on our sweaty skin. The water in the fountain made a wonderful echoing sound in the morning stillness.

As we sat there, Earl got a devilish look in his eyes. He looked at me with a big grin on his face and said, "Why don't you and Sam go into the bedroom for a while."

I looked at him in disbelief. He was giving me permission to have sex…with a woman? All I wanted to do was to have sex with him that night.

"Earl, I…"

"Come on. Try it. What do you say, Sam?"

She took a sip of her drink and looked at me. "I'm game if you are, honey."

"Sure he's game. Right, Milton?"

"Okay," I said with drunken bravado, and then I downed my drink. "Let's go."

Sam took my hand and led me to the bedroom. Earl and Gina stayed on the patio drinking.

Even though I was drunk, I was a little anxious. I had had sex with several men, but never with a woman. I had never had the desire. As sexy as Sam was, I was sure nothing was going to happen between us. I probably wouldn't even be able to get it up.

"Why don't you sit down on the bed, hon?"

I did.

She knelt down in front of me and unzipped my pants. She reached in, took out my penis, and started to stroke it. "Ooh, you are quite a man," Sam said. She was a pro, after all, and knew what she was doing. To my great surprise, I started to get hard.

"You *are* a big, strong man," she cooed. She certainly knew what to say. Then she started going down on me. I closed my eyes, imagining it was Earl. It felt good.

After a while, she stopped and pushed me down on the bed. She kissed me and started to take off my clothes. When I was naked, she did a striptease for me. I had not seen a naked woman before. Sam was beautiful and had a great body. She joined me in bed and ran her tongue up and down my body, rubbing her soft body on mine. By the time she got near my penis, I was fully erect. She sucked me a bit more, then switched positions and pulled me on top of her.

"Touch me," she whispered as she guided my hands to her breasts. This was certainly a different sensation for me, but I was beginning to enjoy it.

"Lick them," she whispered.

I followed her lead, and she seemed to enjoy it. I started rubbing my hard penis against her crotch. She moaned and tossed her head from side to side. She grabbed hold of my penis and put it inside her. The sensation of entering her felt so hot and wet, and it almost made me explode immediately. I started pumping her. The more I pumped, the more she moaned. Then I came.

We lay there awhile, catching our breath.

"Well," she said, lighting a cigarette, "did you like it?"

"Yes. Thanks." I didn't know what else to say.

We dressed and went back to the patio. Gina was gone. I thought I would see Earl smiling, eager to find out what happened, but instead, he was passed out in the chair. Sam kissed me and left. I helped Earl to bed and slept next to him.

The next day I asked Earl, "Why did you want me to go to bed with a woman?"

"I thought you should have the experience."

Earl was like that, always pushing me to have new experiences. I loved him for that.

Thirty-Four

Van had lived in Greenwich Village before he came to New Orleans and could not stop raving about the lifestyle and opportunities that New York City had to offer. I remembered how exciting it was from my Christmas visit with Magnolia several years before and had to agree with him. Earl had never been to New York, and the more Van talked, the more interested he became. We all started to talk about moving there together.

There was one problem. I was still on probation and would be for the next two and a half years. Even though I was no longer a minor, I couldn't leave the state without the permission of my probation officer and my parents. It was so unfair. As the talk about New York became more serious, I was worried that just because I had made one stupid mistake, I might lose my lover and a chance of a lifetime.

It had only been a couple of weeks since the initial talk of moving when Earl announced that he was making the big move to New York with his roommates with or without me. As the days progressed, Earl's excitement about the big move escalated. They were making plans, and all I could do was sit back and listen. My world became dimmer and lonelier at the mere thought of Earl's leaving.

The three of them made plane reservations to fly together. I watched as he started packing. I held back my tears, trying to be strong. Earl planned a special night before he left, just the two of us in a quaint little restaurant in the Quarter, candlelit, white tablecloth, the works. After dinner, we took a stroll through Jackson Square. I wanted to hold his hand but didn't dare. The night air was warm and humid. A typical New Orleans night. We walked around for nearly an hour and ended up at his house.

We went directly to his bedroom. We undressed each other at the same time. He planted a big wet kiss on my lips, just like the first time we met. He guided me to the bed, laid me down, and gently started kissing me all over. We made love for hours. It was the hottest sex we ever had.

The next day I watched as they got into a taxi. "I'll see you soon, baby," Earl said with a twinkle in his eye. My heart broke as they drove away.

Over the next few weeks, Earl and I communicated by long-distance telephone. Our conversations were short because of the expense. Usually, he called me because he made more money. Hearing his voice made me miss him all the more.

He told me that they had found an apartment on Jane Street in Greenwich Village. Van got a job in television, and Richard a job as an assistant to the famous photographer Richard Avedon. Earl had a job in a chic salon on the fashionable East Side of Manhattan. It all sounded so glamorous and exciting. I had to find a way to join them as quickly as possible. I always ended our conversations with "Save me a big wet one."

I shared my plan to move to New York with my probation officer. Of course, at first he said it was impossible, but as I continued to mention it at each meeting, he knew I was serious. He told me that it might be possible to transfer my time to the authorities in New York, provided I continued to maintain good and responsible behavior—and, of course, if my parents agreed. I was overjoyed at the prospect. I discussed it my parents. My mother was sad about it, but she and my father knew how much it meant to me. They agreed to grant their approval once the authorities had certified the transfer.

I worked as much as I could at the salon, knowing I needed to save enough money to finance my move to New York.

Earl was happy to hear about the possibility of the transfer of my probation to New York. I promised to let him know as soon as I could. I could tell by the sound of his voice that he missed me as much as I missed him. He assured me that by the time I arrived, he would help me settle in.

The months dragged by slowly. My probation officer said the paper work was being processed, but I would have to be patient. I started going out, trying to fill the loneliness, seeing old friends and going to parties.

After six months, my probation officer informed me that the paper work had been accepted and my transfer was official. The only stipulations I had to abide by in New York were to have my own residence and a steady job, and to report to a probation officer once a month. I immediately called Earl with the good news. He was beyond delighted. He called me the next day and said that there was a one-room apartment adjacent to theirs that would be available in a couple of weeks. I told him to get in touch with the landlord and to let me know how much I needed to send him to rent it.

My parents were concerned now that my move to New York was approaching. But they knew my mind was made up, and there wasn't a chance of changing it. They reluctantly granted their approval. While they would miss me, they realized that New York offered more opportunities than New Orleans. It took a few weeks to make the arrangements for the move. I said good-bye to all my friends in the Quarter, who were happy for me because they knew I was joining my lover in the most exciting city in the world, but they would miss me. My colleagues at the salon all wished me well.

As for my family, Mom and Dad were sad, but I promised to visit for the holidays and call often. I promised that once I had a steady job, I would send money home monthly to help pay the tuition for my younger brother's and sister's educations. Ronald and Carolyn were both married and had families of their own, and they wished me luck. Bonnie and Glenn didn't understand why I was moving, but they would miss me.

Thirty-Five

Trying to save as much money as I could, I decided the perfect way to enter New York was to drive there in my gorgeous MG two-seater convertible sports car. It would save me that expensive plane ticket. Despite my good intentions, I hadn't really thought it through. First, I had never driven that far before alone. My friend Pete was itching to see New York and offered to accompany me on the trip. He was a very funny guy, and I knew the trip would go quickly with him. However, there was one problem: he was over six feet tall and heavy. When he sat in my car, he made it look like a toy, with two flat tires on the passenger's side. I wasn't sure my poor little car would make it carrying us both.

The next challenge was luggage. The trunk could hold only one overnight case and one small suitcase on the luggage rack. I would have to ship my second suitcase to Earl. Fortunately for me, Pete was traveling light. He planned to fly back. It was a tight squeeze, but we made it work.

I was so excited that I didn't even think about having the car checked before the trip. It ran well enough around town, after all. I filled it with gas said good-bye to my folks, and off we went, full of enthusiasm about the trip and the sights we'd see on the way.

Several hours later, we were driving through a rural part of Mississippi when we heard a loud sound, like metal hitting metal. The car rolled to a complete stop. Neither one of us knew what was wrong or what to do. We hadn't passed a town or gas station for hours. All we could do was wait and hope for a patrol car or someone drive by to get help.

After forty minutes, a motorist stopped and said he would report our problem to the nearest gas station. We must have waited two hours before a tow truck appeared. He checked the car but could not tell us what was wrong and suggested he tow it into town. By the time we arrived in this one-street, one-gas-station town, the gas station was closed. We had no choice but to stay in the town's only motel and wait until morning to have the car checked.

The motel consisted of three separate log cabins. Each cabin had one large room with walls made of logs, and timber ceilings. The bathroom was open to the rest of the room except for a small partitioned wall for the toilet. The room didn't have a closet, just pegs on the wall to hold one's clothes. There were two bare windows placed so high up the wall that even Pete couldn't look out, one double bed, and one wooden bedside table and lamp. The whole place was rather spooky. I wasn't sure what frightened me most—the room or trying to find space to sleep in a small bed with a six-foot-two, three-hundred-pound man with whom I was not intimate.

Morning came, and Pete and I had breakfast in the only diner in town. When we arrived at the gas station, we were met with more bad news. The place didn't fix foreign cars. The only suggestion the station owner had was to tow it back to New Orleans to see if we could have it looked at there. I loved my car and didn't want to give it up or abandon my plan. But the price for a tow truck back to the city was out of sight. I would blow most of the money I'd saved for New York. One of the service guys suggested I call his brother, a farmer who had a large truck that transported livestock. Maybe he could help. I contacted his brother, and he showed up within the hour.

He drove up in an old, beat-up truck with a large, open flat bed covered with dried manure about four inches thick. The bed was enclosed with slatted wooden walls. Disgusted but desperate, I agreed on a reasonable fee for the trip.

The next challenge was how to get my car onto the bed. There was a small, dry riverbed outside of town contained by a levee. He suggested we back the truck up to a height even with the levee down the block and roll the car into the truck. It took five of us to push the car up to a level part of the levee and roll it into the truck. But it worked.

At that point, the townspeople had gathered to see the event and applauded our success. The owner of the truck thought it best to tie all four corners of the car with rope to secure it from rolling out.

Pete and I climbed into the truck. I sat between the driver and Pete. As we drove to New Orleans, every now and then I had a peek out the window and checked the car. The mature smell was almost unbearable during the entire trip.

We caused quite a sensation arriving in the city. I directed the farmer to drive to a repair shop near my family's house and drop off the car. Fortunately, the garage was equipped with a portable ramp, so we could roll the car out of its bed of cow shit. I asked the repair shop to check the problem and fix it. My mother fixed the driver a meal and after I paid him, and then he was on the road back to Mississippi.

The next day, the mechanic told me that the car had thrown a rod and needed a new engine. The cost was beyond my means. Disappointed, I told my dad to put an ad in the newspaper, sell it as is, and keep any profit. I called and made plane reservations that very same day. Pete decided not to come along.

On July 5, 1961, I could hardly contain myself as I boarded the plane in New Orleans bound for New York. I was thrilled, not just because I was going to see Earl but also because I was about to start a new life as an adult, living on my own in one of the most exciting cities in the world. Just as they had done for my first trip, my family drove me to airport and waved good-bye as I boarded the plane. This time, I was neither frightened nor intimidated by the flight. I was too excited for my new life. I knew in my heart it was my destiny.

Thirty-Six

Earl greeted me with open arms at LaGuardia Airport, and those arms never felt so good. I wanted to jump on his bones right then and there but restrained myself until we got to his apartment. During another hair-raising taxi ride from the airport to Greenwich Village, I told him all about the MG fiasco, and we laughed. I missed hearing his laughter.

We arrived at an old, narrow, four-story building on Jane Street. Earl had described the apartment to me as something called a "duplex." I'd never heard that term before. It sounded so New York. Van, Richard, and Earl shared an apartment on the third and fourth floors. It was a walk-up, so we had to carry my luggage up three flights of steps. We entered on the third floor into a small living room with a staircase off to the left. Under the staircase was Earl's bed, built on a high platform with storage underneath for clothes and shielded by a curtain for privacy. Up the staircase to the fourth floor was a small kitchen, bathroom, and Van and Richard's bedroom. The place looked comfortable for two people but a bit cramped for three. Or should I say four, as Lancelot, their Great Dane, lived there also. I soon found out that living in New York was all about improvising.

Van and Richard were there to greet me, drinks in hand. We had a wonderful reunion. I called my parents using their phone and told them I had arrived safely. I gave them the number in case they needed to call and promised to send a note with my address.

I'd done it. I was reunited with Earl and about to make New York City my new home.

The first few nights, I slept with Earl in his makeshift bedroom. I didn't care. I was so happy to see him. Earl had made arrangements with their landlord for me to rent the apartment directly next to them. It was like a small hotel room with a stall shower and basin but no kitchen. Despite the size of the room, I was grateful to be so close to Earl and have a legal address to call my own. I purchased a bed the very first day after signing the lease. Just as we had done in New Orleans, Earl and I started using my apartment as our bedroom and our friends' apartment as our communal living space. Life was complete. I could not have been happier. I started looking for work immediately.

I made arrangements to report to my probation officer that week. His office was on Chambers Street, in the Wall Street area. Earl introduced me to the intricacies of the New York City subway system map and told me what train to take. I walked into an office marked Probation Office, gave my name, and was told to have a seat. I was so nervous. Luckily, I didn't have to wait long before a pleasant man came out to get me. He introduced himself as Mr. Sanders and ushered me into his office. He reviewed my file and asked for my New York address and my job status. I gave the address and said I was currently looking for work.

"Be sure to contact me as soon as you get a job and report to me the first Wednesday of every month. Good luck." He shook my hand, and that was that.

I was so relieved that there were no complications and that Mr. Sanders was friendly.

Unfortunately, the summer was the worst time for a hairdresser to look for a job in New York. The people who could afford it fled to the shore on weekends, leaving their upscale beauty salons empty. I searched the want ads daily and even walked around Manhattan checking into every salon I encountered, with no luck. The other challenge was that I didn't have any dedicated clientele in New York, an important factor for any salon owner in hiring a hairdresser.

After a couple weeks of searching, I noticed an ad in the local newspaper for a hairdresser in someplace called Astoria, Queens.

"What part of Manhattan is Astoria, Queens?" I asked Earl.

He laughed. "It's across the East River from Manhattan. Queens is one of New York's five boroughs. You can get there by subway."

I was desperate for a job and decided to go for the interview. Earl helped me figure out how to get there. I had to take three different subway lines to get to the salon. The trains were not air conditioned then, and it seemed to take forever. After walking five blocks from the subway stop, I arrived at this tiny beauty shop called Giorgio's, located on a busy corner of Broadway and Crescent. The shop had only three styling chairs. The neighborhood was very middle class, not chic at all like the area in which Earl worked.

I never cared for my given name. Milton was my father's name. Now that I was in New York, I created a new persona as a hairdresser and settled on the name Jason. Earl thought it was a wonderful idea. So when I set up the interview, I used my new name.

The receptionist introduced herself as Gladys. She said the owner was not in at the moment. I was disappointed after having traveled all this way. However, there was a young woman in the chair waiting to be done. Gladys asked if I would mind demonstrating my skills on her. She was a walk-in client, not a regular. I had nothing to lose and was confident I would do a great job. I turned on my Southern charm and chatted with her about what she'd like, and then I gave her a current hairstyle. The client was so pleased, she gave me a big tip and assured me she'd be back. Gladys was so impressed that she hired me on the spot and told me to report in the next day. I was surprised she had the authority, but who was I to question? I thanked her and said I'd see her tomorrow.

I returned to the apartment with news of my new job. Earl gave me a huge hug. "It may not be what you were looking for, but it's a start. Something else will come along. Hang in there." We celebrated with a dinner at small Italian restaurant nearby.

The next morning I reported for work. Gladys introduced me to Giorgio, a short, middle-aged straight man of Italian descent. He told me the charges for hair-styling services. A shampoo and set was $2.50, a haircut was $3.00, and so on. I was rather shocked how low the charges were. I had been used to higher prices at the salons in New Orleans. My deal was 40 percent of the price. I kept my tips. He set me up with my own chair and equipment.

Later that morning, another walk-in client came in, and Giorgio gave her to me. As I worked, I was aware how closely he watched me. It was as if I were back in Miss Ruby's class. But the customer went away happy with her do. Giorgio didn't say a word.

After the woman left, he took Gladys into the small back office and starting yelling at her for hiring me. He said I was much too polished for his shop and that I would probably leave in the fall for some fancy Manhattan salon. Of course, I could hear every word, but I didn't let on when they came back. Although I did not feel comfortable there after that first day, I stuck it out. Giorgio was not an easy man to work for, but I liked Gladys and my clients.

After two months, tired of the long commute and Giorgio's penny-pinching ways, I answered an ad for a hairdresser in Manhattan on the Upper East Side, not far from Gracie Mansion, the official residence of the mayor of New York. Earl said it was a neighborhood full of upscale clientele.

The salon was called the East End Beauty Salon, and it had just opened, with four styling chairs. The owner's name was Katie, a first-time owner. She did mostly hair coloring. There was another hairdresser named Thomas, about my age and very quiet. I found Katie to be a delightful and generous person. When I told her I had at least a dozen faithful clients who would follow me from Astoria, she hired me. I worked out a fifty-fifty deal for each customer. I informed Giorgio the next day and started the following week.

Word of mouth spread quickly about the new salon. Before long, the salon was doing great business, and I developed a faithful clientele.

My biggest fan was Cherie, a lady who lived in the neighborhood. She became my client after admiring the hairstyle I did for her neighbor. She walked into the salon; asked for Jason; and had a cut, shampoo, and set. To this day, fifty or more years later, I am still cutting and styling her hair.

Cherie had a great many friends and recommended me to all of them, including her husband, Jim. At the time, it was unusual for a man to have his hair cut in a woman's salon, but Cherie persuaded Jim to give me a chance. Since he wasn't comfortable coming to the salon, I made an arrangement to go to their apartment after work to cut his hair.

Jim was a tall, handsome man with curly hair, which most regular barbers didn't know how to style. I, on the other hand, having curly hair myself, knew how to handle his hair, and both Jim and Cherie could not have been more pleased with the result. He never went to a barbershop again. Cherie also asked if I would cut their two sons' hair. I became their family hairdresser and close friend.

When their sons became teenagers, Cherie started sending them to my apartment for haircuts. As young teenagers, they wanted to wear their hair longer, just like kids their own age. They tried to offer me money for not cutting their hair but telling their parents I did. It was the late sixties, after all, and all the boys wanted long hippie hair. Not wanting to disappoint Cherie and Jim, we compromised with a trim.

Thirty-Seven

Life was finally falling into place. I was living in Greenwich Village with the man I loved. I had a job I enjoyed and continued to get better at my trade. I even changed my look and surprised Earl with a fashionable new hairstyle. He approved and sealed it with a kiss.

Earl, Van, Richard, and I spent a great deal of time together, much as we had in New Orleans. From time to time, I had the unique pleasure of walking Van and Richard's Great Dane, Lancelot. Walking around Greenwich Village with an animal as large as that always drew a great deal of attention.

All four of us had dinner together in the apartment most weeknights. It was a bit awkward because not only was the kitchen on another floor, it was tiny. Preparing a meal and serving it took time and planning. A table was set up under the staircase, where Earl's makeshift bedroom had been. Every plate, glass, and piece of flatware had to be carried down from the kitchen. It was quite an operation, but we got used to it.

While we made the bar scene on Christopher Street, we didn't need to hang out there for hours, as we'd done in New Orleans. The four of us preferred going out to dinner on weekends in one of the many neighborhood restaurants. One Saturday night, Van suggested we try a place I had never been, but the rest of them had. The restaurant was dimly lit and crowded with mostly gay patrons.

Shortly after we sat down, a young guy in a white jacket came over to our table with a pitcher of water and filled each glass. I couldn't help notice how he stared at Earl. I didn't think much of it at the time because

Earl, being very attractive and sexy, often had other men stare at him. As dinner continued, the guy diligently returned to our table and filled our glasses with water, never taking his eyes off Earl. I thought that this guy was either taking his job too seriously or coming on to my lover. Earl was eating it up. I pretended not to notice.

After dinner, the four of us took a short walk around the Village before returning to the apartment. Earl and I said goodnight and retired to our own place. He sensed something was bothering me and asked what it was.

"Do you know that guy serving water in the restaurant?"

"Yes, I have seen him a few times at the restaurant."

"Are you screwing that water boy?"

"He is not a water boy; he is a busboy. His name is Roger. He's an actor."

"Well, he's a water boy to me."

Earl's answer made it clear that something was going on between them. The rest of the night was filled with tension and sleeplessness. Earl finally admitted he'd had sex with Roger. He said it was nothing. But it was the first time this issue of infidelity had ever came up between us. I had assumed we were so in love that we were faithful to each other. I felt betrayed, and I knew our love had faded.

At that point, I'd had two serious relationships in my young life: Andy, who had moved away after my family discovered he was my boyfriend, and Earl, the man who had helped me realize my passion for a career as a hair stylist and my dream of a new life in New York City. When I thought of the many months I had worked and waited to join him and how happy had I thought we were, my heart was broken. He was not only my lover, but my mentor, my role model, and my best friend. At the tender age of nineteen, I had to learn to accept the fickleness of relationships, especially in the fast-paced Manhattan gay scene. I was terribly crushed and feeling all alone in this vast city.

I couldn't stay in the apartment after Earl admitted his infidelity. Earl agreed to take over my lease, making it possible for me to move out as soon as I found a new place. I stayed at the same address, sleeping in the same bed with Earl for nearly a month while I searched for an apartment I could afford. It was one of the most difficult times of my life. Thank God for my job and the friends I'd made there.

Finally, after giving up on renting in the Village because it was just too expensive, I found a studio apartment in a brownstone on East Twenty-First Street near Gramercy Park. At the time, the area was not considered as charming as it is today, but the price was right.

The place was on the fourth floor of a small four-floor walk-up that had just been newly renovated. It was shaped like a railroad boxcar, long and narrow. The hardwood floors were stained dark, and there was an exterior wall of exposed brick and a nonworking fireplace without a mantel, perfect for putting in flower arrangements. There were two windows toward the end of the room facing north, with a perfect view of the top of the Empire State Building. It had a tiny galley kitchen and a small bathroom. The ceilings were high, an advantage of being on the top floor.

I moved in August and notified my probation officer of the change of address. It was my first apartment of my very own.

After I settled in, I started to decorate. The first piece of furniture I bought was a sofa bed. I felt the high ceiling to be a bit stark and thought the perfect solution was to install beams. At a lumberyard downtown, I found some beams made of Styrofoam with a dark wood-like finish that matched the floors. They looked real and were lightweight, easily glued into place. Little by little, I furnished the apartment, which turned out to be rather charming.

The first few nights in my new apartment were rather lonely. I didn't cook much, so eating in restaurants alone took a bit of getting used to, but fortunately, being young and open, I made friends easily. I did keep in touch with Van and Richard, and eventually with Earl, who remained a friend after the pain of our breakup waned.

Thirty-Eight

Despite its generally more liberal atmosphere, especially compared to New Orleans, I still felt that I could not be as open about my sexuality as I would have liked in Manhattan. Living and working on the stuffier East Side, I missed Greenwich Village and the easy access to the gay bars and gay-friendly restaurants. But even there, one had to watch one's behavior. Hand-holding or other public displays of affection were not legal, and you could be harassed by the police. The bars were raided routinely as well. Dancing was allowed in some gay bars, but touching was not. If you were caught touching while dancing, a flashlight would shine on you to stop, and if you didn't, you would be put out of the bar.

But I soon found out that as long as you were discrete, it was not difficult to meet men, even in my new neighborhood. The gay guys there were more the suit-and-tie type, well educated and successful. When I was feeling "downtown," I could dress casually and hit the Village bars. When I was feeling a bit stylish, I'd dress up and hit the East Side.

Meeting people was not a problem for me. Being twenty years old, having a Southern accent, and being attractive had its advantages. I met all kinds of men in the oddest places. One guy I picked up on the street. We started chatting, and I wound up going home with him. He was in his late twenties, a very good-looking and seemingly wholesome guy. He lived in a brownstone building on the Upper West Side, an area I was not familiar with. We dated for a few months.

The strange thing was that every time we got together, his phone would ring every five minutes, interrupting what we were doing. He answered every time. He would pull out a little notebook, take down a description of the caller and his phone number, and then arrange to call him back in five minutes. As soon as he hung up, he dialed another number and gave an address and time, as if he were arranging an appointment, and then hung up.

Wanting to look cool, I just took it in stride and didn't ask him about it. Finally, after weeks of this weird behavior, it hit me that he was a pimp, running a gay escort service out of his apartment. It didn't bother me that he was a pimp, but I got tired of the calls interrupting the good sex that we were having. Eventually, I stopped seeing him.

I became friends with two guys living on the first floor of my building. I started socializing with them and others I met in the neighborhood. They introduced me to live off-Broadway theater and the many gay underground clubs.

My very first introduction to an official Broadway show was through a guy I met in the neighborhood and started dating. His name was Doug. The show was *She Loves Me,* with Barbara Cook and Barbara Baxley.

Doug was a tall, thin, good-looking man in his middle to late thirties who had taken a liking to me. He was a decorative artist. His main job was designing wallpaper for different upscale textile companies. He was a generous person, always giving or doing something for me. He painted my portrait, which was a rather good likeness. He also did a painting of one of the dozen yellow roses I had given him for his birthday. He painted it on wood, making it look as if it were on the bark of a tree with our initials carved in it, a butterfly poised on the rose. It was a replica of the greeting card with the roses I had given him with my exact signature. I was very touched.

Thirty-Nine

In the late summer of 1962, Doug surprised me with a weekend trip to a beach community known as Fire Island. It was basically a sandbar thirty miles long and a mile wide, off the southern coast of Long Island. Doug said it was a haven for gay men and quite beautiful.

After a long train ride, we boarded a ferryboat for a twenty-minute cruise across the Great South Bay to a place quaintly called Cherry Grove, one of the communities on Fire Island known to be almost exclusively gay. It was a breathtakingly lovely ride, and I could feel my body relax as we sat on the top deck with other gay men carrying beach bags.

As we approached the dock, I noticed gay men and women walking around holding their partners' hands, embracing at times, and enjoying the freedom to be themselves. I could not believe my eyes. This seemed like a fairyland (no pun intended), a magical place where one didn't have to hide one's sexuality. People greeted one another with a kiss on the lips in the most natural way. I noticed a policeman standing off to the side. I found out he was there to protect the peace and not haul you off to jail for being gay. I took a deep breath and felt I had just stepped into a bit of heaven.

Cherry Grove was and is a small community, made up of privately owned summer houses built very close to one another. In fact, some were so close you could lean out your window and borrow a cup of sugar without leaving your house. It had one grocery store, a small hotel, and one restaurant. Some owners rented their houses for the season, month, or weekend. There were no cars on the island. Everyone walked to their destinations on boardwalks built above the sand. People transported their groceries and bags in little red wagons, which I thought was quite charming. Everyone ran around in bathing suits or shorts and tank tops. It was a welcome relief from the frenzy of Manhattan.

We checked into the hotel. Doug had reserved a room facing the pool. There was some kind of fashion show going on around the pool with a bunch of drag queens. It looked like fun, but instead of watching, we went to the beach. After spending time cooling off in the ocean, we showered and dressed for dinner.

We entered a restaurant called the Seashack. The dining room was spacious, with windows all around, and filled with attractive men, all with a bronze glow from the sun. The atmosphere was so friendly, so free. After dinner, Doug took me to a place called the Ice Palace. I noticed everyone dancing together, holding and touching each other. This truly was a special place, free of prejudice, so close yet so far away from the restrictions of the city. I thanked Doug for introducing me to this wonderful island. We spent several weekends there that summer.

Winter arrived, and Doug planned another trip, this time to San Juan, Puerto Rico. He asked me to join him—his treat.

I'd never heard of this place and asked Doug about it.

"It's a Spanish-speaking tropical island country, south of Florida, a two-and-a-half-hour flight from New York."

I was thrilled with the invitation and started packing. It was the first time I'd been to a place outside the United States. He told me to apply for my passport just in case I might need it and showed me how to do it at the passport office. I arranged for a few days off work. We flew to San Juan from the other New York airport, named Idlewild International at the time.

We stayed in Old San Juan, a charming city with cobblestone streets and quaint alleyways. The hotel was small and intimate. Most of our days were spent on the beautiful beaches during the day. In the evening, we dressed and enjoyed fine dinners and strolled through the town, listening to street musicians singing in Spanish. One day, we took a trip to the rain forest. It reminded me of the steamy bayous back home, but with more exotic animals and less swampy waters. It was stunningly beautiful. Doug was sweet to share this experience with me.

After that trip, I knew I wanted to begin traveling to other exotic and foreign places.

Forty

That spring, I became restless at the salon and started to search for a new place. I mentioned it to Earl, who remained a friend and mentor, and he recommended me to a salon named Briand, located in a popular East Side building in the upper sixties. With my long list of loyal clients, I had no problem getting the job. The salon, a duplex, was five times larger and busier than where I had been working. I gave notice, which saddened my boss, Katie, but she understood my move. I said I would stay on until she found my replacement. I contacted all my clients about the new location. I was confident that they would follow me, and they did.

It was not long before I started at Briand that I had all the business I could handle, especially on weekends. I usually had one or two people waiting before finishing a customer. Time was never an issue with me, but perfection was. Being a Southerner, I was still working in my comfort zone, slow and easy. However, as I got busier, I realized that some of my newer clients were getting increasingly concerned about the wait. I tried stepping it up, but I never seemed to get any faster. My regular customers got used to the wait because they knew the outcome would be worth it. Whenever I had a new customer in my chair, I would begin by asking, "Are you in a hurry, dear?" Most of them said no because my reputation had preceded me.

The usual procedure for doing women's hair at the time was shampoo first, cut (if needed), set the hair in rollers, dry under the hair dryer, tease, and finish with lots of hairspray.

Clients often asked me, "What is the best way to keep my hairdo during the week?" I would quip, "Hang your head off the bed during sex or sleep alone." That always got a laugh. The secret, of course, was wrapping one's hair in toilet paper at night. It would make the style last all week, but it didn't inspire much romance, I expect.

Saturdays were the hardest and longest days, especially with nearly all the clients wanting the latest up-dos (long hair swept up off the neck and piled high on top of the head). All the teasing, the curling, and the bigness of it all was exhausting. I called them "construction dos." One afternoon, I was running so late that my last client, Madeleine, called her boyfriend to bring us cocktails to the salon. That soon became a routine every Saturday with her appointment.

Women in general would tell their hairdressers the most amazing personal stories. By the end of the day, after hearing ten to fifteen different stories, my head was just as tired as my feet. When blowouts (hair blown out with a hand dryer) became popular, the stories did not stop. But I could no longer hear what they were saying because of the noise from the dryer. It didn't seem to matter. I just nodded and smiled.

I was so busy at Briand that I began to spend less and less time with Doug. He understood, and we parted as friends. However, I still found time to go out. I had a brief affair with a guy I met in passing at some party. Billy was twelve years older than I, handsome, and loads of fun. He worked for a famous fashion designer on Seventh Avenue and knew everyone in that fashion world. He referred many of the high-fashion models to me as clients at the salon. It was not long after meeting Billy and having an affair that our lives intermingled to such a degree that we became lifelong friends.

Forty-One

Many of the men I met in New York were older and interested in the arts. As a poor kid from New Orleans, I had never been exposed to such things as opera and the ballet, and these older men were only too happy to introduce me to them. The ballet soon became my favorite. The costumes and dancers were so exquisitely beautiful, they often took my breath away. It was a fantasy world made real onstage.

I met Robbie, a very attractive man in his early forties, at an East Side cocktail party. Robbie was extremely charming and had the most beautiful twinkle in his eye. As a young man he had been kept—or should I say "sponsored"—by a wealthy gentleman. He had made a fortune by developing a popular men's cologne and was independently wealthy. Robbie pursued me from the very first night we met. Not long afterward, we became an item. He introduced me into his chic circle of friends in the arts and fashion.

Robbie loved to throw parties. He insisted on having a party to celebrate my twenty-first birthday. The party took place in Robbie's posh East Side apartment on a Friday night. Most of the people were Robbie's friends; a few were mine. Everyone dressed formally in suits and ties. Robbie's devoted housekeeper, Drew, a thin, six foot-two black lady with dyed red hair and several teeth missing, served us all champagne in elegant fluted glasses. All during the night, the champagne flowed, and the party got wild. I got so drunk that I had no memory of what happened, but by all accounts, I really let loose.

I woke up late the next morning at Robbie's place with the biggest hangover I had ever felt. It suddenly hit me that it was Saturday, and I was already forty-five minutes late for work. I found my clothes, gulped a glass of water, raced out of his apartment, and jumped into a taxi. Suddenly, I started feeling drunk all over again. I didn't know that one shouldn't drink water after a champagne hangover.

I went directly to the salon in my wrinkled party clothes because there wasn't time to stop at my apartment for a change. Both salon receptionists, after noticing me stumble out of the taxi, came running out to help. I tried to explain, but they said I had to hurry because I had three clients waiting. One of the receptionists had to escort me up the stairs, as I was unsteady on my feet.

My first client was waiting in my chair, already shampooed with a towel wrapped around her head. There were two more women off to the side. I apologized for being late, saying I had been out celebrating my twenty-first birthday and had gotten a bit carried away. My regular clients were so sweet. They smiled and wished me happy birthday.

"I think I need a full cut and style," she said, looking at me in the mirror.

I took one look at her hair and realized she was right about the style. I panicked. My hands were not steady, and my head was throbbing. The last thing I trusted myself to do was a full cut. I tried to convince her, with all the charm I could muster, that a new style and cut could wait until next week, but she insisted. I had no choice but to comply. I managed to get though it on my auto skills, and she was ecstatic. "I will pay you to go out and celebrate the night before my next appointment every week. This is the best cut I have ever had." We laughed.

I don't know how I got through the rest of the day. It was well past closing time when I finished my last client. Lesson learned: never party before a workday.

Despite my busy social life, I kept in touch with my parents. I called my mother once a week and listened politely as she rattled on about people

I did not know. I visited them twice a year. I always made one of my visits during Mardi Gras, which was double fun because I got to see my friends in the Quarter dressed in their finery. I enjoyed taking my parents to elegant restaurants to which they had never gone before.

Forty-Two

After my first visit to Fire Island, I longed to get back there every summer.

In the summer of 1963, I rented a house in Cherry Grove with Billy, my friend from the fashion world, and a few of his friends. We each had our own bedroom and got along wonderfully. My weekends consisted of a mad rush to get out there Saturday night after work, having fun all night and all day Sunday, and then another mad rush to return to the city on Monday evening. It was a typical hairdresser's weekend because most salons were closed on Mondays. My days were spent mostly on the beach walking, swimming, camping it up with my housemates, and, if I got lucky, meeting a hot number. There were occasions when I met someone in passing on the beach who made my head turn. We would connect and have some hot afternoon sex. Then, after dinner on Saturday night, I usually went to the Ice Palace, which had the best DJ and music on the island.

One weekend, I had just arrived and was standing alone on the dance floor when I was approached by two guys in their early forties. They introduced themselves as Arthur and Donald. Arthur was attractive but rather aggressive, and Donald was the total opposite—quiet, classically handsome, and more reserved. We talked and danced for quite a while. I got the impression Donald was interested in me even though Arthur was doing all the talking. They told me about the house they had just finished building in the Pines, which was in the next community, east of Cherry Grove. They invited me to come back to their house, and

I accepted. It was clear to me that the invitation was for sex but not clear whether it was just with Donald or with both of them.

There were only two ways to get around on the island at the time: walking or waving one of the infrequent jeep taxis that were allowed to run on the oceanfront between the communities. We were lucky that night and waited only a few minutes for a beach taxi. During the ride along the bumpy shore, I started to wonder how I would react if this turned out to be a threesome. I'd never had one before and didn't know how comfortable I felt about it. I'd just have to wait and see.

We arrived at the very last boardwalk in the Pines on the oceanfront and took a two-minute walk across the island to their house, which faced the Great South Bay. The house was very modern, built on stilts with a roof shaped like a star. We entered into the upstairs living room, a large space with glass all around and a wraparound outside deck, and had a drink.

Donald motioned for me to follow him downstairs to a bedroom, where we started undressing. By the time I dropped my jeans, I had a huge erection. Donald went down on me almost immediately. It was getting serious when Arthur popped into the bedroom naked, sporting his own erection. We made our way to the bed.

The situation became uncomfortable. I found the bed too small for three people. I was crushed in the middle, and I had a difficult time turning around to have sex. Arthur, realizing that this was not working out, left the room. Donald stayed, and we continued carrying on. After we were done, he got up and wished me good night. He disappeared into the bedroom he shared with Arthur, and soon I heard them having sex.

I woke up later in the morning, alone in bed and hearing noise upstairs. Feeling embarrassed, I wanted to leave from the back door, but a voice at the door asked me to come up for coffee. I put on my best face, adjusted last night's clothes, and went upstairs. I was greeted cheerfully by Arthur and Donald and introduced to two other friends staying with them. Ronnie was an exotically handsome man and very friendly. He had very dark, straight hair, fair skin, and beautifully shaped eyes. The other man was tall, blond, and seemed quite urbane. He introduced himself simply as Halston. I recognized him as the famous hat designer who had created Jacqueline Kennedy's pillbox hat. I didn't let on, even though I was dying inside.

Both men were in their early thirties and seemed pleasant and interested in what I did and where I lived. Later, their comments turned bitchy. It was a game they played, making jokes at your expense. I was getting ready to leave when Arthur invited me to a luncheon party he was hosting that afternoon. I thanked him and agreed to attend.

Later, I returned to Arthur and Donald's house for lunch. The party, already gathered on the outside deck, was in full swing. Ronnie was the first to get up and introduce me to the rest of the guests and offer me a drink. I was accustomed to being around an older crowd, but as I listened to the conversations, I started to feel intimidated. All these people seemed well established, creative, and sophisticated. I was the youngest man there and realized that that was the reason I had been invited. Eye candy for this older crowd. Ronnie was my savior and spent most of his time with me. We got along so well that we agreed to meet up in the city.

As I walked back to my house in the Grove, I realized the difference between the two communities. The Pines was new and expensive and seemed to be populated with an older, wealthier gay crowd who owned their homes. The Grove was more affordable and had more rentals designed for a younger, less established crowd.

Ronnie and I did get together in the city that week and had dinner. I was intrigued by his background. His mother was Indonesian and his father Dutch. He had grown up in Holland and spoke Dutch as well as English. Ronnie had grown up in Europe but didn't talk much about his circumstances. He lived modestly in an old building in Manhattan on First Avenue.

However, I asked him about his friendship with Arthur and Donald. He said they were friends, and he acted as their unofficial " man Friday," driving them to various locations because neither one of them drove a car. Ronnie didn't seem to have a job and liked their company, so he was happy to oblige. He told me Arthur worked as the art director at House of Revlon, one of the biggest makeup companies on Fifth Avenue, and Donald designed and built houses in the Pines and collected and sold antiques.

After a few dates, Ronnie and I had sex and became an item. We saw quite a lot of each other in the city and on the island. I found out that the reason he didn't work was that his family was extremely wealthy. He had gone to expensive private schools in Europe with the children of royalty and maintained friendships with them and other rich people from around the world. He introduced me to his circle of Eurotrash and jetsetters living or visiting New York. He took me to posh parties in the beautifully appointed houses of fabulously wealthy people in the Upper East Side. Before I knew it, I was living in that fast lane—and loving it.

I was invited to many of Arthur's parties in the Pines as Ronnie's guest. Arthur had a reputation in the Pines, and so did his house. It was called the White Web, and those under its roof were under the spell of the queen spider, Arthur. From what I observed, the rumors were not that far off. Arthur was quite controlling, but it didn't affect me. Ronnie knew how to handle him.

Fire Island, especially the Pines, was notorious for having the grandest costume parties. Arthur and Donald were always invited to the best ones and brought their houseguests. For one party at a house on the bay side, Arthur prepared a dramatic entrance. He and his group pulled up to the private dock in a yacht decorated to look like the pharaoh's royal barge. They were dressed in Egyptian attire. They walked off the barge carrying a rolled-up rug and placed it on the deck. Then they proceeded to unroll the rug, and out came a beautiful girl dressed as Cleopatra. I was sorry I missed that event.

This new life with Ronnie went on for nearly a year, until I came to realize how phony most of these people were. The way they lived and what they talked about were vapid and selfish. None of them worked or did anything constructive. As I became more familiar with this scene, there were times I argued with Ronnie about being around them. One time, on the way home in his car from yet another party, I became so enraged over something one of his friends had said about someone who was supposedly his friend that I couldn't contain myself. We argued about it in the car home. When we stopped at traffic light, I bolted out of the car as the light changed. I ran into the corner phone booth and called my friend Billy to bitch about it. He was always such a good listener and calmed me down. I called Ronnie later to patch things up.

Summer arrived once more, and even though Ronnie and I were together a great deal of the time, I still retained my independence and once again rented a house on my own with a few friends in the Grove. He spent most of his time with Arthur and Donald, and I would only see him on Saturday night and part of Sunday before he returned to the city with Arthur and Donald.

One Saturday night I was out partying with my housemates. It was the wee hours of the morning, and the dance bar was closing. I was getting ready to go home when a friend asked if I was going to the after party at a mutual friend's house. I told him I was too tired.

"But it's going to be a great party," he said. "I'll give you something to wake you up." He pulled out small pillbox and offered me a pill.

I told him that I was not into drugs, but he assured me it would just make me feel good. Not wanting to appear like a prude, I took the pill and swallowed it with a gulp of beer.

"See you later," he trilled and walked away.

A few minutes later, Ronnie showed up unexpectedly. He asked about the guy I had been talking with and what I was doing with him. He said the man had a reputation for being a druggie. We got into a huge argument and ended up screaming at each other on the beach. Suddenly, my head started spinning, and it seemed as if I had no control over my body. I was frightened and told him about the pill I had taken.

We headed back to my house, with me stumbling all the way. We got to my house and fell into bed. Ronnie passed out, and I just lay there with my eyes wide open, grinding my teeth. I felt as if I were on the end of a rope, being spun at a tremendous speed but not moving. It was like a waking nightmare.

When daylight came, I tried to get out of bed, but the floor looked as if it were at a slant, and I fell back into bed. When I finally got to the bathroom and looked into the mirror, I thought my whole face had caved in. I was scared out of my wits. Later that day, I realized that the guy had given me a form of mescaline and I had experienced a bad hallucinogenic trip. It took days for that drug to get out of my system and for me to feel normal again. Ronnie was furious with me for being so naïve. I decided we needed a break from each other.

Forty-Three

By sheer coincidence, I got a call from Robbie, my old flame, a few weeks later. We hadn't seen each other much since I had started dating Ronnie, but it was pleasant to hear from him. We went to dinner to catch up.

Our meeting couldn't have come at better time. Robbie was planning a trip in February to Mexico and invited me to join him, all expenses paid. My relationship with Ronnie was a bit shaky, and a trip to Mexico sounded just like the kind of break I needed. Robbie said we would be staying in Acapulco for a week and would later tour towns in Mexico.

I was very excited. It would be my second trip to a foreign country. I knew that Acapulco was the in place to be at the time from all of Ronnie's jet-setting friends. I accepted the invitation and informed Ronnie. While a bit surprised, he seemed to agree with me that the trip would give us the space we needed.

Robbie and I began seeing each other during the winter. He had made all the arrangements for the trip. I only had to show up at the newly named JFK International Airport with my luggage.

We arrived in Acapulco and were met by a car and driver. I thought we were going to one of the tourist hotels on the beach, but the driver drove us into the hills and stopped at a wrought-iron gate with beautiful hanging flowers. We opened the gate and climbed a winding staircase through beautiful lush plants until we reached the entrance to the house. The foyer was open and airy. I looked to my left and saw the most breathtaking view of Acapulco Bay. We were actually standing at the outer edge of the living room, with no roof or walls, totally open to the sky.

A distinguished Mexican man walked up to greet us.

"Buenos dias, senor. Welcome to Casa Flores. Allow me to show you to your room. Miguel will bring up your luggage."

I was both impressed and intimidated. I'd never had servants before.

"Are we the only guests?" I whispered to Robbie on our way up.

"Yes. My travel agent told me about this place. We do not have to do a thing. We have a family of five taking care of us."

I felt like royalty.

After sundown, we sat outside having cocktails, watching the city lights glow around the bay. All of a sudden, there was a boom, and the sky lit up with the most beautiful array of color. Robbie informed me that it was a political holiday in Acapulco. The fireworks went on for thirty minutes. It was so exciting, and it lit the spark between us that night. It was a glorious way to begin our vacation.

Every morning we were greeted by the cook, an older Mexican woman with a lovely smile. She served us a full breakfast overlooking the bay. Afterward, we got into our beachwear, and the driver took us to the beach. Acapulco had many beautiful beaches, but Robbie took me to his favorite, which was gay friendly. We went every day and met loads of attractive guys. We started socializing with them and inviting them back to the house for parties. Robbie was very social and free spirited. He said if I wanted to go to bed with anyone else, I could, as long as we were together at the end of the day. I took advantage of Robbie's generosity on more than one occasion that trip.

After dinner, most evenings we ended at the hottest club in Acapulco, the Whiskey-a-Go-Go. It was not a gay club, but it was full of trendy young people who loved to dance.

One night, while we were partying in the club, a well-dressed group of Americans made a dramatic entrance. At first, I did not recognize them, but it turned out to be the well-known singer Eddie Fisher and his entourage. They were all dressed in white, looking as if they had just stepped off a yacht. Acapulco was a magnet for the rich and famous.

Robbie and I toured a couple of other small towns before returning home to New York City, but Acapulco was the most memorable. The whole trip was idyllic.

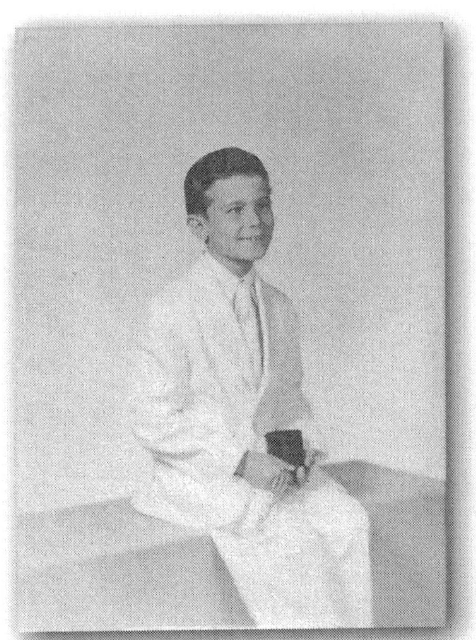

1949. My first communion, age seven. All boys were required to wear a white suit and tie.

1955. My thirteenth birthday party. I was quite popular with all the girls.

1957. All of fifteen years old and dressed in my usual James Dean outfit, I delivered papers with my big Schwinn bicycle.

1957. At fifteen, I sat for a professional photo as requested by Eddie, an older man with a white Cadillac convertible.

1957. My first boyfriend, Andy. He was eighteen.

1957. I dressed in drag to attend a Halloween Party with Andy. My mother was not pleased.

1957. I'm in drag with my handsome sailor, Andy, and his mother at Mardi Gras.

1957. My evening Mardi Gras outfit. My eyebrows are as high as the McDonald's arches.

1945. My father, Milton, in his navy uniform during World War II.

1958. Mother and Dad on the day of my graduation from Holy Trinity Grammar School.

1958. I'm standing in my graduation outfit next to Sister "Cruella de Vil."

1962. Earl, 25, was my second serious boyfriend. He persuaded me to move to New York City.

1957. In Central Park on my first trip to New York City. I had to buy an overcoat for the cold New York winter.

1963. Mother and Dad on their first trip to New York City to visit me.

1965. On my first trip to Europe with Ronnie (right).

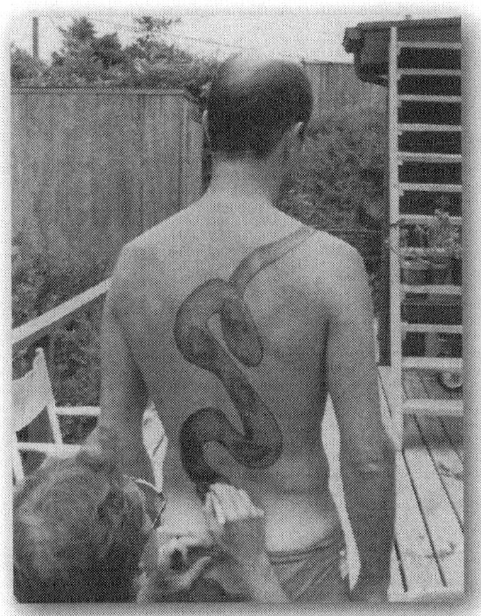

1981. My talented artist friend Teddy putting the finishing touches on my temporary snake tattoo for our wild tattoo party on Fire Island.

1982. Terrence (right) and me sharing a romantic moment on Fire Island shortly after we met.

1984. Terrence and me at Billy and Paul's home.

1993. New Year's Day at our country home in Shohola, Pennsylvania. Me (left), Terrence (center), and Bobbie, the makeup artist I worked with at *The Today Show* (right).

1994. The house we bought and restored in Yonkers, NY, overlooking the Hudson.

1996. Terrence (right) and me on camels near the pyramids in Egypt.

1984. I had the honor of working with Linda Ronstadt for her appearance in *La Boheme* at the Public Theatre.

1985. Working with Jane Curtin on her hit TV show *Kate and Allie.*

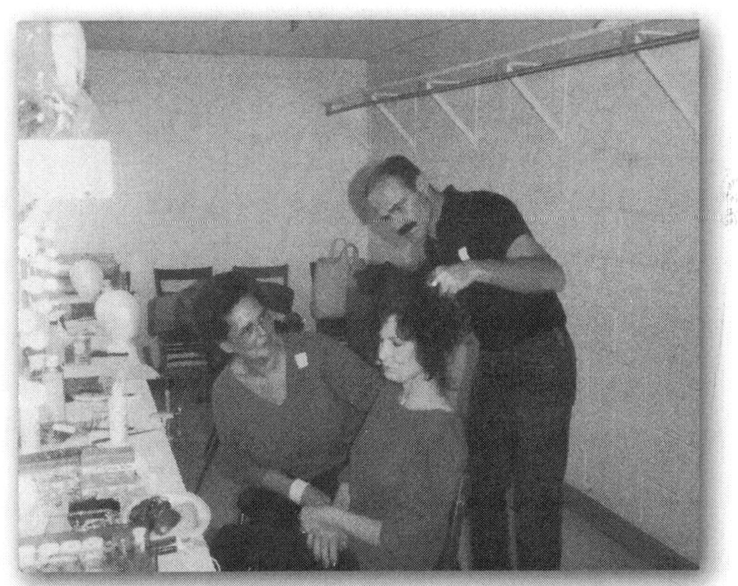

1986. Working with Loretta Lynn for her appcarance on a *Night of a Hundred Stars.*

1987. Jack Nicholson on the set of the film *Ironweed*, flanked by me (far left), his personal makeup artist and dresser.

1989. Linda Ronstadt during her *Canciones de Mi Padre* tour. I styled her hair for every performance.

2004. Working with Rachel McAdams in the film *The Notebook*.

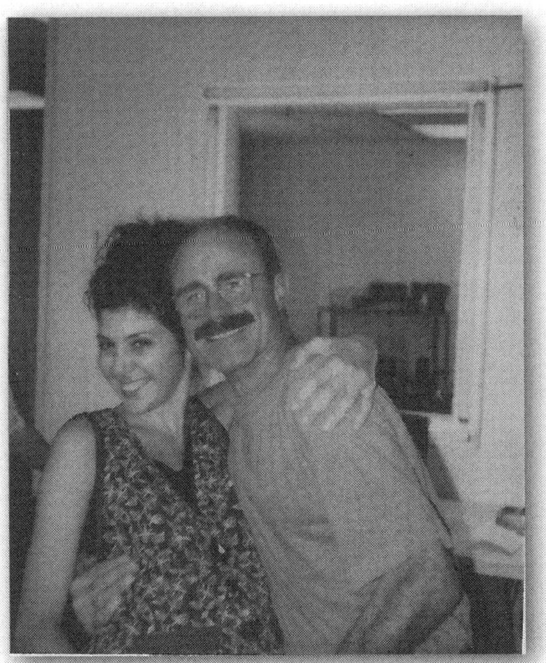

1993. Working with Marisa Tomei in the film *The Paper.*

2004. My reluctant debut in the film *The Notebook.*

2005. I worked with Elisabeth Shue in the film *Hide and Seek.*

2005. I played Howard Hughes toward the end of his life in the film *The Hoax.*

2008. My costume at the Mardi Gras party on my first gay luxury cruise was a big hit.

Forty-Four

Soon after I returned from Mexico, I received a call from Ronnie. He wanted to get together for dinner that very evening. He sounded a bit anxious, so I agreed. I missed him and wanted to see him as well. We met at one of our favorite restaurants after I got off work.

Ronnie looked fabulous as usual and greeted me with a warm smile. During dinner, he asked me about my trip to Mexico. The whole evening could not have been more pleasant. It was as if nothing had gone wrong between us. That was Ronnie's way of dealing with a situation. He hated confrontation and just let things work themselves out. I felt much better after our talk and even slept with him that same night.

My life with Ronnie seemed to be back on track. We had dinner out almost every night. We agreed that he would attend some of the parties with his friends without me to avoid another argument. It was all quite pleasant and civilized.

Ever since my trip to Puerto Rico, I had become interested in going to Europe. Before our falling out, Ronnie and I had planned a trip to Europe. I had done some research and discovered that there were educational clubs one could join at Cooper Union, a college downtown, that chartered planes to Europe. The fee to join was nominal and the fare affordable, but you had to be registered and booked eight months ahead. I chose the educational group that chartered a round trip to Paris and registered us both. Of course, Ronnie had been to Paris many times, but I was so enthusiastic about going that he wanted to share it with me.

Ronnie didn't need to economize, but he realized that it was the only way I could afford to go, so he had agreed.

After my trip to Mexico with Robbie, I wanted to go on the trip more than ever. Now that Ronnie and I were back together, we renewed our plans. I was so relieved that he still wanted to go.

The charter flight was only a round trip to Paris. But I thought from Paris, we could make plans to visit other cities while in Europe. I wanted to see London, Venice, and Rome. Ronnie suggested including Amsterdam, his home city as well. He said we could stay at his mother's house there. She would be in her home in Malaga, Spain. I could visit Rome and Venice on my own after Amsterdam while he flew to Malaga to visit his mother. I would join up with him after touring Italy. It was a perfect plan.

I had told my boss about the trip months before, when I booked it. When I reminded him that I'd be leaving in a few weeks, he was concerned about my leaving my clients for almost a full month. I assured him that I would inform my clients and arrange for them to see other stylists at the salon who I knew would take care of them well.

Forty-Five

Shortly before our trip, Ronnie told me about a four-room apartment that had just become available directly across the street from him on the East Side. I had been living in my tiny Gramercy Park apartment for several years, and Ronnie knew I was interested in finding a new place. He was enthusiastic about it because the new apartment was rent controlled, a rare find in that posh neighborhood even back then. Our friends Donald and Arthur had an antique shop in the same building.

The apartment was another fourth-floor walk-up. The rooms were small and the entire apartment needed a great deal of work, but it was four times the size of my present studio apartment. Despite all the work that it needed to make it livable, I decided to sign the lease that very same day, thinking I would deal with it when I got back. But Ronnie said that he was sure Donald would help me find workmen to do the renovation in the apartment while we were away in Europe, so I could move in upon my return.

I contacted Donald. Ronnie had already discussed the place with him, and he was more than happy to help. He told me to meet him at his antique shop the next day, and he would go up with me and look at the apartment.

Upon seeing the apartment, Donald made some great suggestions about how to open up the space and patch up the place. He had just the right contractor in mind and said he would set up an appointment in the next few days.

We met with the contractor, and Donald explained the work that needed to be done. We all agreed on it and settled on a price. I asked the contractor if he could finish the job during the time I would be away. He said he didn't see why not but gave no guarantee. Later, Donald said he would watch over the job while I was away and make sure everything was done correctly before giving them my final payment. I gave the contractor a down payment and trusted Donald to take care of the rest on my behalf.

I made plans to move what little furniture and other belongings I had into one of the rooms in the new apartment that was not being worked on just before my trip. It was sad to give up my first apartment in New York, but I was excited to have more space in a new neighborhood. I packed for my trip and stayed with Ronnie for a few days. Excited about my first trip to Europe, I didn't give the renovation a second thought, trusting that Donald would be on top of it.

Forty-Six

Ronnie and I boarded the plane for my maiden voyage across the Atlantic. I could hardly contain myself. The flight was long, but for me, it was the beginning of one of the most exciting trips of my life. In those days, flying was such an adventure. I loved the meals they served and how courteous the flight attendants were.

We arrived in Paris in the early morning, but according to my body clock, it was twelve midnight. I'd never experienced jet lag before, but I was so wired, it didn't matter. We got into a taxi, and Ronnie gave the driver instructions to the Hotel du Princess En Montmartre in perfect French. I hadn't known that Ronnie had planned on what hotel we'd stay in. He was always full of surprises.

He told me that Montmartre was a popular artist area on the right bank of the River Seine. The city was awakening with the morning activities as we drove along the narrow, winding streets. The taxi driver pulled up to a small hotel. Ronnie told me that small hotels in Europe were called *pensions*. I was rather surprised it was so modest a place. Given Ronnie's tastes and the rather royal-sounding name of the place, I had expected something grander. But I didn't care. I was in Paris! We checked in and walked one flight up to our room and fell into bed.

One hour later, Ronnie was fast asleep, but I was up and out of the room, exploring. I didn't want to waste a minute. The hotel was old, with dark, narrow hallways and no elevator. The toilet was located on the second floor, one floor above us, and the shower on the third floor. There was a small basin and a pitcher of water in our room to wash and shave. It was all so new to me, but I enjoyed every minute of the experience.

By the time I returned to the room, Ronnie was up, and we got ready to start our tour of Paris. He knew his way around the city and was a wonderful tour guide. We began with the most famous sights, such as the Eiffel Tower, Notre Dame, and the Champs Elysees. We had lunch at one of the famous cafes there. At the end of the day, we wound up back in the Montmartre, walking along the streets filled with artists and their paintings. I felt as if I were in one of my favorite movies, *An American in Paris.*

The first night, we had dinner in a local bistro in Montmartre, not far from our pension. We sat at a table on the sidewalk. The air was warm, and the stars shone above. There was a waiter walking around singing and playing an accordion. It was terribly romantic and a perfect way to end our first day.

Two young, attractive men sitting at a table smiled at us as we left the bistro. I could tell they were gay. I got the impression they wanted a little action. Ronnie and I were flattered but were too exhausted to be interested. We got back to our room and looked out the window; there they were, waving to us. They had followed us to our pension. We waved back, but we did not join them.

After a few glorious days of sightseeing and delicious food, our next stop was London. Ronnie booked us on a train that took us under the English Channel. Traveling took most of the day, but it was a thrill to see the French countryside. Our hotel, located in a central area of the city called Piccadilly, was modest and clean. It was a treat to have a bathroom in the room after the rigors of our Paris pension. The underground subways were quieter and cleaner than New York, but Ronnie preferred the English taxis to get around town.

Of course, I had to see Buckingham Palace, Big Ben, and the Tower of London, with all its history and those shiny crown jewels. The food was very different, not as tasty as French food, but afternoon high tea was delightful. Ever the dedicated stylist, I noticed a huge difference in the hairstyles in both Paris and London. Men's hair was longer at the neckline. The Beatles were just coming into vogue, so most of the younger men wore their hair even longer, letting it fall down on the forehead. Young women on Carnaby Street, the center of the new mod craze, had all kinds of strange angular cuts, accented with several colors. The older women sported the standard up-dos I did in New York.

I asked Ronnie about the gay scene in London. He said that in order to get into gay bars in London, we had to join private clubs. His taste was always on the upscale side. I couldn't believe that there weren't bars that catered to regular working-class gays, but Ronnie wasn't interested in cruising the "rougher" spots. Since we were staying so short a time in the city, we never visited any of the bars.

After three wonderful days in London, we flew to Amsterdam, Ronnie's hometown. We stayed at his mother's house, in a lovely residential area away from the tourist sites along the canals. It was a simple but beautifully appointed two-story house. Ronnie's parents were divorced, and, from what I could see, she lived a rather simple life.

All I knew about Amsterdam was what I remembered from the Danny Kaye movie *Hans Christian Andersen*—ice skating, wooden shoes, cheese, and tulips. Of course, there was so much more. The first night, Ronnie took me to an Indonesian restaurant. I'd never had this kind of food before, but I enjoyed it. Then came the biggest shock of all, the infamous Red Light District. Ronnie explained to me that prostitution was legal in Holland. The only experience I had had with prostitutes was back in New Orleans, where they worked in the shadows. In Amsterdam, the prostitutes would sit behind a glass window with a red light on, waiting for walk-in business. The girls were dressed seductively in variously colored lingerie, just like beautiful window treatments. The red glow coming from the windows went on for blocks. Out of all the prostitutes sitting in their windows, I only saw one male prostitute. Not surprising, but a bit disappointing for me.

The next day, Ronnie showed me the wonders of this water city. I loved the Dutch architecture and the colorful houses on the canals. We also paid a visit to the Anne Frank House and the Van Gogh Museum. I found his paintings disturbing.

The following day, Ronnie had some business to take care with his brother, Hio, whom I did not meet, so I was on my own. The men in Amsterdam were mostly blond. I enjoyed walking along the canal, just taking in the sights as they walked by. I noticed one beautiful guy in his early twenties standing at the tram stop. We exchanged a look. I walked up to him and smiled. Luckily, he spoke English, and we chatted. His name was Hans, and he lived on the other side of the city. The sparks were flying, and he invited me to his place. I hesitated, thinking of Ronnie, but found it difficult to refuse such a warm Dutch invitation. So I accepted.

We were standing together waiting for the tram when I noticed Ronnie passing in a taxi, looking directly at me talking with this cute guy. What were the odds? Ronnie and I had not been exclusive for some time, but he was a jealous person, and it would be awkward since we were traveling together. But I decided to let this incident play out and deal with the outcome later. Hans turned out to be quite a Dutch treat.

That night I was relieved that Ronnie never brought it up.

Forty-Seven

Leaving Amsterdam behind, Ronnie and I headed for the airport together but separated once we got there. His flight was to Malaga, Spain, to visit his mother, and mine was to Venice. The plan was for me to spend a week in Italy and then join him in Malaga. I gave Ronnie my itinerary, airline, and estimated date and time of arrival in Malaga. Needless to say, I was a bit apprehensive visiting Italy by myself, but it was the chance of a lifetime. Ronnie assured me that the Italians were so friendly and helpful that I would not have any problems.

The trip did not begin on a positive note. My flight to Venice had been scheduled to depart earlier than the original time, so when I got to the check-in counter, it had already left. Disappointed, I tried to rebook a flight but was told nothing was available that day. I spent hours and hours in the Amsterdam airport making friends with the agent and sweet-talking my way into a ticket, any ticket, to Italy. Finally, the agent took pity on me and booked me on a flight to Milan with a tight connecting flight to Venice.

When we arrived in Milan, I informed the lovely flight attendant that I had a connecting flight due to leave in ten minutes. She arranged for me to be the first person taken off the plane, put in a car, taken straight through passport control, and driven directly to my flight, which was already sitting on the runway. I boarded through the rear of the plane, just in time.

It was ten in the evening by the time the plane landed at Marco Polo Airport. As Venice was completely surrounded by water, I was told that I had to take a bus to the ferry station to get to the city. All I had were traveler's checks and US dollars, and the terminal's money exchange was closed. I offered the bus driver a traveler's check, but he shook his head. He accepted lire only. He did not speak English, and I did not speak Italian. We went at it for a while, and he finally relented and motioned for me to get in.

The bus pulled up to the depot. It was an open waiting area with a roof over it. It was well past midnight when a beautiful mahogany motorboat pulled up, and I got in. I showed the motorman that I only had traveler's checks, but he accepted the money. I'm sure I overpaid, but at that point, I just wanted to get to the city. I was the only passenger.

The boat dropped me off at the main dock outside St. Mark's Square. I sat outside in the warm summer air, just listening to the water splashing against the pier and sighed in relief that I had finally arrived in romantic Venice. I had been traveling for nearly twelve hours, and my body was feeling it. I needed to find a place to stay. After wandering around the side streets for a while, I found a small pension and went in. I woke up the desk clerk, who sleepily booked me a room. I collapsed on the small bed.

After a good night's rest, I ate breakfast in a tiny little bistro around the block from my hotel. True to the Italian tradition, all they served was coffee and rolls. Then I roamed through Venice, guidebook in hand, seeking all the sites I had heard about. I found my way through the tiny streets called *calles.* They reminded me of some of the streets in New Orleans. The beauty of this city was breathtaking; I had to pinch myself to be sure I wasn't dreaming.

I spent most of the next day in San Marco Square visiting the basilica, the campanile, and the Doge's Palace, and just sitting in the square, watching people and the hundreds of fat pigeons that seemed to own the place. I even got a ticket to the see an opera at La Fenice, the premier opera house, for the evening. I had no idea that it was the opening performance. Everyone was dressed in formal clothes except me. I was very embarrassed, but since I was twenty-two and looked like an American student, they took pity on me and let me in.

The next day, I took a short boat ride across the Laguna Veneto to the Lido, a sandbar on the Adriatic similar to Fire Island but not nearly as beautiful or secluded. I had lunch in the huge hotel there, ogling some of the handsome Italian men who were staying there, and then headed back to the city. Before leaving Venice, I took a fascinating tour of a glass factory on the island of Murano. It was the first time I had seen glass blown. I bought a few pieces, a couple for me and one for my parents.

After spending three fabulous days in Venice, I was ready for my journey to the Eternal City, Rome. This time, I made sure my flight arrangements were in order and arrived there on time.

Forty-Eight

I arrived in Rome bright eyed and anxious to explore the Eternal City. I used my guidebook and found a hotel near the Spanish Steps, close to the center of everything. I arranged for a tour of the city for the next day. Then I walked around to get acquainted with my surroundings. I stopped in a small local restaurant called a *trattoria* for lunch and, of course, a glass of wine.

Rome was so alive, with its beautiful buildings and cobblestone streets and thousands of tourists milling about in the large squares. I walked through the streets and found my way to the Trevi Fountain, the largest fountain in Rome and one of the most famous in the world. I could not resist my Audrey Hepburn moment and threw a coin in the fountain and made a wish. I strolled back to my room for a rest and to make plans for the evening.

By the time I showered, shaved, and got dressed, the bright light of day had fallen, bringing a soft glow from the streetlamps to the city streets. I roamed around the area around my hotel, taking in the sights until the aroma of food hit me. I stepped into a corner restaurant and asked to be seated outside. The temperature had dropped after sundown, making it perfect for dining alfresco, as the Italians say. After a delicious meal and a half carafe of wine, I headed back to the Spanish Steps. I had heard from Ronnie that at night it was a popular cruising area.

By the time I got there, it was bustling with activity. There were groups singing, couples talking, and loners just hanging around. I went to the top of the steps to get the best view. It was there that I met this gorgeous young Italian guy. We were instantly attracted to each other. He had thick, dark, wavy hair and an olive complexion. His chiseled, handsome face reminded me of Michelangelo's famous statue of David. He had the look of a hustler but the eyes and smile of a friendly person looking to find someone. Regardless of whether he was or wasn't, I was willing to take a chance.

He spoke no English, but his smile encouraged me. The more we tried to communicate, the more we laughed and the more I was attracted to him. Finally, I made a hand gesture for him to come with me to my hotel. He nodded his head and followed. We walked to my hotel, into the lobby, and past the desk clerk. He didn't seem to notice. I had no sooner closed the door than we embraced in a long, sensual kiss.

We had sex for hours, until we fell into each other's arms, totally exhausted. We both had just fallen off to sleep when there was a loud knock on the door. It was the desk clerk informing me that I had to pay double occupancy for my room if my visitor was going to stay. My David had a few words with the clerk and indicated I should tip him. I did, and he left us alone.

However, I didn't trust the clerk to let him stay until morning without the additional charge, and my David seemed to agree, as he started to get dressed. Not wanting our time to end so abruptly, I got dressed and stepped outside with him into the early dawn. He motioned for me to follow him. We entered the nearby Borghese Gardens. There was a chill in the air, and the early-morning dew was hanging from the plants. As we passed the statues there, he told me what they were in Italian. It was like a romantic scene in a movie. I just listened, swept away by his passion and good looks. After an hour of walking through the garden, he gestured to me that he had to leave. I gestured about seeing him again. He shrugged and shook his hand up and down, which I took as a maybe. The next two nights, I looked for him on the Spanish Steps but never saw him again. Sadly, I never did get his name.

I spent the rest of the day on a tour of the Coliseum, the Pantheon, and the other great sights of Rome. The third day was devoted entirely to Vatican City. Entering Saint Peter's Square gave me a chill. It was so vast and breathtaking. There were thousands of tourists filling the square, some taking pictures, others gazing at this wonder and saying prayers. I also noticed different clergy from all over the world. I had never seen anything like it.

But the most overwhelming part of my tour of the Vatican was my visit to the Sistine Chapel. I could not get enough of the frescoes covering the ceilings. I spent so much time looking at them that my neck got sore. I was not religious, but I couldn't help but get a feeling of spiritual faith while gazing at the biblical stories depicted there. During the entire Vatican experience, I thought of my mother and her devotion to the saints. I knew she would have to spend several days in St. Peter's Basilica, saying a prayer in front of each stature there. I bought her a beautiful pair of rosary beads blessed by the pope and sent her a postcard of the Sistine Chapel.

Forty-Nine

The next morning, I left beautiful Rome and flew to Barcelona with a connecting flight to Malaga, Spain, to join Ronnie and meet his mother. By the time I arrived, it was late afternoon. Ronnie was at the airport to greet me in his mother's car, as planned. I was happy to see him. He said his visit with his mother was going well, and she was looking forward to meeting me.

He briefed me on the fact that her house was recently built and the finishing touches were still being worked on. Her house was in a newly developed area in the hills, away from the active seaside and tourists in Torremolinos. It was modest in size and structure—only four bedrooms, perfectly suited for one person and an occasional visit from her sons and grandchildren. She wanted a house she could handle herself without live-in servants.

His mother was standing in the doorway when we arrived. She was a tiny, slim, exotic lady with dark hair, and she wore a simple summer dress. She approached me and held out her hand for me to shake.

"It's a pleasure to meet you," I said. "Thank you for allowing me to stay in your home in Amsterdam. It was very comfortable."

"It is so good to meet you also, Milton. Please feel at home in my house."

I could tell by her demeanor that she was a quiet person. Her English was so perfect that I almost forgot she was Indonesian. She apologized for the unfinished rooms in the house but hoped my stay would be pleasant. Ronnie and I sat down in the living room had a glass of wine and talked while his mother, who preferred to do her own cooking, busied herself preparing dinner.

I told him all about my trip in Italy, except meeting the Italian beauty in Rome. In just a couple of hours, a feast of eight to ten small dishes appeared on the table. I learned that unlike the large portions we had enjoyed in the restaurant in Amsterdam, the authentic Indonesian way of eating was to have a little of each dish. I tried them all, some spicier than others but all delicious. Coming from New Orleans, I'd grown up with spicy food, but some of her dishes brought tears to my eyes. I watched his mother eat a whole hot pepper without flinching.

After dinner, the three of us sat outside on the veranda in the warm air and talked. The sky was so clear, I felt immersed by the millions of stars shining above. The only sounds were the crickets and our voices. It was a lovely way to end the day.

The next day, Ronnie borrowed his mother's car, and we left for a trip farther south toward Gibraltar and Tangier, Morocco. This trip was a total surprise, and I was very excited about visiting a place as exotic as Tangier. I knew very little about Morocco—only what I had seen in the movie *Casablanca*.

On the way to Gibraltar, Ronnie pulled off the road and headed for what seemed to be a mountain. We parked and followed a few other people into a large opening that led into a cave. Leaving behind the bright, hot, sunny day, we walked down a rocky path, passing through dozens of stalagmites and stalactites. The temperature dropped twenty or more degrees. Up ahead, I heard voices and Spanish guitar music.

Suddenly we arrived at a performance space with dozens of people sitting in an audience watching a glamorous pair of flamenco dancers. It was spellbinding to watch them in that setting. I had never seen authentic flamenco dancers before. Apparently it was the La Cueva de Nerja Festival, a newly established annual musical event that is now world famous, performed by a community of Romani who had actually lived in the cavern for decades. We stayed until the end of the performance and then made our way back to the car.

We arrived in Gibraltar, parked the car, and boarded a ferry to travel through the Strait of Gibraltar, passing the lock itself and docking in the harbor of Tangier, a port city in Morocco on the edge of Africa. One of the first things we did was exchange some of our US dollars for *dirham,* the currency of Morocco. Ronnie warned that we needed to use only Moroccan currency in the country to avoid being targeted by thieves who hustled tourists for foreign cash. He said to be on guard at all times because the area was famous for pickpockets.

Every direction I turned, I saw something full of color and mystery. It was the first Muslim country I had ever seen and the first time I had heard the call for prayer, although I did not see many mosques. The language barrier was difficult, but Ronnie seemed to get us around quite well.

I noticed the unique designs on the doors and doorways as we walked through the tiny, winding streets. The men wore long robes, mostly white, with beanie-like hats, and the woman were totally covered except for their eyes. The buildings were old and nestled close together. There were a few beggars milling around, but not as many as I would have thought. I could feel the energy that so many writers, such as Tennessee Williams and Jean Genet, had experienced. Ronnie told me that for many years, it had been a playground for gay men from Europe who were interested in Moroccan boys.

We traveled up the hill to the Kasbah, which I had thought was an exotic bar, but it turned out to be a historic section of the city with a seventeenth-century palace on top, once used by the sultans and now a museum. The artifacts in the museum were fascinating, and the view overlooking the city was spectacular.

We had dinner there. I enjoyed the local food, which was mostly lamb. I had heard of people getting sick, but I was lucky that it didn't happen to me. Ronnie told me to stay away from anything that was not cooked. The waiters served in their traditional dress, which created a wonderful ambiance. Ronnie said that Tangier could be dangerous at night, but that did not stop us from club hopping after dinner. Most of the clubs we went to were filled with Europeans dressed exotically, which I loved. There were pimps on the streets trying to get our attention, offering sex with women or men/boys, but we ignored them. We stayed overnight in a small hotel that had character but not much else. Tangier was by far the most exotic place I had ever visited.

The next day, we boarded the ferryboat back to the mainland, picked up the car, and traveled back to Malaga. We spent a couple more days with his mother before returning to Paris to join our charter flight home to New York.

Fifty

Exhausted as I was from our weeks of traveling, I was excited about seeing my new apartment and the work that had been done while I was away. We dropped our luggage at Ronnie's place and walked across the street to my new building.

I opened the door to a complete dusty mess. There was dust on everything—the stove, refrigerator, windows, and bathroom. The middle room was just as I had left it, with my furniture piled in one corner, also coated with a mound of dust. The inside living room wall was gone and patched but not primed. The new vinyl tile floor was down in the living room but was so dusty that I could hardly make out the color. I was so disappointed, I wanted to cry.

Ronnie took one look and said, "You're staying with me until this is cleaned up."

The next day I stopped in the antique shop to speak with Donald. We chatted a bit about the trip, then about the apartment. I told him it looked great except for the mess the workers had left. He apologized and gave me the name of a cleaning service. I had expected that this all would be taken care of by the contractor, but apparently I was mistaken. Within a few days, the apartment was free of dust and ready for me to settle in.

The first piece of furniture I needed to purchase was a bed for my long-awaited new bedroom. The small table and chairs I had in my old apartment fit perfectly next to the kitchen area. I used a cardboard box as a coffee table in the living room with a few folding chairs until I found something suitable. On weekends, I started painting, room by room, with the help of friends.

Donald made several visits, helping me arrange things. I looked forward to those visits because I was still quite attracted to him. He felt the same, and eventually we wound up in my new bed. I was sure Arthur seemed to know nothing about our little tryst. If he did, he never let on. Donald was very discreet. Ronnie might have suspected also, but he never said anything about it.

In a couple of months, I had my apartment together enough to start entertaining. I enjoyed cooking again, now that I had a larger kitchen. My favorite foods to prepare were the dishes I had grown up with in New Orleans. I remembered the recipes from watching my father cook. Gumbo filé was a favorite. I also got several "gourmet" recipes from Madeleine, one of my clients who loved French cuisine.

I usually allowed myself an hour or so after I arrived home from the salon to straighten up the apartment and start preparing a meal before my guests arrived. I made the first drink for everyone and chatted for a moment and disappeared into the kitchen. I always invited one person whom I could count on to entertain the room while I cooked. Every now and then, I would pop into the living room to see if my guests needed anything. By the time I served dinner, which was never before nine fifteen or so, people were ravenous. My reputation for serving late traveled among my friends, but it never stopped anyone from refusing an invitation. Everyone loved my Southern dishes.

Ronnie and I were still together, but not with the same intensity. I stopped going to parties with his jet-setter friends. As a result, we didn't see each other as often as we had before. Our relationship became less sexual and developed into a good friendship. We still shared holidays together. Occasionally I slept at his apartment, but I started meeting new people and attended parties without him.

I spent a great deal of time with my friend Billy. Billy and I shared the same sense of humor. On weekends, we rented bicycles and cycled all over Manhattan even to Staten Island. We went to the movies together.

We had great fun just sitting in the park goofing on all the characters milling around. Because our friendship was strictly platonic, I was able to share my most intimate secrets with him. I became more knowledgeable of the arts through Billy, who was far more educated than I was.

Fifty-One

I heard, through a friend, of a position for an experienced hairdresser at R. Keith Coiffures, a fancy salon just off Fifth Avenue, on West Fifty-Sixth Street, just around the corner from Tiffany's. My first meeting with the owners was successful, and I was hired. I gave a two-week notice to Briand and moved to my new position. The salon was smaller than the one I was leaving, but it catered to a very wealthy clientele. Most of my clients followed me to the new location as well.

The owners of the salon, Keith and Thom, were an interesting, sophisticated couple. Keith was a tall, attractive, blond man in his forties. He was a very talented hair stylist. Keith had an unusual approach to hairdressing. He enjoyed creating a style for a client but was not interested in maintaining it on follow-up visits. He would hand his client over to another hairdresser in the salon instead.

Thom, his partner, ran a dress shop, designing formal gowns on the floor above the salon. Thom was the total opposite of Keith—shorter and heavier, with thinning dark hair and a very flamboyant manner. They had been together forever and took a shine to me. We became friendly.

I enjoyed working at the new salon. The clientele was upscale and loads of fun. Ginny and Nancy were among my favorite clients. I took them over from Keith, and they became two of my best friends. They were in their late twenties. Both were divorced and held high positions at Gimbels department store. Ginny had a remarkable resemblance to

Elizabeth Taylor. Nancy was short and very funny, similar to a Fanny Brice character.

The other hair stylists in the salon were professional and very nice, but my favorite was Margo, a tall, statuesque Swedish girl, single, in her late twenties with bleached-blond hair and a great sense of humor. Margo loved to hang out with the gay boys and have cocktails after work.

Mrs. Robinson, an elegant lady in her sixties, was the receptionist. She wore original designer clothes and had a refined demeanor with clients. She also enjoyed letting her hair down after work in the cocktail lounge and had a wild sense of humor. All in all, it was like a happy family, and it was a delight to work with them.

Keith and Thom introduced me to the Hamptons, a string of exclusive summer communities on the south fork of eastern Long Island. The rich and famous had fabulous estates hidden behind huge hedgerows there. It was totally different from Fire Island. It was not so exclusively gay and informal. People dressed in their best to go out and drove to dinner at expensive restaurants in their expensive cars. It wasn't unusual to see celebrities from the film industry there.

Keith and Thom rented a weekend house in East Hampton each summer. One weekend, they invited Margo, Ginny, Nancy, and me to be their guests. The girls had been out there several times before and filled me in on the place during the two-hour train ride on the Long Island Railroad. Thom picked us up at the station. Their house was lovely, nestled several yards off a quiet road not far from the beach. The two-story house was surrounded by a charming log-rail fence and beautiful, lush trees. The outside of the house was covered in classic cider shingles with white trim. It had five bedrooms, four baths, a cozy living room with fireplace, a dining room, and a gourmet kitchen.

We spent the day at the beach playing in the surf in the morning and then riding around looking at all the mansions and going to one of the fishing docks to buy fresh lobsters for dinner. By five o'clock, all were bathed, coiffed, and ready for cocktails on the comfortable wraparound porch. Cocktail hour lasted till eight and was followed by a feast of barbequed lobsters and delicious wine.

I spent many weekends at their house in East Hampton. Keith and Thom were elegant, generous hosts, and I learned a great deal from them. Unlike Ronnie's condescending, vapid jetsetter friends, they were kind and unpretentious despite their wealth.

Fifty-Two

Working in the new salon, I broadened my interests a great deal. I was making more money than ever and could afford to go to the opera and ballet regularly. I entertained a great deal as well. I remained in close contact with my family and continued to send them money monthly. I didn't see much of Ronnie, as he was spending more and more time in Los Angeles. My sex life remained quite active, although I didn't have a steady boyfriend at the time.

Ever since I returned from Europe, I had been thinking about learning another language. The entire time I was in Europe, I felt like a parochial American, able to speak and understand only English. I enrolled in a basic French course at the French Institute on East Sixtieth Street. I had lessons twice a week. My teachers commented that my accent was rather good. I think that was due to my father's Cajun ancestry. I often heard my father speak in that singsong, French-inflected Cajun dialect among his friends or relatives and must have absorbed it, as children often do. I took lessons for a year and a half but didn't get to use it much in conversation outside of class, so I decided not to continue.

Thanks to Thom, I took up another hobby: horseback riding. Despite his weight, Thom was an accomplished rider using an English-style saddle. He had an Austrian instructor who worked out of Claremont Stables on West Eighty-Ninth Street near Central Park. After hearing him talk about it at the salon, I became intrigued, so he agreed to get me started.

My first riding lesson was a disaster. I had made the mistake of partying the night before and had a terrible hangover. Thom picked me up at the unearthly hour of 6:00 a.m. and drove uptown to the stables. The stench of the stables almost made me throw up, but I managed to contain myself. Thom introduced me to his Austrian instructor, a tall, lean, stern-looking gentleman in his early seventies who agreed to teach me the basics. It was torture, mostly because I was so hungover, but I stuck with it. I was so dizzy at times that I nearly fell off the horse. But after the lesson was over, Thom complimented me on my being able to remain on the horse throughout the lesson. Apparently, most beginning students fall off frequently until they get the hang of it. Encouraged, I continued to take lessons at the stable and eventually became a fairly good rider.

Truth be told, I was more interested in the proper English attire—high boots, riding pants, riding helmet, and a crop—than the riding itself. I loved the way I looked in that outfit.

Billy introduced me to boating. He had been a navigator in the navy and loved the water. One of the first boating trips was across Great South Bay from Sayville to Fire Island Pines in a Sunfish sailboat about eight feet long. It was a chilly but sunny day in May when we set out. I sat up front while he handled the stern. We were drenched by the time we landed. I was freezing but exhilarated. Throughout that summer, we made the trip several more times and enjoyed it so much that we bought a twenty-one-foot speedboat together and started water skiing.

Fifty-Three

In the late sixties, I decided to return to Europe on my own. I mapped out the trip with a travel agent friend I knew. I told him I wanted to arrange for train and plane reservations, leaving hotel accommodations to chance. In those days, it was easier to find rooms in Europe on the fly, and it made the trip more of an adventure for me.

I planned on returning to Rome and Venice and then to move on to Athens. After that, Vienna and Dubrovnik, a chic hot spot at the time, and then I would end with Zurich. The whole trip would last eighteen days. Keith and Thom were thrilled about my vacation and even planned a big bon voyage party. Keith and the other hair stylists would take care of my clients in my absence. Billy gave me two European travel guidebooks, which proved to be invaluable.

It was July when I arrived in Rome. It took most of the day, but I finally found a small pension near the Spanish Steps. It was an odd but welcome coincidence to be in the same area in which I had stayed on my first trip. Unfortunately, the room was available for the following night only. The clerk was kind enough to help me, offering me a bed where the workers often slept for the night. I followed him into the dining room. He stopped at a large cabinet and pulled down the front, revealing a single Murphy-style bed. I had never seen anything like it, but I decided what the hell. I had slept in worse places. I thanked the clerk with a generous tip.

I disappeared into the restroom, where I pulled out a fresh change of clothes, washed, shaved, and dressed. Then I returned my things to my suitcase and stashed it behind a settee. There was no room behind the front desk.

With sweet memories of the good-looking Italian guy I'd met on my last visit on the Spanish Steps years before, I decided to set out to find another. As I was leaving, the desk clerk said, "What time shall I wake you?"

"I get up early," I replied.

"The dining room opens at six in the morning for breakfast, so you would have to be out by then."

I smiled and assured him I would.

I had a wonderful night roaming around Rome, but alas, I did not find another beautiful Italian guy. Rome was Rome. Just being in one of the most romantic cities in the world watching couples enjoying each other, sitting and strolling hand and hand, was thrilling. I noticed how the people in Rome lived outside in the summer, not like a lot of us Americans, inside in front of the TV. Of course, the food was delicious and the novelty of eating in the outdoor cafes a pleasure. After several hours of rest, I woke up in my pullout bed in the dining room, and there on the ceiling were white, puffy clouds and a blue sky. I felt as though I were in heaven. The following day I took a tour of the ancient ruins I had missed on the first visit.

After two lovely days, I boarded a train to Venice. My second-class ticket did not include lunch, but I was able to purchase it on board. The restaurant could rival any fine restaurant in ambience. It had white tablecloths, silver cutlery, and wine glasses. I was seated at a table in the dining car with three other passengers, two French and one Italian. All three spoke perfect English and were friendly. The meal and wine were superb.

By the time the train pulled into the station in Venice, I had found three inexpensive pensions in the trusty guidebook Billy had given me. I took one of the water taxis to the central part of the city and asked the handsome boatman for directions to the first pension on my list. He was more than gracious, and I found the place without too much difficulty.

Luckily, they had a room. Since I was familiar with the city from my first trip, I was able to enjoy my two days in Venice in a more relaxed manner than the first time.

I strolled through the magnificent sites I had seen before and discovered new ones. I learned from other travelers to visit the small local restaurants instead of the touristy ones. I did a little shopping for my parents and friends. I visited the Lido once again and found the gay section of the beach. I had brought a white boxer-style swimsuit, very popular on Fire Island but a novelty in Europe at the time. I noticed all the Italian men were in bikinis. I usually like to blend in and not draw attention to myself, but after I changed into my American swimsuit and hit the beach, I seemed to catch the eyes of most of the guys lounging there. I soon found out why.

I went for a swim in the warm sea. As I walked out of the water, I noticed several of the guys on the beach pointing at me and smiling. I looked down and realized my swimsuit, dripping wet, was clinging to my body in a way that left nothing to the imagination. At first, I was embarrassed and could not reach my towel fast enough, but all the guys were so good natured, I decided to relax and enjoy the attention. Sad to report, nothing came of it.

Fifty-Four

I flew from Venice the following morning and arrived in Athens around noon, fully prepared to begin my tour of that ancient city. After a bus ride from the airport to the central part of the city and a short taxi ride, I arrived at Hotel Plaka, one of the inexpensive hotels mentioned in my guidebook. It was first on my list because it was near the Acropolis. The hotel was far from luxurious, but the location was perfect. After checking in, I was on a tour that very same day, eager to get a general feel for the city. I returned to the hotel exhausted and hungry. I freshened up and went in search of dinner. The hotel clerk was kind enough to recommend a wonderful little tavern a few blocks from my hotel. The food, different from anything I had ever eaten, was most enjoyable, and the service friendly.

The following morning I set out on my own. I spent the whole day roaming through the Acropolis, the Parthenon, and many other temples. I stood in awe of the magnificent structure with its giant columns and imagined how beautiful it must have been in its day. I sat in the Theater of Dionysus and wondered what it must have been like to see productions there, and I strolled through the museum.

Walking around the city, I occasionally became confused by the street signs, which were in Greek. Very few people spoke English in Athens back then, so asking directions was a challenge, but I managed. It was all part of the adventure. I had the name and address of a gay bar in Athens, given to me by a friend back in New York. But the address was in English, and I could not find it on my own. I was too uncomfortable asking the hotel clerk for directions, so I never got there.

Everyone I knew who had been to Greece told me I had to visit the island of Mykonos after seeing Athens. I packed an overnight bag, stored my suitcase with the hotel, and purchased a first-class round-trip ticket on a large boat that sailed to the island. The boat was fully packed, mostly with tourists. The approach to the island was truly spectacular. The whole shoreline and hillside was a sea of whitewashed houses, one or two stories high, and windmills. The symmetry, the balance of it all, was so beautiful, so pure.

We were taken ashore in small boats because the day cruisers were too large to dock in the port itself. I had read in a guidebook that local residents rented out rooms in their homes for a small fee to tourists who chose not to go to one of the tourist hotels. I thought it would be a quaint and inexpensive way to find a place to stay. I approached a man on the dock who appeared to be offering rooms. A young American couple approached him just before I did and got the last room available in the man's home. The man, eager to make a buck, told me the kitchen was available. I looked at him and thought, "Is he serious?" But I decided to check it out just for the fun of it. The young couple introduced themselves as Dennis and Garda. They were from Cincinnati, Ohio, and were warm and friendly. I could tell immediately that we were going to be friends.

We walked to the house together. The living room was perfect for the two of them, but the kitchen was the size of a New York closet, totally empty, with only a sink on one wall and a small window with shutters. The owner said he would put a cot in the area. It was just for one night and I liked my new friends, so I took it. I was traveling back to Athens the next day.

I spent the rest of the day and evening with Dennis and Garda, wandering through the tiny streets of the village. There was a sense of calmness and simplicity everywhere. There were flowers bursting with color. The people were friendly and helpful. We found a tiny restaurant and had a great meal, with lots of local wine and even more laughs. They said they had just finished college, had gotten married, and were on their honeymoon. That sparked a toast and another bottle of wine. I told them I was a hair stylist working in an upscale salon in New York. By the end of the evening, we were drunk and stumbled back to the house.

The next morning, I was awakened by the sound of a man singing outside as he rolled his cart over the cobblestone streets, selling fresh fruit. After washing up and shaving as best I could in the little kitchen sink, I met up with Dennis and Garda, overnight bag in hand for breakfast in a small tavern in town. The warm, fresh bread; cheese; and rich, dark coffee were delicious. After a relaxing breakfast, we ventured up the hill to the very top and had a magnificent view of the sea and the rich side of the island. We strolled down to the beach sat down in the fine white sand and talked. They were such a delightful couple and so much in love.

They were traveling back to Athens on the same boat as me that day, but in second class. I decided to cash in my first-class ticket to sit with them. With the difference, I bought a couple of bottles of wine and shared them with Dennis and Garda and other people around us on the boat. I noticed most of the travelers in second class were locals, and after a little wine, they let their hair down and broke out into song and dance.

Most everyone on deck, including us, were having a good time, except an old Greek woman sitting across from us. She was dressed in the traditional black mourning outfit. She had a couple of cloth bags filled to the top around her feet and was holding a rope with a goat on the end of it. I offered her some wine, but she turned her head in a rather rude manner. I shrugged and went back to partying with the rest of the passengers. An hour and a half later, I tried again and offered the old woman a little wine, and this time she accepted. After a few sips, she smiled and started clapping, but she never let go of that goat.

By the time we pulled into port, I was one happy drunk. Dennis, Garda, and I exchanged information and promised to keep in touch. They hoped to visit New York someday soon and promised to look me up. My trip to Mykonos was one of the highlights of my trip to Greece.

Fifty-Five

The following morning, I flew to the next stop on my trip, Dubrovnik, on a small propeller plane. It was one bumpy ride, but we arrived safely. I asked a taxi driver at the airport to take me to a hotel/pension. But he didn't understand English, and, mistaking me for an American student, he took me to a youth hostel up in the hills, miles from the city. It had thirty beds in a few big rooms and was full of young people living on the fringe. I didn't have anything against youth hostels per se, but it just wasn't for me. I wanted more privacy and security for my belongings. I was outside in a minute, looking for another taxi driver to take me back to the city, when a man from across the road approached me. Seeing my bags, he pointed to a house down the road and said in a thick Croatian accent, "Room?"

I was tired and hungry and anything would be better than the youth hostel, so I decided to check out the house. I nodded and followed him. The house was simple in design, with two floors, and built mostly of cement. His family was talking on the side porch. They waved at me, and I smiled and waved back. The man, who I assumed was the father, showed me to a small room. The window faced the porch, where I could see and hear the family talking. It was clean and comfortable, so I nodded, accepting his offer. I paid the man a small fee, dropped my bags next to the tiny bed, and then went into the kitchen.

There were two young women speaking in English. I introduced myself, and we chatted for bit. They were perfectly lovely and gave me information on the area and how to get around Dubrovnik. I made my way to the village center, which was crowded with local people because of some kind of annual feast. I enjoyed a taste of the local food and then took a bus to Dubrovnik. It was a lovely small city, full of charm and history.

Later that evening, it was pitch dark when I returned to the house. I undressed and climbed into my little bed, only to discover that another guy was already asleep there. I was embarrassed lying there nude next to a guy I did not know. There was barely enough room for the both of us, but I was so tired, I didn't care and made the best of it.

Morning came, and my roommate was gone. The lady of the house invited me to the side porch for coffee. It was strong Turkish-style coffee with thick sediment at the bottom. An acquired taste, to say the least. I declined a second cup and made my way to the village for breakfast and took a bus to the city. I picked up a tour to show me the sights of Dubrovnik and the old fort.

When I returned to the house, my student friends were on their way to take a swim in the local river. An excellent idea, I thought, because it was beastly hot. I followed them to a fairly large swimming area filled with local families and loads of kids. Remembering my experience at the Lido, I made sure to take a towel with me to cover up as soon as I got out of the water.

I boarded a plane to Vienna the next day. As I bid farewell to Dubrovnik, I couldn't figure out why the city was so popular. It was pleasant enough, but certainly not chic. Perhaps there was an exclusive section of the city itself that catered to rich tourists I had missed because I had stayed in a tiny room in a tiny house in a tiny town outside the city. It was an experience nevertheless.

Fifty-Six

Vienna was the total opposite of Dubrovnik. It was a beautiful and regal city, rich in history and architecture. I was lucky to find a room in a charming little hotel in the center of the city and began my walking tour. I found the Viennese to be friendly and sophisticated.

Since I had become interested in the horseback riding, I visited the renowned Spanish Riding School, where the world-famous Lipizzaner horses trained. The inside ring where the horses performed was on a grand scale, decorated with antique mirrored walls trimmed with gold leaf, crystal chandeliers, and plush velvet chairs for viewers to sit. It was truly a magnificent place to put on a show. Unfortunately, there were no performances while I was there because the Lipizzaner horses were on tour in another country.

The Vienna State Opera House was the grandest building I think I had ever seen. As I walked around the lobby, I imagined how elegant it must have been to attend performances in the mid-nineteenth century, with the men dressed in tuxedos and the women in fine gowns. Unfortunately, the performances were sold out for the days of my visit.

After three wonderful days in Vienna, I took a train to Zurich, my final destination before returning home. The train passage through the mountains was breathtaking. I could not help feeling especially fortunate as I had lunch in the dining car while looking out on the magnificent scenery.

I arrived in Zurich in the late afternoon, and I found lodging in the Old Town section of the city. I freshened up and went out exploring the town. I reached what looked like one of the main town squares. There were lots of restaurants and pubs to choose from. I fell in love with the old Tudor-style houses there. Feeling hungry, I popped into a restaurant and had a delicious German meal of bratwurst, German potatoes, and cabbage.

That evening, I was feeling rather lonely and a bit homesick. On my way back to the hotel, I met a handsome man as I waited to cross the street. He was tall with darkish-blond hair, blue eyes, and winning smile.

"Bonsoir," he said, looking directly into my eyes.

"Bonsoir," I responded in my best French accent.

"You are an American, non?" he asked. "You have a nice accent."

"Oui…yes. Thanks," I said. "From New York."

"My name is Lucky."

"Milton."

I could feel the chemistry between us. He invited me to join him for a beer in the bar across the square.

Lucky turned out to be a native of Zurich and worked as a watch and clock designer. He was in his middle to late thirties and spoke English quite well. We talked for several hours and drank several beers. I told him of my travels. He had visited some of the places I had, and we share observations. It was near closing when he invited me back to his place. I accepted and enjoyed a delicious night of lovemaking that lasted till dawn. Wonderfully exhausted, we fell asleep.

We woke up that Sunday morning to hear the chiming of church bells. Lucky offered to give me a tour of the city. I returned to my hotel shortly before noon only to change, and then I met Lucky in the lobby. We had a lovely day. It makes such a difference to tour a city with a person who lives there. Later that night we went on a cruise up the Limmat River, with a spectacular view of the Fraumünster Church. We finished the evening back at his place for another delightful interlude.

He took off work, and we spent the next two days together, just enjoying the city. He showed me the best restaurants, and we toured some of the lovely gardens. The evening always ended at Lucky's place.

I returned to my hotel each morning to change before meeting Lucky. I even got to practice my French and learned quite a few mots d'amour from him in bed.

He was kind enough to accompany me to the airport when I had to leave. It was sad saying good-bye to Lucky because I really liked him. We exchanged addresses and promised to keep in touch.

I was happy to be home after all those weeks away. My apartment. My friends. Even my clients. While I missed the adventure and excitement of being in Europe and experiencing so many different places and people, I agreed with Dorothy. There was no place like home.

When I returned to work in the salon, I enjoyed sharing my stories with my clients and colleagues. I even got to try some of the styles I'd seen in Europe on my clients. I had my friends over for dinner and caught up with Billy on all the gossip.

Fifty-Seven

Nineteen sixty-nine was an exciting year. The Stonewall Riots ushered in a new era of empowerment for gay men and women in New York and around the country. Stonewall was not one of the bars I frequented, but I applauded their stand. There's one thing you should not fuck with, and that's a drag queen. After the riots, the gay lifestyle exploded and sex was everywhere. From the discos to the popular backrooms, the trucks and the docks, it was a free for all—if you wanted it. Studio 54, Flamingo, the Saint, and the Garage were the main dance clubs in Manhattan. The same crowd that went to the city clubs in the winter went to the clubs on Fire Island during the summers. It was hot!

I got caught up in the disco scene—the drugs, the music, and the late hours. Fortunately, I did not have an addictive personality. I took drugs to party and have sex and was conscious of which drugs I took. I would often leave my apartment at midnight, dressed in my disco outfit of tight button-fly jeans and T-shirt and dancing boots. Not too different from the Jimmy Dean look I had sported as a kid back in New Orleans. I was slim, and I could still pull it off.

My T-shirt came off after the first half hour of dancing. Most of the guys did the same, until the whole floor was a sea of naked, well-developed, sweaty bodies. It wasn't uncommon to have a hot body rub up against you while dancing and not skip a beat, in total sync with your rhythm. On disco nights, I never got back to my apartment until dawn, if at all. I was careful not get too drunk or stoned so I could function at work the next day.

Right around this crazy time, I attended a party in the Village. I spotted a very handsome German guy around thirty-two years old sporting a sexy mustache. We started chatting. His name was Werner. He was born in Germany and had been living and working in New York for the past eight years as a hair stylist on Broadway shows. That's right, another hairdresser in my life. I was intrigued with his accent and European manners.

I was instantly attracted to him, and I got the feeling it was mutual. He suggested that we leave the party and continue our conversation over dinner in a little bistro he knew on Christopher Street. We spent the rest of the evening getting to know each other. After dinner, he invited me to his place. That night was the beginning of a romantic relationship that lasted several years and developed into a lifelong friendship. Werner wasn't a disco person, so I spent less and less time in that scene.

Werner lived in the Village and worked nights in the theater, so it was a bit difficult for us to see each other, but we made it work. I even got to go backstage at shows to watch him work. It was a whole new world of hairdressing to me, very different from the salon. Each style had to be exactly the same for each performance and sturdy enough to last through the hot lights and dance numbers. It was hectic, and Werner worked hard.

Shortly after I met Werner, I invited my parents to New York for a visit. It was a grand event, the honeymoon they never had. I made all the arrangements. My mother had never traveled anywhere outside of New Orleans or flown in a plane. She was a little anxious, but Dad calmed her down. I picked them up at JFK and took them into town. They insisted on staying in my apartment instead of a hotel to save money, and I was worried that walking the four flights of steps would be too tiring for them. But they were fifty years young at that time and took it all in stride. Going up and down the flights of stairs took a toll on Mother's feet, though, so she wore slippers and Dad carried her high heels.

Werner arranged three tickets for *Mame,* the show he was working on at the time, complete with backstage passes to meet Janis Paige, the star of the show. My parents were over the moon with excitement.

After the show, Werner joined us at Joe Allen's, the well-known restaurant in the theater district, for supper. The dinner could not have gone better. Werner was a perfect gentleman and charmed them both with all his Broadway stories.

I took a few days off work and showed them the sights, including the Empire State Building, the Circle Line, the Lincoln Center, Radio City Music Hall, the Statue of Liberty, and Central Park. On their last day, I managed to get two tickets through Werner for *The Tonight Show Starring Johnny Carson.* Mother watched the show nightly, so it was a big event for her to attend it live. I gave my dad money and instructions to take a taxi after the show to one of my favorite restaurants, where I planned to meet them for dinner.

When I walked into the restaurant and saw them sitting at a table in the dimly lit room looking around and smiling, it nearly brought tears to my eyes. I was happy to give them such a wonderful experience. I had never seen them happier. I accompanied them to the airport and hugged them both before they boarded. It was bittersweet to see them leave to return to their sparse life back home. But I knew that they were grateful to me for giving them a once-in-a-lifetime experience.

Fifty-Eight

Werner and I were together for several years. I introduced him to horseback riding English style in Central Park, and he taught me how to ski, or did his best to teach me. We rented a house one winter with a couple of friends in Killington, Vermont. After two weekends struggling to stay upright, I finally got the idea. Later that year, we traveled to Augsburg, Germany, Werner's hometown, for a vacation. I got to meet his lovely mother and two sisters. From there, we took a train to Munich, stayed a few days, and then trained it to Saint Anton in Austria, a beautiful ski resort in the Alps, for two fantastic weeks. By the time we left Saint Anton, I was almost a pro.

The summer of 1972, Werner and I rented a house in East Hampton with Thom, Keith, Billy, and Paul, his new boyfriend, a window-display designer for the posh department store Bergdorf Goodman. It was an old Hampton shingled house on Three Mile Harbor Road overlooking the water. Ginny and Nancy had decided to move to East Hampton together permanently and were renting a darling little cottage not far from our house. Werner couldn't make it out several Saturdays due to his work schedule, but usually he was there on Sundays and Mondays. Toward the end of the season, it was my thirtieth birthday, and they threw me a party. Ginny surprised me with thirty wrapped gifts to open. Reaching thirty was not as traumatic for me as for many of my friends. My life was grand at that point, and I embraced it.

After designing hair and working many shows on Broadway, Werner moved over to working in TV. He did *The Today Show* with Barbara Walters and traveled with her extensively on her various shoots. He also headed the hair department on *Saturday Night Live* for a season. His schedule shifted to working days, and we had more time to see each other.

Werner was smart and very ambitious. After working an intense schedule in TV, he shifted his career to feature films. His first film was *Stardust Memories*, a Woody Allen movie. He went on to work on other Allen films, such as *Radio Days* and *Zelig*. Some of his movies sent him on location away from New York for months at a time. His frequent absences began to take a toll on our relationship.

We both started to wander. Fortunately, while our romance ended, our friendship remained strong, and over the years, Werner has been a best friend, a mentor, and someone I have looked up to with respect.

After Werner and I parted ways romantically, I started spending more time with my friends Billy and Paul. Paul was totally devoted to Billy and a true friend. We did so many things together. We rented a house in Vermont during the winters and skied. We rented houses on Fire Island Pines during the summers. Billy and I still had the speedboat and used it often to commute to the island. We docked the boat in Sayville during the week. It was also great for hopping to other communities on the island. We even made trips to East Hampton to visit Ginny and Nancy and, of course, Keith and Thom.

One summer, Billy, Paul, and I chartered a thirty-five-foot sailboat out of Greenport, a small seaside town on the northern coast of Long Island, and sailed to Nantucket and Provincetown. Billy was an excellent sailor and served as the captain of the boat. Paul's cooking abilities made him our galley chef. I became the trusty first mate and tried to help whenever I could.

Ptown was the gay summer mecca in New England, as Fire Island was in New York. It was a free and open town. The bars were crowded with great-looking guys. One night, Billy and Paul stayed on the boat while I made my way through the crowds in the bars and met this guy named Jack—good looking, around my age. We talked and danced and drank brandy stingers till it was near closing. I was waiting for him to invite me to his place when he dropped the bombshell: he lived with his mother. Just my luck. We just kissed goodnight.

One evening that same summer after work, I was walking down Third Avenue and made eye contact while passing this sexy-looking young guy. I walked a few feet and stopped to see if he would turn around. To my surprise, he did. For a moment, we both stood looking at each other, waiting to see who would make a move. He seemed rather shy. I started walking toward him as he walked toward me. We chatted a bit and introduced ourselves. His name was Brad. He was around five foot nine, with light-brown hair clipped short, a boyish body, and the most kissable-looking lips. I suggested we go for a drink, and he accepted.

At the bar, I got to know a little about him. He said he had recently moved to New York from Los Angeles and was working part time at Bloomingdale's and going to FIT (Fashion Institute). I invited him to my place and had the hottest sex I'd had in a long time. He was as sexy in bed as he had looked on the street. That first encounter with Brad was the beginning of a long, sexually charged affair.

Brad lived in a small apartment on Fifty-Eighth Street with a roommate named Stefan. In the beginning, we got together only on weekends, but that changed to several times a week. I'd never met anyone as sexually adventurous as Brad. He was willing to try any position, and we did. I introduced him to my friends, who all thought he was quite a number. We went dancing in the clubs in the city, and he started spending weekends on Fire Island with me at the house I'd rented. That winter, he went skiing with me in Vermont. Even though we were together a great deal, I kept my independence, and he kept his. Our affair lasted until he moved back to California, but our friendship has remained till this day.

Fifty-Nine

In the early spring of 1976, I accompanied Werner to the Pines because he decided to buy property there. We had remained friends, and he trusted my opinion. I was not interested in buying anything myself; I preferred renting. But when the real estate broker showed us a two-bedroom duplex unit in the Co-Ops with a balcony facing the ocean, I fell in love with the idea. The Co-Ops was a complex of a hundred or so apartments in the Pines directly across from the downtown harbor area. Impulsively, I told him over dinner that night that I would go into partnership with him and buy the unit. He was pleased and agreed.

I don't know what had gotten into me. I was in my early thirties, reasonably successful at the salon, having a ball, and had managed to save a nice little nest egg. I had never planned on ever owning real estate. The sale price was $40,000.00. It was the largest amount of money I had ever seen on paper. Of course, my share was only half that, but still, I had had to do a lot of heads of hair to save that amount.

We were approved by the co-op board of directors. The sale went through, and I was part owner of a lovely apartment in one of my favorite places in the whole world. It was scary but exciting to embark on this new phase of my life.

The timing was right because Billy and Paul had moved to Pound Ridge, New York, in the country and were no longer renting on the island. I had bought out Billy's share of the speedboat we still owned and rented a boat slip in the harbor directly across from the Co-Ops.

In late spring, Werner and I spent the first few weekends decorating the apartment. It would be our first summer there, and we wanted it to be perfect. We each had our own bedroom, his downstairs and mine upstairs.

I had had no idea how good it would feel to own a place on the island after so many years of renting. It made me wonder why I had waited so long. I was still seeing Brad at the time. In the beginning, he was out there often, but our affair had started to cool down and it became on-again, off-again, leaving me freer to party on my own. Werner never went to the discos, but I was out there all the time, especially at the new disco, the Sandpiper, in the harbor area in the Pines.

The Pines was still *the* place to be during the summer. There were several parties happening each weekend. The most talented and beautiful people had houses in the Pines. Tea Dance was the highlight of the afternoon in the harbor area at the only hotel-club there. It used to be called the Botel (now called the Blue Whale), and it was always teeming with good-looking guys and well-known actors and designers.

People would freshen up and go out at five in the evening, looking their best, to drink, dance, be seen, or hook up with a date for the evening. It was a wild scene. Nearly everyone was stoned on something, and I certainly had my share. You could hear the snap of poppers (amyl nitrate) on the dance floor. It was so popular; you could get a contact high just by dancing next to someone using them.

One of the most memorable experiences I had on the island at the time was with a hot guy named Jim who had a house near the Co-Ops. Jim was much taller and quite a bit younger than I was. He had dark-blond hair, cut short in a buzz cut, and was a little rough around the edges. I was neighborly but not very interested in dating him. But he courted me relentlessly. Every weekend, when I arrived on the island, there would be a present on my doorstep from him and an invitation to get together. I always thanked him and was flattered by his gesture.

On one Monday afternoon, usually a quiet day in the Pines because most people had left, he invited me over. I wasn't leaving until later, so I decided to accept. When I arrived at his house, he suggested we go out in the sunshine on the outside deck and have a drink. His deck was totally secluded by a ten-foot solid wooden fence.

"Do you mind if I get comfortable?" he asked.

"Sure. It's your house."

He stripped and lay down on a chaise. He had a great body and was quite well endowed.

After a bit, he said, "Why don't you join me?"

I knew where this was going, and I took off my clothes as well. The sun and the gentle breeze hitting my naked body felt incredible. It didn't take us long before we started to have sex. We carried on for hours. Afterward, all we could do was lie there in total exhaustion. I was beginning to gather my things to leave when we heard a burst of applause coming from the adjacent house, slightly above his deck. I had had no idea we were being watched, but the men living there seemed to enjoy the show.

Jim became my late-summer affair that season. He was creative sexually, and I loved to play along. One Saturday night, he arrived at my place to pick me up to go dancing in Cherry Grove. He was no sooner in the apartment when he asked me to drop my jeans. I did, thinking he wanted to get it on before we went dancing. He had another plan.

He took out a piece of thin leather, about three feet long, and proceeded to tie one end around the base of my penis and testicles, causing me to start to get excited. Then he tied the other end around his. We stood there, our cocks connected. He then said, "Pull your jeans up. We're going dancing."

"You're kidding, right?"

He shook his head. I could see he was serious. We were both wearing button-fly jeans, making it easy for the leather string to come though the space in the buttons. Curious as to where this was going, I followed along. As we walked, the tiniest tug on the leather around me got me aroused, which I realized was Jim's intention.

Connected crotch to crotch, we walked side by side to the harbor for a water taxi to the Grove. Jim walked confidently with his arm around my shoulder, but I felt self-conscious, thinking everyone we passed noticed the leather connecting us. If they did, they didn't seem to care. That's the way it was on the island.

I thought there was going to be a problem for us stepping down into the water taxi, but Jim said we would just do it together. We got a couple of comments like "You guys look hot."

We danced for hours, taking breaks every now and then, never farther than three feet apart. We even peed together at the same urinal. That leather tied around my penis and balls kept me aroused all night. It was the sexiest night of dancing I ever had.

Sixty

After eighteen years behind a salon chair, I had become increasingly irritable servicing the same clients, doing the same cuts, hearing the same gossip week after week. In the salon business, you either get tired of your clients or they get tired of you. The writing was on the wall for me. As much as I loved what I did, I needed a change. And I was beginning to notice that all the new hairdressers were younger than I was. That started me wondering about the future. One couldn't stand eight, sometimes ten, hours a day forever, after all.

It was the late seventies when Werner, a veteran in show business hair styling, gave me the best advice I had ever received from anyone. "You cannot stand behind the styling chair all your life, Milton. You either own your own salon or do something else with your talent. Like show business."

It was an eye opener. I never wanted my own salon. I had seen too many failures. The responsibility of running a business, dealing with bitchy clients and haircutters, was not something I was interested in. Werner led such a glamorous life, styling stars of stage, screen, and TV. He was not part of the daily grind of salon work.

"You may be right, but how can I break into that world? I've only worked in salons."

"Don't worry. I'll keep my eye open for you. Something will turn up."

True to his word, Werner called a month or so later. At that time he was working on the hot new TV show *Saturday Night Live.* It was the first live TV show in decades and a hectic gig, but it was exciting and paid well. They needed another hair stylist to help out that weekend. He was able to use me, a nonunion member, because no other members were available at such short notice.

I went directly from the salon that evening to the eighth-floor make-up room of the NBC studios, where Werner briefed me on the workings of the show. I would be taking care of Jane Curtin's hair changes. My stomach started to gurgle. I had never watched *Saturday Night Live*, much less knew how it worked. But I knew she was one of the big cast members.

"How much time is there for each change?"

"Sixty."

I breathed easy. "It'll be tight, but an hour will work."

He laughed. "Sixty *seconds*, Milton! It's live TV."

One minute per style! My stomach dropped to my feet. I'd never done *anything* in sixty seconds.

"Werner, I'm not sure I can—"

"I know you can handle it. It's a quick change."

It was grueling, but somehow I managed to pull it off. When the show wrapped, I was exhausted and went home and collapsed. That was my introduction to a hair change in the performance world. Despite the anxiety of working the show, I could see that was why Werner loved it so. Working with stars in a fast-paced, creative environment beat the boring routine of the salon. I was ready to make the change at the first opportunity.

In the summer of 1979, Werner told me about a position at the hot new Broadway musical *Dancin'*, a Bob Fosse extravaganza. I interviewed with Romaine, the hair designer of the show, and she hired me on the spot, despite my lack of theatrical experience. Of course, I had a strong recommendation from Werner, who was well respected. I had a few days to get it all together.

The decision to leave my secure salon position was a difficult one. I was making a good salary and made my own schedule. Working on a Broadway show, I would be bound by its hectic schedule, make only half the money with no tips, and would have to make new friends. I knew I would have to make time in the off hours to supplement my income by doing clients on the side. Many of my longtime clients were excited for me and were ready to follow me, but some felt abandoned.

Keith and Thom were not only my bosses but my friends. Having to give them such short notice made me feel guilty. However, Keith and Thom had been fighting on and off for quite some time, and their partnership was dissolving. It made my decision to leave easier. While they felt a bit put out by my leaving so suddenly, they were excited for my big break into show biz and wished me well.

After nearly twenty years of hairdressing, I thought I knew a lot about hair, but I discovered that the world of theatrical styling was entirely different from the salon. I had a lot to learn, but I was ready for the challenge. After my experience at *Saturday Night Live,* I had the confidence that I could work under pressure.

On my first day, Romaine gave me a tour of backstage and the makeup room, located under the stage where the hair and wigs were styled. She introduced me to Gary, the hair stylist I was replacing, and to Steve, the one I would be working with. Romaine had designed the hairstyles of the show; she did not work it. She also gave me some tips on doing the wigs. They all seemed nice and very professional.

I spent the next two days following Gary and learning how he worked backstage during changes and how he kept each hairstyle fresh during the show. Working backstage in the dark looked challenging, but I was certain that I would master it.

It was exciting meeting the dancers, especially Ann Reinking, who was the featured dancer. I found out that dancers were lots of fun. They usually did their own makeup and loved to joke around with one another. Most dancers, I noticed, warmed up before a show and avoided eating anything heavy. Ann Reinking was the only dancer in the show who could go onstage after a big lunch and kick up high without warming up. I know this to be a fact because Ann, Steve, and I would have big lunches together between shows.

My first day on my own was nerve racking. Steve was extremely helpful and encouraging. Werner was busy working on a movie but wished me well. I learned to listen to the music and wait in the wings for my cue to make a hair change on stage right or left. I got used to working in the dark and working on demand. In a very short time, I learned a great deal about wigs and hairpieces and how to maintain the style the designer required. The wigs had to be washed and redressed once a week. It was all new and refreshing. Wigs do not talk back at you like salon clients.

During most every show, there was some hair disaster backstage. I would have to fix it so the audience would not notice. One time, one of the dancer's hairpieces came loose as she shook her head back and forth dancing onstage. She grabbed it with one hand and held on till the end of the number. It was quite embarrassing for me, and I made sure it never happened again.

During intermission, I had to go into the girls' dressing rooms to make their hair changes. I was the only male allowed in. Everyone knew I was gay. Two of girls had just had breast implants and were topless, massaging their new breasts as their doctors ordered. The two of them sat there, natural as could be, as if they were sitting having tea with Her Ladyship as I did their hair.

I found working on Broadway exhilarating because it was live, in real time. Unlike salon work, where I was used to taking my time until I got the style the way I wanted it, there was no time for that level of perfection. The show had to go on no matter what, and I had to make sure the players looked their best. Unlike salon cuts, which had to last until the next appointment, performers' hairstyles only had to last for the performance. Fortunately, I was a fast learner.

My personal life changed drastically after I started working the Broadway show. My work schedule switched from day to night. I had to report for work at seven thirty, a half hour before curtain. Instead of dinners with friends, I ate alone at six o'clock or grabbed a sandwich on the way in. Wednesdays and Saturdays we had both matinee and evening performances. Since there was little time between shows, I usually hung around, grabbed some dinner, and did a couple of haircuts for the crew. Sunday was a matinee day only. The curtain came down at five o'clock, and I had the evening free to go out to dinner and party or go to Fire Island. I was able to stay on the island until Tuesday afternoon because theaters were dark on Monday. My affair with Brad was still on at times. We would meet at my apartment after the show and party until one or two in the morning. And, of course, I had fun on the island. It was exhausting but fun.

Sixty-One

I suppose one could say that Werner loved to stay as busy as possible. He worked films and in his downtime worked TV occasionally as well. He advised me that since most Broadway shows don't run forever, it would be smart for me to hedge my bets for the future and introduced me to the manager in charge of scheduling hair, makeup, and wardrobe at NBC studios. Sadie was a longtime friend and former employer of Werner's. With my experience on Broadway and my one time on *Saturday Night Live,* she agreed to book me for fill-in work as a nonunion freelancer when union stylists weren't available. The TV industry was totally unionized. Money was tight, and I was more than happy to accept the extra work.

The days I worked both TV and Broadway were long, grueling days but were worth the time I put in. The shows Sadie put me on sent very favorable reports to her, asking her to schedule me again. I managed to fit in my private clients between four and six or on Mondays. The hardest days were when Sadie booked me on *The Today Show* because I usually had to start before dawn.

Working in TV was another adjustment, but I rolled with it quite well. In TV, the talent comes in freshly shampooed and cut, ready to be blown out and styled. The styles usually followed the current trends and the personal taste of the hosts, actors, or actresses. Working with celebrities could be a challenge, but I learned how to charm them. After all, I had spent twenty years dealing with demanding clients at the salon. It was a whirlwind time for me, both exciting and fascinating work.

After I had been working about a year as a freelancer, Sadie offered me a full-time staff position at NBC. I was assigned to *The Today Show* in the morning and the soap opera *The Doctors* in the late morning. While I hesitated to give up the glamour of working on Broadway, working in TV paid better, and, as a full-time employee, I would be able to join the union as an apprentice. Broadway had not been unionized at that point. I gave two weeks' notice at *Dancin'*. The cast was sad to see me go but gave me a great going-away party.

Werner, who had worked at *The Today Show* for years, prepared me for the rigors of working full time on a morning news show. He said my life would change radically. He was right. Working on a morning news show was brutal. Monday through Friday, I had to be there at 4:00 a.m. to get the hosts ready in time for their 7:00 a.m. appearance. Tom Brokaw and Jane Pauley were hosting when I started. The entire *Today Show* family was a delight to work with, which made arriving so early in the morning bearable.

Gene Shalit, the film critic, always arrived in the makeup room in good humor and with his trademark bushy head of hair. Willard Scott, always telling jokes, never could sit still while having his toupee put on. As I had discovered on Broadway, all the fun stuff happened in the makeup room.

While my first responsibility was to help the hosts of the show, it was also part of my job to help any person of interest, famous or not, who came through as a guest. I got to work on some rather impressive, important people. One of my big faux pas early on was when Jane Fonda appeared on the show. While fixing her hair, I mentioned that I had loved her in the movie *Chinatown*. She replied graciously that Faye Dunaway had starred in the film. I blushed and apologized.

I had the pleasure to work on guests such as Sofia Loren and Bette Midler. Most male guests did not need much help. One male celebrity, who shall remain nameless, brought his hair in a box expecting it to be washed and styled before the show. When Bob Hope was a guest, I had to go to his hotel to do his hair. It was another learning experience in celebrity protocol. In the limo back to the show, I sat in the back beside him instead of the front with the driver. That simply was not done.

I worked closely with Bobbie, the makeup artist who had been with *The Today Show* since its inception. Bobbie was a true Yankee, with a tough outside and a generous, soft inside. An attractive woman in her middle fifties, very stylish, she chain-smoked and was never caught without wearing her mink eyelashes.

Bobbie had started doing makeup when TV shows were all live. It was her life. She was a supreme professional and knew where and how much makeup to use on a person, and she did it with the greatest of ease. Everyone who knew her respected her expertise. Bobbie did not take any crap from anyone, especially from people appearing on the show trying to be divas. She was a woman of few words and always spoke frankly. One time, Ann Miller, the famous tap dancer, made an appearance on the show. Miller came into the makeup room with heavy stage makeup she'd done herself. "Do I need any more makeup?" she asked Bobbie. Bobbie looked at her and said, "I wouldn't know where to put it."

Sixty-Two

My second show, *The Doctors,* started at 9:00 a.m., immediately after *The Today Show.* It was a relief because the show was taped and a bit more leisurely than live TV. The makeup room was directly across the hall, which made the transition easy. Lee, the senior staff makeup artist at NBC, was scheduled on the show. It took me fifteen minutes to set up my equipment to do the cast. Rehearsal and camera blocking started at 9:30.

The cast would arrive promptly with clean, dry hair. I would either set the hair in hot rollers or blow it out and style. This process usually took the greater part of the day because I had access to the actors only during the scenes they were not rehearsing. The actors did not have to be in their costumes for rehearsal. I was responsible only for the main characters; the background actors had to do themselves. The number of people I had to do on a daily basis varied depending on the storylines.

By 3:00 p.m., the cast was camera ready to tape the half-hour show. Lee and I did our final touch-ups, and the cameras rolled. The last part of the day was spent watching the videotape of the show in case anything had gone wrong and we had to reshoot. That was the hardest part of the day for me because having been up before 4:00 a.m., my body was ready to shut down. I often dozed off in the dark viewing room. Luckily, no one noticed.

Some of the most well-known actors started their careers working on soap operas, and *The Doctors* certainly had its share of rising stars. Kathleen Turner was one. When I started working on *The Doctors,* she was appearing in the show *Gemini* at night at the Little Theater on Broadway and working on *The Doctors* during the day. That kind of schedule is hard on anyone's body, especially actors who have to appear on camera. Kathleen was a striking woman and could wear a variety of hairstyles better than most.

She came into the makeup room one morning looking as if she had had no sleep. She looked into the mirror several times, up close and then farther away, and said out loud, "You are beautiful!" I guess she had to psych herself up for the show. By the time the camera rolled, we had her looking perfectly lovely.

Alec Baldwin started his career on *The Doctors* as well. He was a young, charismatic, cocky guy, very friendly and comfortable around people. The makeup room came alive when he walked in. My biggest challenge with him was cutting and styling his bone-straight hair and keeping it out of his eyes. We got along quite well. I would tell him, "Sit down, doll, and let me do something with that mop of hair." "Doll" was a pet name I used for many of my actors.

One morning, Alec walked into the makeup room just as I was taking a vitamin pill. He asked, "What are you taking?"

"It's niacin. Good for your blood flow. Want one?" I said.

I must have taken more than my dose because I turned beet red and got tingly all over right before his eyes.

"Not if it does that to you!" he said, laughing.

It became a running joke between us. To this day, whenever I see him, he asks, "How is the niacin working for you?" We've become friends over the years.

This hectic schedule changed my work life dramatically. I missed the excitement working on Broadway, but working in TV was less stressful and more varied creatively. The best part of working in TV was that my evenings were free again. My early arrival to work became routine, and after a quick nap at home, I took full advantage of the wild scene in town. There were times I would not get home from partying until 1:00

a.m., got a few hours of sleep, and then showered and took off for my 4:00 a.m. call at NBC. Luckily, I didn't seem to need much sleep.

Many mornings, I had to wear sunglasses to hide my bloodshot eyes, which miraculously cleared after the first hour of the show. Bobbie, knowing the party animal I was, said, "Honey, don't come in until four thirty. I'll plug in your hot rollers for you." That half hour made a big difference, and I was grateful for her help.

Sixty-Three

Several glorious summers had passed since Werner and I bought the apartment in the Co-Ops. After I started working a normal five-day week at NBC, I joined the usual Friday-Sunday weekend rush. Werner would often join me at the house, since he was working films exclusively at that point and had most weekends off when he was in town. However, over the years, we did find that living in the Co-Ops, right smack in the center of the harbor area, had its disadvantages. While the ocean, with its spectacular beach, was directly in front of our apartment, we were too close to all the action, making it impossible to have any quiet time. Usually, I had to go farther up or down the beach to a less crowded area just to have a relaxing swim.

It was during our fourth summer there that we decided to look for something in a quieter area of the Pines. After seeing several properties, we found the perfect house. It was a small, two-bedroom house with a partial view of the ocean, located on three lots at the far end of the Pines just outside Cherry Grove. There was enough property to build a pool and a large deck. The living room was large, with two sets of sliding doors and a fireplace. There was also a back deck with an outside shower, which I knew would become a favorite of mine.

Werner and I decided to buy it. We put the Co-Op apartment on the market and it sold immediately for double the original price. We used the entire amount as a down payment on the house and took out a mortgage for the balance. I had never taken out a mortgage before, but

I knew we were getting a good deal and felt more settled in my career then, so I decided to take the risk.

We took possession of the house in the middle of October, just as most people were closing their summer houses. We decided to celebrate with dinner at the Monster, a popular restaurant in Cherry Grove. Before leaving, we lit a fire in the fireplace and had a toast to our new summer home—then another, and another, until several bottles of wine were gone. We were so drunk that we almost forgot our dinner reservation, and we stumbled along the beach to arrive late. The host/hostess was a tall, bald, heavyset queen dressed in a caftan with enough attitude to fill a room. He looked us up and down and said, "Follow me…if you can!" We just laughed and had a wonderful meal despite that bitchy queen.

Werner and I opened our new house in late April of 1980 and spent most of the spring fixing it up. We were settled in well before the beginning of the season. The neighborhood seemed quiet despite the closeness of the houses. Our house was two walkways down from the edge of the notorious wooded area that separated the Pines from Cherry Grove, known as the Meat Rack. It was the place people went to have anonymous sex at night under the stars, hidden by trees and bushes.

My friend Teddy told me about his experience one foggy night roaming through the Meat Rack looking for some action. Teddy's vision was particularly poor, and he refused to wear his glasses in the dark of the night. He could barely make out shapes. He stopped abruptly when he came in view of a husky-looking shape of a guy. He waited for any sign of movement. Finally, he got up enough nerve and walked closer and said, "Been here long?" Getting no response, he reached out and discovered it was a dead tree trunk, with two branches shaped liked husky arms. He said he was disappointed, but the following night was hot.

While it was exciting to hear all the hot stories of sex alfresco, I preferred more comfort and privacy.

Since we were new in the neighborhood, we decided to give a party and invite all our friends and neighbors. Theme parties were all the rage. Tattoos were in vogue, so we decided on a tattoo theme. The invitation had a drawing done by Teddy, our artist friend, of a hunky guy sitting on a tree branch with a snake tattooed over one shoulder all the way down to his ass.

The turnout was fantastic! Some people sported their quite elaborate tattoos. Others had drawn temporary ones on their bodies just for the party. One guy, who loved showing off his perfect ass, had a beautiful butterfly tattooed on his right cheek.

Teddy gave me my temporary tattoo. He drew a snake similar to the one on the invitation, starting on my front shoulder and going all the way down to my ass. It took him nearly three hours to complete. I had to cut my jeans down so the head of the snake would be visible. It was quite a hit.

We loved the house so much that we made plans to build a deck and pool on the side. A crew of workers started breaking ground immediately after the summer season was over. The building and construction continued until the first snowfall and started again in March. By April of 1981, the deck and pool were nearly finished. We were pleased but amazed at the size of the new additions. The deck and pool was nearly twice the footprint of the whole house. The deck included a bar, an eating area, and a lounging area with a six-foot fence for privacy. The new decking surrounded the built-in pool. As a result, our house became known as the Pool with the House.

Werner was especially happy that summer because he was with his new boyfriend, Stephen. They had met during the winter through a mutual actor friend. Between films, Werner was designing the hair for a short live Broadway show, *Bring Back Birdie.* Stephen, younger than Werner, had worked in a salon for several years and expressed interest in doing the hair on the show to a friend in the cast. Werner noticed he had talent and put him in charge of doing hair for the chorus. That turned out to be the beginning of an illustrious career for Stephen and a beautiful relationship between the two of them.

Since our house was built on stilts, like most houses on Fire Island, we decided to build a small room under the house to use as a third bedroom and rent it to our friends Tony and Bobby D, fellow hairdressers from the theater world. The room was accessible from the back staircase. All five of us were hairdressers and had a lifetime of stories to share about the business. We became known as the House of Hair. During that summer, Stephen, Tony, and Bobby D worked on *Bring Back Birdie.* Since there was no Sunday performance, they hired a limo after the curtain came down on Saturday to catch the last ferry to the Pines. Werner and I, already on the island, greeted them at the ferry dock. The weekends were filled with Sunday pool parties and drop-in friends.

Sixty-Four

Ever since the huge success of the porn feature film *Deep Throat,* the porn industry, once the province of sleazy Times Square theaters and peep shows and eight-millimeter home films, became more mainstream than ever before. And with the later introduction of home videos, porn was exploding in bedrooms across America. Gay porn was no exception. The male porn stars became minor celebrities in their own right. Men threw parties in which they watched their favorites perform onscreen, which led to all-night orgies. I wasn't an avid fan initially, but after meeting a few of the men off screen, I could understand the attraction.

My first encounter with a real-life porn star happened quite innocently. While walking along the beach one summer afternoon in the Pines, I saw a stunningly handsome guy sitting alone on a towel looking out at the ocean. He was beautiful, with dark hair, deep-blue eyes, and an amazing body. I could not resist and walked over to him. He motioned for me to sit next to him on the towel. His name was Bo. We chatted for a while. I wanted to jump his bones, but for some reason, I suggested we go water skiing. He said he did not know how, but he would like to try.

I briefed him on water skiing while we walked to the harbor to my speedboat. The boat was ready to pull out as soon as I put the top down and loosened the lines. Bo had a big smile on his face when he got aboard and said he had never been in a speedboat. We motored out of the harbor. Great South Bay was calm that day, perfect for water skiing. I motored a safe distance from the harbor and cut the engine. I gave Bo some pointers, equipped him with a life preserver, put the skis and tow line in the water, and told him to jump in. I started the engine, but Bo couldn't get the hang of standing up on the skis. We tried a number of times before we finally gave up.

He got back in the boat, and I motored to the center of the bay, cut the engine, and let the boat drift. There were no other boats around that day. I laid a towel on the seat, grabbed Bo in my arms, and guided him down next to me. I pulled his swimsuit down and then mine. The sun and air felt fantastic on my naked body. It was electric. The bobbing up and down of the boat added another sensation to the moment. We started making passionate love. It got hotter and hotter, and we lost all sense of time and place.

Suddenly, I heard the sound of a boat. We had drifted into the channel, and the ferry boat, blowing its horn, was passing us just yards away with a full load of passengers on the top deck, waving at us and clapping. We hurriedly got our suits on. I started the boat and headed back. I saw Bo later at Tea Dance, and we kissed. A friend of mine came up to me afterward to ask how I had scored one of the hottest porn stars. I was shocked—but not surprised, judging from his sexual expertise.

My sexual thrills with porn stars were not limited to just weekends on Fire Island but carried on in the city as well. One of the best-known porno stars at the time was a hot number named Calvin, who had starred in *Boys in the Sand.* We met on a subway platform in Manhattan in front of a men's room. The men's rooms were open in those days and famous for cruising. We made eye contact, chatted a bit, and then made a date to meet that very afternoon at my apartment. Calvin had an all-American boy look and the most beautifully shaped ass I'd ever seen. When he told me he was a porn star, I could understand why. Later I found out that he was a superstar in that world. Lucky me.

We had been dating for a while when Calvin invited me to a special party he was giving at one of his fans' Upper East Side apartments. That evening, I had tickets to the Metropolitan Opera, so I told him I'd come over after the performance. I arrived at the party location still dressed in suit and tie and rang the bell. Calvin opened the door totally nude, with a big smile and an even bigger erection. I have never felt so overdressed.

"Good, you are finally here. Take off your clothes and join us upstairs."

The apartment was huge and lavishly appointed. I left my clothes in the living room and walked up the stairs feeling a little self-conscious and not knowing what to expect.

There was a huge orgy going on in the bedroom. Some heads popped up briefly when I walked in, but for the most part, everyone just continued what they were doing. Calvin was in bed screwing this tall, good-looking guy who, I later found out, was a well-known feature-film actor who was not out at the time. Apparently, he was a big fan of Calvin, and was invited as the guest of honor. Calvin motioned for me to join them. I joined them for a while, but threesomes were not really my thing. I was there for Calvin, after all. At some point, Calvin strapped on a huge dildo, and I just left. That was my last foray into the world of porn stars.

Sixty-Five

In 1981, the whole world changed. Word spread throughout the United States of an unknown disease that attacked the immune system. It became known as HIV (Human Immunodeficiency Virus), which led to the deadly disease called AIDS (Acquired Immune Deficiency Syndrome). At first, it was thought to affect only gay men, but as the epidemic grew, it affected nearly every community, gay or straight. One of the principal ways to contract the disease was through unprotected sex.

This epidemic caused panic in the gay community. Unprotect sex had been the norm for years. With the advent of this disease, health professionals urged everyone to engage in safe or protected sex and to be tested to prevent the spread of the disease. But many people were afraid to get tested. At that time, testing positive was tantamount to a death sentence, as there was no treatment available. Because of my own sexual behavior, I thought about getting tested, even though I did not show any symptoms. However, I decided against it. The more I learned about the practice of safe sex (a term coined in because of AIDS), I realized that my own activities fell squarely within its bounds, so I continued to be increasing careful about what I did and with whom and practiced safe sex.

This epidemic hit the arts and entertainment industry, where many gay men worked. I had friends coming down with the symptoms and dying months later. It was heartbreaking to watch these vibrant and creative men slowly deteriorate. Brad's roommate, Stefan, came down with the symptoms of HIV/AIDS and had blood transfusion after blood transfusion. It worked for a while. But he lost most of his hair and body weight.

Lesions from Kaposi's sarcoma started appearing on his body. He had to be hospitalized. I went to see him quite often. Because they knew little about this disease, the hospital compelled you to wear protective gowns, gloves, and hats. When Stefan saw me all covered up, he turned his head in disgust at what he had become.

One time, I stayed though the night, giving his niece a break. I sat alongside his bed. At some point during the night, he turned and looked at me. I saw the sadness in his eyes; it was almost as if he were saying he was sorry for getting this disease. Early that morning, his niece came to relieve me. He died later that afternoon.

I am fortunate to have survived, considering my lifestyle. Many of my friends did not make it. I miss them so.

It was the spring of 1982, the beginning of a new season on Fire Island. Werner, Stephen, and I opened the beach house at the beginning of May. Bobby D and Tony, our friends who had rented a room last season, decided to rent again. The five of us knew one another quite well and looked forward to a wonderful summer. I never felt like a third wheel with this group because I often invited a friend for the weekend, and, if not, I knew enough guys on the island to party with.

Despite the news about HIV/AIDS on everyone's minds, the island teemed with men looking to escape the heat of the city. While the atmosphere was a bit subdued, everyone still partied till the wee hours. Safe sex was the topic and practice that summer, although it was still not necessarily the norm. I continued to party but made sure to stay safe.

Sixty-Six

One morning, while I was cleaning the leaves out of our pool, our neighbor in the Pines, Earhart, an attractive Swiss-German man, appeared on his deck with a good-looking guy. He was tall and lean, with a fair complexion and quite handsome features. He was conservatively dressed for the Pines, in pants and a sport shirt. I assumed it was his new boyfriend.

We exchanged hellos. Earhart introduced him as Terrence, his houseguest for the weekend. Our houses were built close, no more than a yard apart, so it was easy to conduct a conversation. Terrence commented on how murky and green the water was in our swimming pool.

"Yes, I know. We don't know how to fix it."

"Use more chemicals to shock and stabilize the water," he suggested quite confidently. "And keep the pump running. By afternoon, it should be crystal clear."

"Terrence is a contractor," Earhart added. "I'd take his advice."

"Then I certainly will. Thanks."

I went straight down to the supply store and picked up what we needed, and the pool was clear in no time. Earhart's guest was not only handsome but also quite knowledgeable. I was impressed and wished he were my boyfriend.

Later, that afternoon, while my housemates went to Tea Dance, I had a swim in the pool and a shower on the outside deck. Feeling fresh and clean, I took a walk to the beach with cocktail in hand for an afternoon gaze at the ocean. There wasn't a soul on the beach, and it was peaceful.

Standing at the top of the dunes and watching the surf roll in and out as dusk begins to take over the sky is one of nature's gifts.

In the distance, I noticed one lone person walking along the surf. He started to walk toward the steps on which I was standing. As he drew near, I realized he was Terrence. He was wearing a forest-green shirt and light pants—not the usual bare-chested-and-tight-trunks look most of the other men on Fire Island sported.

"Hi," he said, and he smiled as he walked up the steps.

"Hello. It's Terrence, right? We met this morning."

"Yes. How did you make out with the pool?"

"Your advice was perfect. It cleared up nicely."

"Happy to help."

As we talked, the attraction between us was obvious. I invited him to the house for a drink. By then, my housemates had returned. I introduced Terrence to the others. He had the kind of wit that seemed to fit into the group quite well. After the first drink, Werner, noticing the attraction we had for each other, whispered in my ear, "Invite him to dinner." I did, and he accepted.

That night, we went dancing at the Ice Palace in Cherry Grove. After a couple of hours, we left and walked back to my house along the ocean, stealing a kiss every now and then. It was a beautiful night, made for lovers.

No sooner were we in the front yard than we started to paw each other. We could hardly wait to get inside, leaving a trail of clothes behind on the way to the bedroom. We made love till the wee hours of the morning. We could not get enough of each other. Despite our wild abandon, we made sure to practice safe sex. It was glorious.

The following day, he went next door and collected his things, and he spent the rest of the weekend with me. Earhart was not offended by his houseguest leaving. After all, it was part of the free lifestyle on the island.

Terrence was from Canada and had been living in Manhattan for a couple of years in an old building in the East Village, on the corner of

Astor Place. He had a roommate named Frank, an antique dealer. That week, we spent nearly every night together at my place in town.

Every day, I looked forward to our next meeting after work. For the first time in a long while, I did not have the desire or interest to go to bed with anyone else. When I was with him, I felt totally content, socially and sexually. He was eight years younger than I was, smart, creative, and insightful. I introduced him to my circle of friends. They all accepted him with open arms. I invited him to the beach house the following weekend. I realized I was in love.

Our relationship grew stronger and stronger over the fall and into the winter that year. We continued to see each other nearly every day. There were times I had to have an early night because I was still working on *The Today Show*, but it did not stop us from sleeping together. Most of the time he stayed at my apartment, but on occasion I stayed with him at his place.

In the early eighties, the East Village was just beginning to become hip. People were fixing up the run-down tenement buildings and turning the neighborhood around slowly. The first time I visited Terrence, I could not find the door to his apartment. The entrance was alongside a smoke shop that had crazy psychedelic posters; the outside walls and doors were painted with Day-Glo colors. Everything blended together. It was crazy.

I finally found the door; I climbed one flight of rickety steps to the first floor and entered into a room filled with incredible antiques. The contrast from the outside to the inside was remarkable. The second floor was mostly living quarters with a roof garden. It was under renovation by Terrence. That was when I became aware of just how talented he was in design, decorating, and building. He had even built a workshop for himself in that tight space.

Six months into our relationship, I knew I was ready to settle down with him. Not since my relationship with Earl had I felt this strongly about another man. We started talking about moving in together in a place of our own because he felt my apartment was not comfortable enough for two. We agreed to start hunting for a house. I was bit surprised, as I had lived in apartments since I had gotten to Manhattan, as did all my friends. No one ever talked about moving, let alone into a "house." But Terrence yearned for more space, and I was willing to explore it with him. One day he announced that he had found the perfect house in Long Island City, directly across the bridge from Manhattan. I was skeptical. Living in Queens? I remembered the long commute I had had to my first job in Astoria. Terrence assured me that it would be an easy commute for me to the NBC studios. That weekend, we went to see it.

At first, I thought it would never work. The house was old and not very attractive. But after hearing the plans Terrence had to fix it up, I went for it. Normally I would procrastinate for days, weeks, but I was sure of our relationship and believed it was the right thing to do. I trusted Terrence. We made an offer, and it was accepted. We became joint owners, sharing equally the purchase and expenses. We set up a joint bank account just for the house expenses. We agreed that I would keep my apartment on First Avenue. The rent was cheap, and I could use it see my private clients. Terrence gave up his place, put his things in storage, and moved in with me in my apartment. It was the first time I had lived with anyone since my short time with Earl. Living together every day strengthened our relationship.

Soon after the closing, he started gutting and redesigning the house. He was a fast worker, and within a month, we were able to move in. Within months, we had the nicest house in the neighborhood. Terrence turned the bottom half of the house into a two-bedroom apartment, which we rented immediately. Having a place of our own meant we were building a life together as a couple. I felt secure and happy.

Sixty-Seven

Working on *The Today Show*, I had gotten used to meeting celebrities and dignitaries coming into the makeup room. Most were polite but distant, in a hurry to do their interview and leave. In 1982 Linda Ronstadt made an appearance on the show. She was a superstar, had just released her album *Get Closer*, and was about to go on tour. The whole studio was abuzz. While I knew of her, I was not familiar with her music. I was expecting to see yet another diva walk into the makeup room. But I was taken by surprise when she entered. She was so friendly and soft spoken. She treated me like a friend, not just a studio hairdresser. I helped her with her hair, which was already lovely, and we chatted. After I was done, she thanked me for the beautiful job. Just before she got out of the chair, she asked me if I was available to do her hair for her upcoming concerts at Radio City Music Hall that week.

I didn't know what to say. It was the first time a *Today Show* guest had asked me to do her hair outside the studio.

"Thank you, but I have to get up so early to do this show; I..."

"Don't worry," she said, smiling. "After you do my hair, you can leave."

With that kind of offer, how could I refuse? I went home and told Terrence. He was so ecstatic, he could hardly contain himself. "Linda Ronstadt! I have every one of her albums. She is the hottest singer right now!" He immediately put on one of her records. I listened and fell in love with her voice.

The concert was the following night. I felt like a lost puppy arriving with my workbag at the stage door on the first night. The backstage area at Radio City was huge, much bigger than any Broadway theater I had worked in. It was a good thing I was taken directly to the right dressing room; otherwise, I would have been roaming for days.

Working with Linda was a delight. She gave me the freedom to style her hair differently for every show. As she had promised, I had her permission to leave after doing her hair, but instead I went out front that first night, saw the show, and became an instant fan. I was too naïve and embarrassed to ask for a ticket for Terrence, but I did have an opportunity to introduce him to Ms. Ronstadt at the stage door the following evening.

Months later, I got a call from Linda's manager asking if I was available to work on a music video she was shooting in Los Angeles. I was to work with the background characters but not Ms. Ronstadt. He said she would consider it a personal favor to her. Of course, they would pay all expenses and a fee. I didn't know what to say and told him I'd get back to him later that day.

It was the first time I would have to travel for business. I would have to miss several days of work at NBC, but it seemed like a great opportunity to do something different. I discussed it with Terrence, and of course he encouraged me to do it. I spoke with Sadie, who was kind enough to help me work out the schedule for my replacement. I called back Linda's manager and accepted. He took care of all the travel arrangements. Terrence came with me to the airport to see me off. I was excited but a bit anxious. I'd never been to LA before, let alone to work with a huge celebrity on a music video.

From the moment I landed, it was hectic. After dropping off my luggage at the hotel, I was driven to the set. I met with the director and makeup artist to get a sense of what they wanted for the cast. Linda greeted me personally and thanked me for agreeing to work on the video. I worked nearly nonstop for the next few days and then was on the red-eye back to New York. I called Terrence every day.

Later that year I had the pleasure of working with Ms. Ronstadt again, in the production of *La Boheme* at the Public Theater in New York. I was very flattered that she asked for me, knowing she had her pick of dozens of expert stylists at the theater. She did only three shows per week. That schedule worked for me because I could do *Today* and *The Doctors* and be at the Public Theater by six o'clock. This time I was able to get a ticket for Terrence, and we met her after the show. Needless to say, he was overjoyed. Sadly, the production ended, but we remained in touch.

That summer, I invited my parents to New York a second time, and they accepted. I was a bit worried about their meeting Terrence and seeing that we lived together, but the meeting between Terrence and my parents went quite well. Mother adored him. My father was his gentle, quiet self and was impressed with Terrence's expertise as a builder. They could not get over how beautiful the house was. They stayed in our bedroom, and Terrence and I stayed in my apartment fifteen minutes away in Manhattan.

Terrence had just finished landscaping the garden that spring. We gave a garden party in my parents' honor and invited all our friends. It did my heart good to see them smiling and laughing, comfortable with me in my new life. We even brought them to the house on Fire Island for the day. They had never been to a place like that and enjoyed it immensely. It was a wonderful visit, and I was so thankful for our loving relationship.

Sixty-Eight

In 1984, I was still on staff at NBC doing *The Today Show. The Doctors* was over, and I was assigned to an afternoon news show, *Alive at Five.* I was in one of the studio makeup rooms working with Lyn, a fellow hair stylist, when I received a call from Linda's manager. We hadn't been in touch since her performance at the Public Theater, but I had followed her career. He asked if I was available to go on Ms. Ronstadt's month-long *What's New* tour in Japan and Australia as her personal hairdresser. I nearly dropped the phone. One month away from NBC and Terrence, on a tour with Linda Ronstadt's new show singing the standards halfway around the world? Me? I didn't know what to do.

I had committed to take over for Lyn on a new show called *The New Show,* a takeoff on *Saturday Night Live,* while she was away doing a film. I thanked him and Ms. Ronstadt for the opportunity but had to decline due to a prior commitment. He gave me his number just in case I changed my mind.

After I hung up the phone, I was a bit dazed.

Seeing my reaction, Lyn asked about the call. I told her that it was a job offer to go on tour with Linda Ronstadt for a month in Japan and Australia, but I didn't want to leave her show in the lurch, so I had declined. Her jaw dropped. When she recovered, she said, "Get back on that phone and tell him you are available. Don't worry about the show. I'll get Sadie to find someone else to take over while I'm away. It's a once-in-a-lifetime opportunity."

I called Terrence, and he agreed with Lyn. No way I should pass up this chance to travel on tour with Linda Ronstadt. He could not have been more supportive and proud that I was going on tour with his favorite singer halfway across the world. A bit nervous, I called back and got the job. I went to see Sadie later that day to give her the news. It was a long time to be away, and I was a little worried she would not let me come back. Supportive as ever, she arranged for a replacement at *Today* and Lyn's show.

I was very excited but at the same time worried about being away from Terrence for a whole month. It would be the first time we'd been apart for that long. When I got home, he greeted me with big hug. He was proud and happy for me. I promised to call him every other day while on tour. We celebrated with dinner and a hot "desert."

Since I was traveling with the entire tour company from New York, Terrence decided not to accompany me to the airport. Before I left home, he held me tight and wished me a safe trip and speedy return.

After an eleven-hour nonstop flight, we landed in Tokyo, the first city of the tour. Tokyo was fascinating, with a culture totally unlike any I had ever experienced. I spent the first couple of days recovering from jet lag, getting acclimated with the rest of the company, and doing a little sightseeing. I called Terrence every other day, mostly to hear his voice. I missed him so.

I had the honor of being included in Linda's entourage. I got along with the rest of the company extremely well, especially her backup singers and the famous conductor/arranger Nelson Riddle. I even had the pleasure of trimming his hair. Compared to the constant touch-ups I had done while working on Broadway after each number, working on a music tour was much more relaxed. Getting Linda ready for the show was a favorite time for me. I could sense her mood—whether she wanted to talk or prepare for the show. After finishing her hair, I always stayed close by for any last-minute change. Every night during the performance, I popped out front to see the show. Linda not only sounded incredible but looked beautiful. The audience went wild for her each night.

After several successful shows in Tokyo, we traveled by bullet train to Osaka and Kyoto. The train travel was a lot of fun because the entire company occupied the same car. It was like one big family traveling together. We chatted and ate together. I French braided all the girls' hair, one after another.

The company flew to Australia after the last performance in Japan. We landed in Sydney, another place I had not been. Again, I found the culture different from my own, but at least I was able to understand the language. We had some downtime before rehearsals began, so several of us toured the sights. Linda was generous and thoughtful, always making sure I was included in the day or evening festivities. I looked forward to our show nights. The excitement never paled.

We finished our tour of Sydney and flew to Melbourne, our last city before returning home. Melbourne was smaller than Sydney, cozier, rather artsy, and easier to get around in. The one thing that impressed me most about Melbourne was its zoo. It was a vast area containing hundreds of species. Linda and a few of us in the group spent an entire day roaming through the well-tended grounds. We had the privilege of a personal guide showing us around.

I did get a chance to experience gay nightlife in both Melbourne and Sydney thanks to Linda's bodyguard, who was Australian and knew both cities well. He was not gay but happy to point me in the right direction. It was a wild scene. Australians loved to party and had a particularly physical style of dancing that was rather intimidating. I just sat back and watched the show. I enjoyed being part of the gay scene halfway across the world. But it made me miss Terrence even more. I was more than happy to get back to him after the tour was over.

Sixty-Nine

I returned to my job at NBC. It was a pleasure to be back with my friends there but a little of a letdown getting back into the same routine after working on the tour. Lyn had returned to resume the hairstyling on her show. In addition to *The Today Show,* Sadie put me in charge of the hairstyling on the TV series *Kate and Allie,* starring Susan Saint James and Jane Curtin. Bobbie, the makeup artist on *Today,* worked with me. The schedule was light, only two days a week. Thursday was a rehearsal day and Friday the tape day at the Ed Sullivan Theater. Our call to work was 10:00 a.m. That gave us both an hour to relax after we had finished at *Today.* I knew Jane Curtin from my work on *Saturday Night Live,* and we all got along quite well.

By this time, I had fulfilled my apprenticeship as a hair stylist and became a full member in Local 798 Makeup Artists and Hair Stylists Union, which enabled me to work on TV shows, commercials, and films. As a full member, I was able to accept work on unionized shows in any one of the three categories as a freelancer as well. Film and commercials had a higher base pay rate than TV, so my goal was to get into those areas eventually. Werner was a great help in helping me break into this new career.

Now that I was a union member and able to explore other opportunities, I expressed an interest in getting into film work to Werner over dinner one evening. He said he was just beginning another Woody Allen film, *Bullets over Broadway,* shooting in New York, and he would see if he could get me on the team to work part time. True to his word, he did hire me for several days during that shoot to do the hair on the extras. It was set in the 1930s. He gave me some pointers on the period styles, but I had already done my own research and was ready. Sadie was good enough to find a replacement for me on my shows for a few days so I could work on the film.

It was my first time on a film set, and it was a whole new world. I'd been a movie fan since I was child, and being on the set was a dream come true. I came to understand just how much went into filming one scene. Every aspect of the shoot has to be in perfect sync, from the weather and set to the lighting, acting, and, of course, the hair and makeup. I watched carefully how Werner, as department head, delegated the work to each hair stylist. I walked away from that shoot with more knowledge than I had ever thought there was to know. I loved it and knew that was where my career was headed. After that, I worked on three or four other films Werner was in charge of and became rather good.

By then, I had gotten enough experience working in film that my reputation grew. I started getting offers regularly to work on films, so I decided to leave my full-time staff position at NBC and enter the freelance world. I was a little frightened to leave a secure position, but I felt ready to move on. Terrence, a lifelong freelance builder and designer, supported me wholeheartedly.

Most of the stylists I met in the film world got their jobs through agents, who took a percentage of their fees. I was lucky enough to get offers through personal connections and never felt the need to have an agent. I learned how to negotiate my own fees and kept every penny.

Early on, most of the films I worked on were shot in or around New York City. However, that would change. I was recommended by my good friend and well-known hair stylist Paul LeBlanc, who had designed the hair in *Amadeus,* to serve as department head, or "key person," on a film in Wilmington, North Carolina. The film was *The Bedroom Window,* starring Elizabeth McGovern, Steve Guttenberg, and Isabelle Huppert. From what I could understand, it was a remake of *Rear Window* by Alfred

Hitchcock, set in contemporary time. Paul and I had worked together on several films in the past, and he felt I'd be perfect for the project. I had not served as key person before, but I was confident I could do the job.

I hadn't been away from Terence for any prolonged period of time since my tour with Linda Ronstadt. This project entailed my being out of town for two to three months. Despite the fact that it was a great opportunity, I did not want to leave Terrence and my home for that long a period. I discussed it with Terrence, and he thought I should take it, provided they paid me for the inconvenience. He said he would visit from time to time.

I quoted the producer a pay rate I thought was beyond their budget, half hoping he wouldn't agree. To my amazement, he accepted it, and I was hired. I soon found out part of the reason for his agreeing to this high rate. It was a nonunion film and didn't need to follow the union's strict staffing guidelines. I would be working alone, without an assistant or any other stylist, as is required on union projects. I was responsible for styling the hair for the entire cast. The cast was wonderful, but the hours were grueling. It was difficult, but it proved to be a fantastic learning experience. It was a career builder for me and led to many other projects.

Seventy

The mid-1980s were exciting years for Terrence and for me. Our relationship was closer than ever, and our careers soared. We were both recognized as talented artisans in our respective fields and had a steady stream of projects. Terrence was a very talented contractor/builder. Each job he completed led to another job just by word of mouth. He had a keen sense of design and color. He was able to walk into an empty room/space, sit down, draw a new design, and build it.

Sadie was kind enough to put me back on *Kate and Allie* two days a week as freelancer. I started to break into TV commercials also, a whole new field for me. Commercials were similar to films, but they were local. The time on set was only one or two days, but they paid the most. I enjoyed working on them because it was fast and easy money. I also worked on films when local projects became available.

Linda would call me from time to time to work on her concerts and videos in Los Angeles. I usually stayed in her house as her guest, and we became close friends. One benefit of my gigs in LA was that I got to visit with my old friend Ronnie from New York and my first boyfriend, Andy. Both had settled in Tinseltown, and it was a joy to reconnect with them. It had been twenty-two years since I had seen Andy, but we always remained in contact. That reunion brought back many beautiful memories from our youth. On one trip, I even introduced my old flames Andy and Ronnie to each other, and they became friends. I wish I could have been a fly on the wall to hear what each one said to the other about me.

I made arrangements to travel home with Terrence to visit my family during Mardi Gras. It was the first time we'd visited New Orleans together. I booked a room in a nice hotel in the Quarter, but they would not hear of it. They insisted we stay in their house. Pleased with their acceptance, I agreed, but something told me to keep the reservation until we arrived—just in case.

My father met us at the airport and drove us back to their house. It was a delightful reunion, and my father cooked one of his wonderful dinners. When we were ready to turn in, my mother pulled me aside and asked that we sleep in separate beds. I realized it was coming from her staunch Pentecostal religion. I told her that while I respected her beliefs, I didn't feel comfortable about her request. Terrence was the person I was spending my life with, and I was not ready to be separated from him at night. I said we would stay in a hotel instead and got ready to leave. At hearing that, she relented and let us sleep together. I was not quite sure why she had changed her mind so quickly but was happy she did. Terrence had no idea this conversation took place, and I never told him. My parents were as gracious as ever during our entire stay.

Terrence charmed the rest of my family, and we had a wonderful Mardi Gras. We stayed a few days after Mardi Gras so Terrence could explore New Orleans's architecture and delicious foods. He enjoyed New Orleans so much he suggested we move there. He also gained twenty pounds.

Seventy-One

In 1987, Werner and I decided to sell the Fire Island house. We had been going to Fire Island for more than twenty years, and it was getting a bit old. Werner and Stephen expressed interest in buying a house in Key West because they wanted to spend the winter in a warm climate. Terrence and I wanted to own a country house together someplace not too far from New York City.

Werner and I had a buyer for the beach house shortly after putting it on the market but could not close until we obtained a certificate of occupancy for the pool extension we'd put in years before. Luckily, the buyers were so in love with the place that they agreed to rent it that summer and keep the offer active until the paper work could be resolved.

Terrence and I started looking at properties within a two-hour drive of New York City. After several months, we found the most divine property in Shohola, Pennsylvania, on the Delaware River. It was on five acres and had four hundred feet of waterfront and three buildings. The main house was an arts-and-crafts-style house built in 1920. The exterior of the first floor was built of stone and the second floor of wood, and it had three small bedrooms, one bath, and a wraparound porch. The house sat high above the river's edge, with a spectacular view. There was a separate guest cottage a few yards away and a barn down the road.

As soon as we finished the tour of the house, Terrence's mind was already swirling with plans about how to add design touches. The following weekend we drove back to Shohola, viewed the house a second time, and made an offer. Two months later, it was ours.

That spring, Terrence and I went to Shohola as often as we could, working on our new house and furnishings.

In late November of 1987, I received a job offer to be Jack Nicholson's personal hair stylist on a film called *Ironweed*, directed by Hector Babenco. In the film business, when you are hired to be a personal stylist to an actor/actress, you are only responsible for taking care of that one person. It's one of the best positions to have and is often reserved for people with much more experience than I had at the time. Most of the film was to be shot in and around Albany, New York, in the winter over two and a half months. It would be a challenge, as it got really cold that far north, but I jumped at the chance to work with Jack Nicholson.

I started collecting research on the late 1930s, the period in which the film was set. One of the things directors and designers liked about me was that I always was prepared. When it came time to discuss Mr. Nicholson's hair for the character he played, I was ready. I had a serious discussion with Mr. Nicholson and the director on the style and length required for the character. I suggested a short cut appropriate to men of the period. Mr. Nicholson agreed to the style I presented, as did the director.

Confidently, I picked up the hair clipper and buzzed the back and sides of his hair. I thought the director was going to faint when he saw all of Jack's hair fall to the ground. Mr. Nicholson's comment was "Maybe a little shorter." I suggested waiting until the first day of shooting to cut more if needed. Two days later, the first day of shooting, Mr. Nicholson said it was perfect.

It was a pleasure watching Mr. Nicholson act. He was a consummate professional. He always knew what was going on, in front of and behind the camera. His generosity with his fellow actors was impressive. He appreciated my work and even gave me a picture of him in character signed, "Could not have done it without you. Jack."

I was happy to be home after finishing the film, mainly to be with Terrence and to see how our new country home was coming along. Despite the cold Pennsylvania winter, he had been working steadily while I was away. Whenever I called him from the set, I asked him, "What are you building?" And his reply would be "You'll see."

He knew I would love what he'd done. After seeing his work, I gasped with delight. He'd designed and built in much of the furniture, such as window benches with cushions and throw pillows, allowing for a tailored, comfortable look. The rooms looked so much more spacious. He'd replaced the old wood-burning stove, the only source of heat in the house, with a new, more efficient one that warmed the entire house. He installed radiant heating under the stone floor in the kitchen and bathroom, which kept the pipes from freezing in the winter and warmed your feet when you stepped out of the bathtub.

Terrence also resurfaced the exterior walls on the cottage that spring. The barn became his workshop. He loved to garden, so he set aside some land for that purpose and built three compost bins, which created the best soil for planting.

For a city boy like me, country living was a real eye opener. There were all sorts of animals running around—wild turkeys, bears, foxes, raccoons, chipmunks, and so on. The deer constantly chased our Abyssinian cat; I guess because he provoked them or their young. That summer we went tubing or rafting down the Delaware River. The townsfolk were friendly and accepting of us newcomers. We discovered it was a great area for antique shopping as well.

Terrence and I enjoyed entertaining, and once the house was finished, our friends came up to visit on weekends. We got a reputation for throwing good parties. Before long, our weekend house became more like home than our house in Long Island City, and we spent most of our time there.

Seventy-Two

In 1988, I had a call to work with Linda on her latest tour, *Canciones Di Mi Padre.* It was a huge stage show with dancers, sets, costumes, and traditional Mexican songs. The tour was scheduled to begin in early July in San Antonio, Texas. Then we would go on to Houston, work our way through the Southern states on up to Virginia and DC, and end New York. Of course, I agreed to go and did not take on any additional projects for the summer.

I did not know much about Mexican hairstyles when I left home, but I certainly picked up speed the moment I arrived. Her dresser, Arturo, a handsome young Mexican guy, extremely talented in Mexican costumes and dance, gave me some pointers. After seeing her costumes, I was able to style her hair appropriately.

I saw a run-through of the show and loved it. It was my first exposure to authentic Mexican music, played by a world-class mariachi band. Linda also hired the best choreographer, set designer, and dancers. The show was spectacular, with songs rich in emotion and colorful traditional costumes in beautiful settings. Linda's singing was superb, as always. I did not miss a night going out front to enjoy the show.

When we hit New York City, it was the end of July and unbearably hot and humid. We had ten shows to perform. I thought the company would enjoy getting out of the hot city on our one day off, so I invited Linda and the entire company to our house in the country. Linda's manager arranged for a bus to transport those in the company who wanted to come. Thirty-five people signed up.

Linda; Janet, Linda's lovely assistant; and I drove up the night before, immediately after the performance. The rest of the company followed the next morning. The three of us, still wide awake from doing a show, spent the two-hour journey talking and telling stories. We arrived at our house after midnight. Through the late-night summer fog and misty rain, we could see lit candles in all the windows. Terrence had done his magic. Our arts-and-crafts house never looked more inviting; it seemed to glow like a haven in the night.

Terrence had refreshments ready and a fresh-baked lemon meringue pie, which Linda still talks about as the best pie she has ever eaten. She thought the house, inside and out, was beautiful. She was happy for the both of us and thanked us for the invitation. Linda stayed in the guest cottage and Janet in the main house.

The company arrived the next morning, grateful to get out of the hustle and bustle of the hot city. The whole day was spent outside playing volleyball, walking through the forest, and sitting alongside the Delaware River. Some people even went swimming. Terrence and I prepared an elaborate picnic for everyone. The company told me that it was their favorite part of the tour.

The show went on touring the country sporadically for the next three years. I always had ample notice of the tour dates and made myself available. It was truly my favorite project I had ever worked.

Seventy-Three

As I learned over the years, there is nothing regular about movie work. Every project is different and changes your life dramatically during the filming. Everyone who works in film lives by the motto "Make no plans, and there will be no disappointments." Your call to work could be at 5:00 a.m. the first day, and it might be 8:00 p.m. when the day is done. The next day you might start at 7:00 a.m. and return home at 10:00 p.m., and so on. By the end of the week, you could be working through the night until dawn. The movie business is demanding, but it is satisfying professionally, with decent wages. Because of the erratic hours one has to work, having a relationship can be challenging. I was fortunate that Terrence was so tolerant of my crazy schedule and had his own projects to keep him busy.

One of the things that I love about film projects is working as part of the creative team of actors, producers and directors, and costume and set designers. With so many talented and opinionated people, it can be quite a balancing act for the hair stylist to keep good relations with everyone and still achieve the hair design that is appropriate to the character. It takes a certain amount of finesse. I personally found it easier to listen first to whatever demands or direction others had and then offer my professional advice afterward. Some directors will try explaining the general look of what they want for each actor, and then you, as the hair designer, must interpret what they are trying to convey.

Film actors are a breed of their own. Some are easygoing, and others can make you pull your hair out. I understand that actors are concerned over how they look because their faces are up there on the screen, blown up a thousand times. One stray hair can ruin an actor's entire image. An actor's trust in the hair stylist is important because he or she becomes the actor's eyes while shooting a scene. That is to say, the hair stylist must pay minute attention to every movement in a scene to make sure the actor's image remains consistent and complimentary, without disruption to the actor. It is nerve-wracking at times.

The relationship between an actor and his or her hair stylist/makeup artist is intimate and personal. As a result of this close contact, the hair stylist is often on the front line of the emotional ups and downs, and this can often lead to some challenging experiences.

I had a call from a makeup artist to style the hair for the iconic movie star Lauren Bacall. She was doing a publicity photo shoot. I refused right on the spot because I had heard she had a reputation of being a handful. News of difficult actors travels fast among hairstylists. I had heard stories about her temper, especially concerning hair and makeup people. Life was too short to be subjected to that kind of abuse. But my friend was desperate and said it would only be for a few hours anyway. After some persuading, I agreed to do it.

The location to do hair and makeup was in Ms. Bacall's apartment, not a studio. I arrived at her building and was told to take the back entrance to her floor. That should have been an omen of what was going to happen, but I just went along. I heard people talking as I stood at the door. I knocked, not noticing there was a bell. Ms. Bacall opened the door and yelled, "There is a bell, you know!"

I smiled and said, "So there is!" I laughed.

She threw me a look of exasperation and then turned and left, expecting me to follow her.

Over her shoulder, she asked if I had brought any products to style her hair. I said I had and mentioned that they were French products.

That seemed to please her. I later found out that French products were her favorite.

I was told we were to set up in the kitchen. My friend, the makeup artist, was already there and looked anxious.

After settling Ms. Bacall in a chair, I asked politely, "How would you like to have your hair styled?"

"I don't want to look like one of those ladies who 'lunch'!" she shot back at me like a cobra.

"Oh, you don't want a big head, then." I replied, perhaps with a little too much attitude.

She didn't reply but just threw her head back in recognition.

I finished setting her hair without another word. My friend did her makeup. When she was done, I started to comb out her hair.

"You know, you have to tease my hair a little."

"Of course." I proceeded gently.

"Well, you're going to have to do more than that!" she barked.

"So you do want a big head" flowed off my tongue without my realizing it. Normally I keep those thoughts to myself.

Again, she gave me that look and tossed her head back. I decided to give it the old sixties teased-and-packed-down look. By the time I finished, she looked as if she had four times the amount of hair, formed into a solid helmet. She looked into the mirror and shouted, "Look. Look at what he has done! It's wonderful!"

I had not expected that.

The photo shoot went smoothly. Afterward, she told me I had done a superb job and she would call me again. That was the part that scared me. Over the years, I worked with her many times, and we became friendly.

On a film set, the makeup trailer is specially designed with proper lighting and tools of the trade to ensure the final look is appropriate to the scene to be filmed that day. Most actors understand that and have their hair and makeup done there. But not always. On one project, an actor refused to sit in the trailer and required that his hair and makeup be done in one of the hotel rooms we were using as a set instead.

In order to accommodate the actor, electricians had to set up proper lighting in the room, and we had to bring in our hair and makeup equipment. This procedure took hours and put the entire production behind schedule twice. I accepted the situation and followed along, despite the extra work. I hoped that seeing all the problems this actor was causing, the director would put his foot down for future scenes.

He did not.

This actor made the same demand the next day. I lost my composure and went directly to the producer. I was so upset I could hardly talk. I explained to the producer what had happened. "I cannot work under these conditions. It's a waste of my time, and unless something changes, I'm off the project."

Producers are masters at dealing with difficult situations, especially those involving actors' special demands, not to mention the concerns of other professionals they might affect.

"I know this situation is difficult," he said diplomatically. "We're behind schedule already. Why don't you take a long lunch at the hotel restaurant? Take Tania with you, and I will pay the bill."

Still angry but realizing he was not going to change the situation, I accepted his offer. Tania, the makeup artist, and I had a delicious, relaxing meal with a glass of wine in the expensive restaurant of the hotel we were shooting in. The lunch gave me a chance to calm down and think about the situation. I returned to work and got through the rest of shoot without incident.

Wigs are a key element in many films, especially period pieces. I've always felt there should be a book from the hair department of dos and don'ts to give to actors who wear wigs while working on a film production. Wigs are made to order, extremely expensive, and very delicate. Hair professionals know how to handle them with great care. Most actors do not.

On one project, an actress went to a restaurant for lunch with her wig still on, which is not unusual. It takes so long to put a wig on properly that actresses often wear them on and off set during the daily shoot. But when she returned to the makeup room for a touch-up before resuming filming, she looked totally different. Her face and wig were covered with little white flakes, as if she had dandruff. "What's all that flakiness?" I asked.

"My friend noticed my forehead was getting red from the wig lace," she said casually. "So I put some bread under it to cushion it."

That was a first. I looked at her in astonishment. It took a minute or two for me to be able to respond. "Never put bread under the lace of the wig. It stretches the wig so it will not fit properly. And the bread crumbs get all over." It took quite a while to fix the damage.

Seventy-Four

Aside from one or two projects, I was fortunate that nearly all the films I worked on were shot in or near New York City. I got to go home to Long Island City nearly every night and spend the weekends in our country house in Shohola.

During the 1990s, I worked on *Carlito's Way* (1993), styling hair for the leading lady, Penelope Ann Miller; *The Paper* (1993), as personal stylist for Marisa Tomei; *Everyone Says I Love You* (1995), styling some of the principles; *In and Out* (1996), styling Tom Selleck and Matt Dillon; *Picture Perfect* (1996); and *Donnie Brasco* (1996), as department head, styling Johnnie Depp and Al Pacino.

It can be crazy working in the film industry. Sometimes the demands of the producers can be outlandish. When I got the call to work on the film *The Paper* as Marisa Tomei's personal hair stylist, I was happy to accept. I respect Ms. Tomei a great deal and thought it would be great to work with her. However, I told the producer that I had a commitment to work with Linda Ronstadt on her tour in Boston, but he assured me the shooting schedule would not interfere.

The next day, the unit production manager called to ask if I would mind if Ms. Tomei had another hair stylist from Los Angles design her hair for the film. I was not happy. Not only did it make the work more difficult, following in the wake of someone else's design, but it was insulting to me as a professional. My reply was swift and direct: I minded a great deal. However, if it pleased Ms. Tomei, I would agree.

That was when the complications began.

The LA stylist was flying into New York on Saturday for the test, so I had to wait around all day until they were ready. After four or five hours, I got the call to join them at their location and view the styling procedure.

The screen test was scheduled the following day. I did the exact procedure as shown me by the LA stylist on Ms. Tomei's hair. Everyone seemed pleased, and I left to join Ms. Ronstadt in Boston for her first week on tour. The first thing I was greeted with while checking into the Boston hotel was a message from the producer of *The Paper* stating I had to return to New York to reshoot Ms. Tomei's screen test with a different hairstyle. I was not surprised, as I had had my doubts about the hair design.

I called him immediately to remind him that I was beginning the tour with Ms. Ronstadt and that after the Boston show, I would be in a different city every day. But if they could have me on the first morning flight out of Boston into New York, schedule the reshoot to finish no later than 1:00 p.m., and have me on the next flight back to Boston to arrive no later than 4:00 p.m., I would do it. He agreed.

The reshoot went off without a hitch. Everyone approved of the new hairstyle for Ms. Tomei. I got on the plane and made it in time to do Ms. Ronstadt's hair for the show. It was exhausting, but luckily, it worked out.

After I finished Ms. Ronstadt's tour, I started on the film. Ms. Tomei's scenes were shot the first two weeks of production. I was hired to stay on as key hair stylist (first assistant) for the rest of the production to work with other members of the cast. Midway during the shooting, Ms. Tomei was called in for a cast photo. I was shocked when she arrived with her hair cut so short that it had no resemblance to the style she had worn for the movie. The producers were frantic.

In circumstances such as this, a custom wig would usually be required. It would cost $6,000 to $10,000 and take upward of three weeks to make. As there was no time, I came up with a solution. Using one of the hair falls in my wig collection, I colored it to match Ms. Tomei's hair.

Then I styled it to replicate the hairstyle of her character in the film. It took two days instead of weeks and cost a fraction of what a wig would have cost. Ms. Tomei loved the miracle I had achieved just by adding hairpieces. The producer barely even noticed.

Working on the film *Sweet and Lowdown* (1998), starring Sean Penn and Uma Thurman, was much more satisfying. It was a period film set in the 1930s. Working with Sean Penn for the first time was a delight and, I might add, fun, because of the freedom he allowed me to design his hair for his character, Emmet Ray.

It was the first time I'd had the pleasure of working with Uma Thurman as well. She had just given birth to her first child, Maya Ray, and was still nursing her. To avoid holding up the production schedule, she asked me if I could do her hair while she was nursing. I agreed, of course. Her character, Blanche, required a wig done in the style of the period. I prepped for the wig before she finished nursing and then simply adjusted it when I put it on. The only time I needed her full attention was the last five minutes of the process, which meant taking her eyes off her beautiful baby daughter. She pleasantly complied. So did Maya Ray. Over the years, I have had the pleasure of working with Ms. Thurman on a variety of projects, and we became friends.

Terrence and I divided our week between Long Island City and Shohola. We still had my old apartment on First Avenue as well. Always looking to shake things up, Terrence suggested that we think about consolidating, selling both homes and buying one house to live in full time. I was not keen on the idea. The thought of selling Shohola practically brought me to tears. I loved that house and our life there. But it seemed to be the right decision at this stage in our lives.

Terrence noticed in the *New York Times* an ad listing great deals on houses in Yonkers, New York. Yonkers was a suburban community just north of Manhattan, only twenty minutes away by car. I was reluctant to leave the city to live full time in the burbs, but Terrence convinced me to at least take a look. I usually gave into him, mainly because he was mostly right and I loved him. He answered the ad and made an appointment with the real estate broker.

On the first trip, the broker showed us some fixer-uppers and some big old houses not to our taste. However, driving around the area, I was pleasantly surprised. It was a quiet, quite rural area, not like a development-type suburb at all. Its close proximity to the city where I worked on so many of my films made it doubly attractive.

On our fourth trip to Yonkers, we saw a house that caught our attention. It was a majestic home built in 1892. It sat behind a tall iron fence. The first thing I noticed was four large chimneys on the roof. The entrance to the house was off to the side of a charming wraparound porch. I walked to the very end of the porch. It was then that my jaw dropped. There, before me, was the most magnificent view of the Hudson River and the New Jersey Palisades. There were three grassy terraces cascading down the hill to a built-in pool. I was already sold without even seeing the inside.

We entered the house. It was huge. There were double parlors to the left and a dining room to the right. The kitchen had three rooms—kitchen, pantry, and butler's pantry. On the second floor, there were four bedrooms and two baths. I noticed that there was a fireplace in every room—a total of nine. On the third floor, there were four more bedrooms and one bath. The basement was the footprint of the house, large enough to be Terrence's workshop. It had a large detached garage as well.

According to the broker, it had been owned and occupied for decades by a gentleman around eighty-five years old. The house needed some serious work, but it was certainly in livable condition. I loved the place and could see that Terrence was already sizing it up for what he could do with it. We told the broker we were interested and would get back to her.

He made an appointment to view the house a second time the following weekend. After a closer inspection, we made an offer. In the interim, we put the Shohola house on the market and were lucky to a get a buyer quickly. We had two months to vacate after the closing. We had to put all the furniture into storage until we took procession of our new home.

It was a sad day when we left Shohola. I said good-bye and thanked the house, the river, and the grounds for the good times and memories. Our dear cat was not happy about leaving either; he hid in the basement to the bitter end. Our neighbors, Judy and Lloyd, were sad as well, but we remained friends and kept in touch.

Toward the end of that year, our offer on the Yonkers house was accepted, and we closed on the deal. We sold the Long Island City house a few months after we moved into the Yonkers house in November. Another sad good-bye for me. It was the first house we had owned together. It had been a big step in our relationship. But the future was bright and full of promise.

Shortly after we purchased the new house, I received a letter of eviction on my First Avenue apartment. With everything going on, I had mistakenly sent my rent check with my Yonkers address, which gave them proof it was not my primary address. I had kept it all these years but rarely used it except for the occasional private client. While one never gives up a rent-controlled apartment in New York City without a fight, we agreed it was time to let it go. The furniture, what little there was, was moved into the garage at the Yonkers house.

As much as I loved the house, I was a little disappointed with living in Yonkers at first. While it was more rural than most suburban areas, it still didn't have the sense of nature that I loved about Shohola. Houses, lawns, and neighbors were a little too close to one another. While I was used to driving everywhere on our country weekends, during the week I still enjoyed the convenience of walking everywhere on errands in the city. Now, living in Yonkers full time, I had to get used to relying on the car for everything. Even something as mundane as going to the corner grocer to pick up milk involved getting in the car.

Strange as it might sound, the real shock for me was shopping in a mall. I had never been in one before, and it was an eye opener. All those stores packed under one roof; shopping for everything from clothes to cosmetics. I had to admit it was convenient once I embraced the idea, but it took some getting used to.

We settled into our new home rather quickly. Terrence set up his workshop first thing in the basement and was successful at getting renovation jobs throughout the city. He had at least one full-time employee working for him at all times. He concentrated on making our house comfortable, and within a couple of months, the house looked as if we had been living there for years.

Once we were settled, our goal was to return the house to its original turn-of-the-century beauty. We acquired a baby grand piano to add to the ambience. Terence was careful to restore many of its original design elements, such as its period dentil molding. His renderings of the new kitchen and terraces were in keeping with the period of the house. He was not a licensed architect, but he had the ability to draw a room/space to scale and design and build it to function with the smallest of details.

We even joined the local historical society and became active members of the community. Thanks to Terrence's knowledge of architecture and his enthusiasm at meetings regarding Yonkers' historic houses, he was asked to be on the community board. He later joined the landmarks commission in Yonkers. We had finally put down roots and were happy.

After we settled into the Yonkers home, we decided to take our first big vacation together, sort of like a long-overdue honeymoon. We no longer had a second house and an apartment to support, and we were both making good money. I thought the renovations could wait. We already had the best-looking house in the neighborhood. I planned the vacation during the month of January, a slow period in the film industry. My friend Jerry, also a colleague, stayed in the house and took care of the pets.

We flew to the romantic islands of Hawaii. It was the perfect time to escape the horrors of New York's winter. We spent three weeks in Hawaii and saw four islands: Oahu, Big Island, Maui, and Kauai. It was idyllic, and we came back refreshed and ready to tackle the work on the house.

The rest of the year was devoted to rebuilding the kitchen and outside terraces. Terrence designed and built a huge kitchen that any gourmet chef would envy. The three terraces on the property required more time and expense than expected. Steps of bluestone were built cascading down from the house to the terraces. All three levels needed replacing because the rocky cement was old and cracked. We chose bluestone, expensive but classic. Terence's design included a bar/dining area on the first level, a small sitting area on the second, and a pool house on the third level. The pool house, designed in the Greco-Roman style with four columns, was built on a four-foot platform at the head of the pool. It included a sitting area, wood burning fireplace, and changing room. The pool house, when finished, resembled a temple with a pond in front.

Aside from its lovely river views, spaciousness, and close proximity to New York City, the feature I enjoyed most about this house was that the porches were perfect for entertaining outside during the summer. The back porches and terraces overlooked the pool and faced west, treating us all to a glorious sunset at the end of each day. We took advantage of this unique location and entertained outside as often as possible.

Winter entertaining proved to be as wonderful as the summer. The house, with working fireplaces in every room, lent itself to warm and cozy dinner parties and get-togethers. The flickering from the fire and lit candles on the mantels would cast a gentle glow in each room. The library, or parlor room, was perfect for cocktails. The design of this house made it possible for one of us to play host and the other to disappear and prepare dinner without being missed.

Each morning, when I left for work, I went to the end of the porch, gazed over the terraces onto the Hudson River and the Palisades, and whispered, "What a lucky guy am I!" I had dreamed of living like this, but I had never thought it possible. I, the paper boy, owning this majestic home in this incredible location with the love of my life brought me such joy.

Seventy-Five

I remained close with my family and visited them at least once a year. Terence often came along when he wasn't involved in a construction job. My parents were well and happy, firmly involved in their Pentecostal church. My father even retired from his longtime job in the lounge at the Monteleone Hotel because his adopted religion didn't allow him to serve alcohol.

During my visits, I got to see my siblings and all their ever-growing families. By this time, I had well over forty-five nieces and nephews. I had had the honor of being godfather to my brother Glenn's firstborn, Jennifer. Over the years, she had grown up to be smart as well as beautiful. She was the first one in the family to go to college, followed by Robin, my sister Bonnie's daughter. They all went out of their way to see me on my visits home, and I was happy to see them. Most of the kids wanted to hear stories about the celebrities I worked with. They all knew I was gay, and it made no difference to them.

Sometime around 1992, my regular phone conversations with my mother were growing shorter and shorter. I became concerned because she had always been quite a talker. I used to call her and say, "Hello, Mother. How are you?" and she was off. Sixty minutes later, I would say, "Good-bye, Mother." One time I fell asleep while listening to her. I woke up forgetting she was on the line and hung up the phone. My mother called back and asked what had happened. I blamed it on the connection. But over time, she got increasingly less communicative.

I shared my concerns with my father. He said he had noticed it and had taken her to the doctor to check on her health. The doctors diagnosed her with grave depression and possibly early onset of dementia. The doctors prescribed antidepressants and they worked for a while, but she would slide back. As her condition worsened, they suggested shock treatments, which she had had many years before, when we were children. At the age of sixty-four, it was risky, but my father felt he had no recourse but to allow the treatment. I offered to fly back to help him, but he said he could manage. She received treatments for a year or so in DePaul Tulane Rehabilitation Center. My father visited her daily and finally took her back home. Unfortunately, she was not the same woman.

I went home to see her shortly after she got out of the hospital. I found my mother quietly sitting in the kitchen cutting a cardboard box into little pieces. Dad said it was part of her therapy. Mother and I had always had lively conversations about all kinds of things, especially all the show business people I met. Now she was mostly unresponsive. I appealed to her love of religion and suggested she say some prayers, just to get her talking. She looked up blankly, said "Thank you, my son," and continued cutting up the box.

My heart broke. My father was patient and caring, as always, but I could see he was sad about Mother.

The following year, Mother started falling down. It seemed as if she was losing her balance. My father, having a weak heart, could not pick her up. My older brother, Ronald, persuaded my father to put her in a nursing home, where she could get the care he was not able to provide. It was a good thing my brothers were nearby to help my father through this painful process of choosing the proper nursing home. Eventually, Mother was confined to a wheelchair. My father has always been totally devoted to my mother. I have never known a man to have as much love for a woman as he for my mother. She was in a nursing home for seven years. He was at her side, feeding her every meal, 7 days a week, 365 days a year. I never heard my father complain. As always, he was my hero.

I visited as often as I could, always putting myself on his schedule, at my mother's side. I noticed with every visit a decline in her health. Most of the time, while I was there, I brought lunch for the two of us and ate in Mother's room. My father would not leave in the evening until she had fallen asleep.

Mother's memory was nearly gone toward the end. On one visit, I walked into her room and said, "Hello, Mother," and gave her a hug and a kiss. She gave a little smile and looked at me without saying a word. I'm not sure she recognized me. I always took care of her looks, helped her dress, fixed her hair, and put on a little lipstick. I noticed her fingernails needed attention. "Mother, I am going to shorten your fingernails," I said, and I held her hand in mine and started to clip.

She screamed, "Help, police!" That ended the manicure.

My younger brother, Glenn, the dearest guy I know, went to visit Mother one day. Glenn was a hefty guy, weighing over 350 pounds at that time. When he walked into Mother's room, she seemed alarmed, scared of this large figure. She stared at him for several moments, not saying a word. Finally, my father patted her on the arm and said, "Henrietta, this is your baby!"

Mother looked at him and yelled, "Ho, my God!"

Jennifer went to visit Mother one day. She has been especially close to Mother growing up. But Mother just looked at her without saying a word. Jennifer tried telling her a story to help her remember who she was. She finished her story, and Mother looked directly at her and said, "No shit!" Jennifer was shocked. She had never heard her grandmother talk like that. Mother has always lived her life religiously, never swearing or using four-letter words.

Mother's condition took a turn for the worse, and she had to be hospitalized. I flew down to see her and offer any help I could. My brother Ronald, who lived the closest, visited often. My sister Carolyn and Glenn drove in for support. I gave my sister Bonnie an update on Mother's condition because she was unable to make it in. Dad, ever vigilant, was at her side. I felt sad seeing my dad watching his loving wife slowly disappear. She did not speak or open her eyes.

Three months after Mother was admitted, Father had a heart attack and was put into the veterans' hospital, several miles away. His concern was always about her welfare, but in his present condition, he was not able to be with her. Again, Ronald stepped up to the plate and visited Dad almost every day. I flew down, in between film work, as often as I could but could only stay two or three days at a time. Most of my day was spent visiting with my father first and then my mother.

Dad looked frail and lonely, and Mother just lay there in the hospital bed hooked up to all kinds of tubes. My sister Carolyn, just as religious as Mother, was there praying over her. The doctor said she had multiple problems, and without the feeding tube and other medicines, she would die. I prepared myself and my siblings for the inevitable.

Seventy-Six

After visiting my parents in late March of 2000, I flew back to New York. As soon I as walked in the door at home, I received a phone call from my brother Glenn that my mother had passed. While we all had expected it to come at some point, it came as such a shock. Death was so final. Glenn said we could hold off on Mother's burial until I was able to fly back and suggested that we not tell Dad of Mother's passing until my return. Terrence held me as we wept together.

After rearranging a few work schedules, I booked a flight back to New Orleans. Terrence offered to accompany me, but I thought it best that I do this alone with my family.

Mother's appearance had always been very important to her. She was conscious of maintaining a certain style, especially among her church friends, and I knew she would want to look her best at the funeral. Mother had lost most of her hair during her illness. After she went into the nursing facility, the family decided, without my knowledge, to give her clothes away, so she didn't even have a dress to be buried in. Before I left for the trip, I went shopping for an appropriate dress and a wig and styled it in the fashion she had worn. The finishing touch would be a simple silk scarf around her neck. I went directly from the airport to the funeral home and gave the dress and wig, with instructions, to the funeral director. I told him that I wanted to see my mother before she was presented at the church service. Ronald and Glenn took care of the funeral arrangements. Glenn and I picked out a suitable casket, with Ronald's approval.

My sister Bonnie and her daughter Robin arrived from Charleston. Ronald, Glenn, and his daughter Jennifer told Dad of Mother's passing the day before I arrived. He took it quite hard. His only comfort was that she had passed before him, because he had worried about who would have taken care of her without him. His condition had worsened, and the doctors did not allow my father to attend the funeral. It broke his heart.

The morning of the funeral, I returned to the funeral home to see my mother. My nephew Bubba came along for support. I had no idea how I was going to react. I'd always had a problem at funerals, as viewing the dead deeply disturbed me. I was taken to a back room, where my mother's lifeless body lay in the coffin.

I could not contain myself after seeing my mother and yelled at the mortician, "This will never do! The wig is on sideways, and the scarf is tied like Dale Evans, the cowgirl on the TV show!"

My nephew and the mortician were shocked at my reaction. I was surprised myself. It was as if I were on set, giving directions about the look of an actor. Looking back now on my reaction, it was my way of overcoming my grief at that moment. I do not know where the strength came for me to do what I did next. I could only assume that it came from the love I had for Mother and the need for her to look her best.

I asked for help to lift her head so I could put the wig on correctly. When her head rested back on the pillow, it pushed the wig forward onto her forehead, directly above her eyebrows. Mother had no hair to pin the wig to, so I asked for some glue. At first it did not work because her head was so cold. Finally, I got it to stay on. I retied the scarf. I looked at my mother and said, "Now she is ready!"

The funeral services were held in her church by Brother Cupid, their pastor. Our family, relatives, friends, and church members filled the small church. The service was very moving. Glenn and I got up and delivered eulogies. The church congregation gave a lovely reception in their recreation hall. Everyone in the congregation offered their condolences and asked after my father.

Mother was buried the next day. It was a Friday. Afterward, the family gathered around Dad in the hospital and told him how peaceful Mother had looked. My father did not cry but lowered his head and said a prayer. I knew he was feeling pain but trying not to show it. After a short time, I suggested we leave and give Dad some time for himself and return tomorrow.

I was the first to arrive the following morning. Dad was sitting up in bed, his breakfast tray untouched. He looked frail and weak.

"Hello, son," he said sadly.

I gave him a hug and tried to console him, but the tears came rolling down my cheeks.

"What am I going to do without your mother?"

"I miss her too, Dad. We all do." I tried to keep my voice from cracking.

We sat in silence for a while. Then, suddenly, I said, "Dad, if you want to go, it's okay." I don't know what possessed me to say this to him. He looked so sad and lost.

Moments after, Carolyn, her husband Donald, and Bonnie came into the room. I was grateful for the time I had had alone with my father. The next morning at two thirty, I received a call from my brother Ronald that Dad was gone. I knew he did not want to live without her. I was sorry to lose my father but was comforted by the fact that they were together again. The doctors said his heart had given out, but I knew it was because it was broken. I called Terrence with the sad news. He offered to join me, but I said I would need him more when I returned.

Ronald, Glenn, and I made arrangements for the funeral. It was hard to believe that just days ago we had buried Mother, and now we were making arrangements for Dad. The services were held in their church, just as before. Everyone was shocked with the passing of my father so close to Mother's. Somehow, I was not. He had always loved and taken care of her. With her gone, there was nothing left for him. This time, all four children, with the exception of Ronald, rose up to speak about our father. He was the gentlest, most loving man any of us would ever know.

He had never uttered one unkind word to anyone and cared for his family without complaint. There wasn't a dry eye in the house.

As close as they had been in life, we had hoped to bury them together in death. However, there was only enough room in the grave for one casket. Under Louisiana law, we would have to wait one full year and a day before opening up the plot to bury my father, as he had died days after my mother's burial. Fortunately, Ronald's wife had an open family plot, and she graciously offered it to us for my dad. We buried him there, and after the legally designated time, we exhumed his remains and reburied him with his beloved wife. The inscription on their shared monument reads:

MILTON AND HENRIETTA, TOGETHER FOREVER

I will miss them so but will always remember their love and understanding.

I returned home after the funerals to find a surprise addition in our garden. Terrence had built a small pond of bluestone with a fountain above it. On top of the fountain stood a statue of a young girl holding a vase, with water cascading down into the pond. The trickle of water cascading down the stones sounded so peaceful. He called it Milton and Henrietta's Garden. Terrence's gesture of thoughtfulness left me speechless. My eyes filled with tears as I gazed upon this beautiful oasis, this silent, tranquil place in memory of my parents. I put my arms around him and said, "Thank you for this incredible gift. I love you."

Terence said that our dear friends Ginny, Nancy, Billy, Paul, Werner, and Stephen, all of whom had met my parents, had chipped in to pay for this lovely tribute.

Seventy-Seven

Terrence and I were at the top of separate careers; however, it was very difficult to coordinate our schedules. He was able to postpone a job or delay it as he saw fit. I, on the other hand, was bound by the shooting schedules of the films I took on. Ever since we consolidated our residences, we had decided to travel more, but planning vacations had gotten more complicated. We'd had some short vacations together over the years, but nothing really big. Terrence had always wanted to visit Egypt and I loved the idea, so we booked a three-week tour of that ancient land. We blocked out the time well in advance.

Of course, as soon as our itinerary was secure, I received a call to do *The Mirror Has Two Faces,* a major film with an all-star cast directed by Barbra Streisand. It was quite coup to be offered a film of this caliber, but I declined the offer. My time with Terrence was more important.

Egypt, with all its treasures and secrets, was fascinating and full of wonders. Not knowing the language or the culture, we booked a private car and driver with a guide. We took a river tour on a luxury boat down the Nile, past the majestic Valley of Kings and its royal temples. During our stay, we visited Abu Simbel, Aswan, Luxor, Alexandria, and, of course, Cairo. We even rode camels near the great pyramids. While in Cairo, we were drawn to the Gaza market to see and sample the most amazing array of spices Egypt produced. We found Egypt's food rather exotic but tasty.

The one thing the travel guidebooks never mentioned was that when traveling in a conservative Islamic country, one had to adhere to their rules. We experienced this firsthand at the Egyptian hotels. They insisted on single beds for two males staying in one room, due to their religious prejudice against homosexuality. At each hotel we checked into, we had the same battle, fighting for the double bed that I had requested and confirmed when planning the trip. Sometimes we won, and other times we slept apart.

As exciting as Egypt was, it was good to be home and resume the wonderful life we were having in our house overlooking the Hudson River. For our twentieth anniversary that year, we went to Tiffany's and bought matching rings in white gold. We reveled in our good fortune to remain in love for two decades and looked forward to growing old together.

Seventy-Eight

At this point in my career, I thought I had encountered and mastered all the challenges of styling hair on a film set. But I was sadly mistaken.

In 2004, I accepted work on *The Notebook,* starring Ryan Gosling and Rachel McAdams. It was a period film set in the late 1930s and shot on location in Charleston, South Carolina. This required me to be away from home for three and a half months. But on the plus side, I got to visit with my sister Bonnie, who lived in Charleston. The film had its challenges, as most projects do, but this particular project had one I had never encountered before. The director, Nick Cassavetes, asked me to play a bit part in the film. I was in a meeting with Nick before shooting began when he casually offered me a role as an employee of Lon Hammond, Rachel McAdams's finance, played by James Marsden.

I had never been interested in acting and did not feel at all comfortable in front of the camera, so I politely declined. However, he insisted, saying I was perfect for the part. I tried, using every excuse, to get out of being on camera, but to no avail. I had no acting experience and could not understand why Nick was so adamant that I play the part. I found out later that Nick often put a friend or crew member in a film as a favor. That was not the kind of favor I was looking for. But to keep the peace, I grudgingly agreed.

On the day scheduled to shoot my scene, I got the principals ready. Jerry, my fellow hair stylist on the film, styled my hair, and Linda, the department head, did my makeup. I barely had enough time to get into costume and was still tying my bowtie as I ran up the steps to the set. The entire company was waiting. I do not ever remember being as nervous as I was at that moment.

The action of my character was to write random stock market numbers on a large blackboard with chalk while standing on a ladder in an office. As far as I knew, I had no lines and was grateful that my back would be to the camera most of the time.

The cameras started to roll. In the scene, the boss character, Lon, is talking to two gentlemen in his office while I'm on the ladder writing numbers. I could hear them talking but was not really paying attention. All of a sudden, I heard Lon shouting in my direction, "Am I or am I not half an ass?"

I froze like a deer caught in the headlights, not knowing what to do.

"Cut!" the director said. "Milton, your line is, 'Yes, you are half an ass.'"

I turned to Nick and said, "You didn't tell me I have to talk."

There were several giggles from the crew.

"Well, you do. Let's try again. Places...action!"

On the next take, I said my line on cue, but the sound department complained that I spoke too softly. About the sixth take, they got it. The cast had fun with me about the shoot, but in a good-natured way. So did Terrence when I told him what had happened that night on the phone. I hoped it would my last acting role in a film, but it was not.

The following year, I started the film *The Hoax*, with Richard Gere, Alfred Molina, Marcia Gay Harden, Stanley Tucci, and Hope Davis. The film featured Howard Hughes, the eccentric billionaire, toward the end of his life, when he was deeply disturbed and disheveled. I had to secure a long, thin, straggly white-gray wig and beard for the character. I arrived at the production office, slipped on the wig and held up the beard, and said to the AD (assistant director), "Is this what you had in mind for the character?"

"Looks perfect," he said, and then he paused for minute as I started to take it off. "Hold on a second, Milton. Don't take it off. Follow me."

He left the room and knocked on the door of an office where the director, Lasse Hallström, was rehearsing with Richard Gere and Alfred Molina. When the door opened, he introduced me as "Howard Hughes." Mr. Hallström, upon seeing me, went wide eyed. I thought he was just pleased I had gotten the look right.

"We've found our Howard Hughes," he said.

"Excuse me?"

The AD explained that that they were having trouble casting the Hughes character and that I'd be perfect.

Here we go again, I thought. "Absolutely not," I said without any hesitation. "I'm flattered, but my place is behind the camera. I'm sure there are any number of actors who would suit the part. It's mostly makeup, anyway."

Seeing my reluctance, they said they'd continue looking. I left the office thinking that was the end of it.

A week later, I was called into the wardrobe department. Thinking that it has something to do with coordinating the look of one of the characters with the hairstyle required, I entered the room. One of the assistants immediately started to measure me for the costume to be worn by Howard Hughes. I said there must be some mistake and went to the producer. He said that they had been unable to find an actor for the part because it involved only one scene being shot the following week in Puerto Rico. They were on a tight schedule and had run out of time. Personally, I don't think they even tried looking for an actor after seeing me in the wig and beard. Lesson learned: use a wig block next time. I explained that I had declined the part and was not interested in the role. But the producer was desperate, and I finally agreed.

The day arrived, and I showed up to rehearse the scene in a hotel room built on a set. As I had not been given a script for the scene, I assumed I had no lines. The director set up the action in the scene, with Richard Gere and Alfred Molina entering the room and me sitting in bed in a lotus position behind sheer drapes. I told the director I had bad knees and could not fold my legs like that. Mr. Gere, a yoga enthusiast, climbed into the bed and put pillows under my legs to help me get into the position. It made all the difference. But as I knew I would be sitting in this position through multiple takes, I went to the prop department and asked them to build me a backrest. They teased me about being a prima donna, but it was all in good fun. They had it ready for the shoot in an hour.

My friend Lyn, Mr. Gere's hair stylist, did my wig, and Kelly, the makeup department head, did my beard. Kelly also glued long fake fingernails with jagged edges on both my hands. I have to admit, they did a great job. When I was completely dressed and brought to the set, I really looked like what the disheveled Hughes must have looked like as an old man. I assumed my position in bed. Richard Gere, noticing the pillows were not placed under my legs properly, climbed onto the bed and adjusted them himself. I had my backrest in place, out of the line of the camera. Props handed me a bag of prunes. I had no idea why.

My heart was beating faster than I had ever thought it could. I tried not to think that I was acting, or trying to, in a scene with two major stars. The camera assistant clicked the clapperboard and yelled, "Take one!"

"Action!" the director shouted.

I could feel the camera focusing on me first and then on Richard and Alfred entering the room. There was some dialogue between the two of them. The director, while the camera was rolling, said, "Offer him"—Alfred Molina—"a prune."

That's why I have a bag of prunes, I thought. I started digging in the bag, trying to grab a prune. I fumbled around because of my long nails. I only succeeded in making loud noises from the paper bag. "My nails are too long to grab a prune!" I said.

"Cut!" the director said, and then the whole set burst out into laughter.

"Don't worry. You're doing fine. Props!" the director said.

Props added more prunes to the bag, making it possible for me to grab one more easily.

The assistant director said, "Your line is, 'Would you like a prune?' Then you offer Alfred a prune through the bed curtain."

I got a little more confident with every take. Richard and Alfred were very patient with me. We continued shooting take after take for about two hours. Once the director was happy with the main star's performances, the camera was turned on me and my prune. The director set up an extreme close-up shot of me extending my hand outside the sheer bed curtains, holding the prune and saying my line. That one shot seemed to take hours until he was happy. I was totally exhausted, and I never wanted to see a prune again.

The whole crew got a chuckle out of my playing the role. They called me Mr. Howard Hughes throughout the rest of the filming. They were not the only ones kidding me about my performance as Howard Hughes. I heard Richard say out loud to Alfred, "I will never work with children, animals, or Milton again because he is a scene stealer!" I was quite flattered, but I hoped I'd never be asked to be on camera again.

Seventy-Nine

After I finished *The Hoax*, Terrence and I went on a vacation to Greece and Turkey. I loved traveling with Terrence because he was adventurous and had no fear of driving in a strange land. I admired his thirst for the unknown and trusted his choices.

It was his first time visiting Greece and my second, but seeing it through Terrence's eyes made it fresh and new. But for most of our trip, we traveled in Turkey. We rented a car in Ankara, the capital, and drove ourselves from city to city, stopping at places of interest, such as the fairy chimneys in Cappadocia and Ephesus on the Turkish Riviera.. We ended up in Istanbul. It was very exciting and romantic despite the occasional problem with our sleeping arrangements at the hotels.

After we returned, I started work on another film, *Hide and Seek*, directed by John Polson, with Robert De Niro, Dakota Fanning, Amy Irving, and Elisabeth Shue. I did not have the pleasure of working with Mr. De Niro, as he had his own hair and makeup people. Dakota Fanning was the first child actress I had worked with, and she was a delight. I had a wig designed for her character. It was the first time she'd worn one, but after a little adjustment, she wore it like a pro.

Later that year, Terence and I were exhausted from a particularly hectic schedule, and we decided to take a short, relaxing vacation. I had heard about the wonderful time friends had had in Merida, a small, charming old colonial city not far from the Gulf of Mexico in the Yucatan Peninsula of Mexico. Neither of us had ever been to Mexico and thought it would nice to get out of the cold weather. First, we flew to Cancun for a couple of days. Then we rented a car and drove to Merida, stopping at some of the Mayan ruins and a few quaint little towns along the way.

We arrived in Merida in the late afternoon, just before the sun started to set. The light shining on the old colonial homes was breathtaking. There were several hotels available, but we lucked out and found a lovely, charming guest house owned by a gay couple in the historic district.

We spent a few days exploring the city's rich history and local customs. Life seemed so relaxed there. We also discovered the cost of living was far cheaper than in the United States. Over the next few days, Terrence fell in love with the place and started talking about settling there. I loved the place also but wasn't so sure about our moving there. It was in the middle nowhere. How could I get back and forth to work on films? The nearest airport was hours away. Could Terrence find enough contracting work to keep him busy? There were dozens of things to consider. But I knew that once Terrence got enthusiastic about a project, there'd be no stopping him.

After we returned home, Merida was the topic of our conversation for weeks. We discussed all sorts of possible scenarios, from buying a second home there to perhaps even retiring there. Of course, that kind of talk made me nervous. I was not ready to retire. My career and roots were in New York, and I loved our Yonkers home. Terrence had no such concerns and felt he could find work as a contractor anywhere we lived. He was excited about taking on yet another new challenge.

As the year progressed, our discussions on moving to Merida became more frequent. My biggest concern was the impact it would have on my lucrative and satisfying career. If we moved there full time, I would have to give up my American address. Would that prevent me from getting projects? Terrence, always the problem solver, suggested the possibility of renting an apartment just to have an address in the States. There was so much to think about.

That spring, after I finished work on *Anamorph*, a psychological thriller starring Willem Dafoe, we flew back to Merida. We stayed in the same guest house as before. Paul, a local resident whom we had met on our first trip there, invited us to a party. Paul was the gay yenta of Merida and knew everyone's business. He introduced us to some of his friends there. Most of them were retired gay expatriates from the United States and Canada. I was convinced after speaking with them that Merida would be the perfect place for us to retire when we were ready.

The guest house we stayed in had a tradition of serving complimentary cocktails on the roof every evening. It was a time to meet other guests or just celebrate the end of the day. We invited our friend Paul to join us the evening after his party. We talked about the possibility of retiring in Merida. Paul said that Tony, a friend of his, was selling his house directly across the street. He pointed it out. We had admired that house every day as we left the guest house. Paul said the owner was out of town, but he could get a key and show us the house tomorrow if we wanted. It was early in our plan to settle in Merida, but both Terrence and I were eager to see it.

The next day, Paul brought us into the house. It had a small foyer with beautiful tiles that led to a lovely courtyard with tall palm trees and lovely pots of flowering plants. Two of the four bedrooms were off the courtyard. The master bedroom and bath were a separate unit overlooking the courtyard. There was a small pool and running fountain at the far end. The kitchen, dining, and entertaining area also opened onto the courtyard. It was spacious, quaint, and comfortable. Terrence and I fell in love with it. We met the caretaker, who was living on the premises, as the owner was away frequently.

After the tour, we said that we would be interested in meeting the owner. Paul was delighted and said he'd arrange for us to meet him as soon as he returned at the end of the week.

Tony was an American from North Carolina who purchased houses in the area, renovated them, and then sold them at a hefty profit to rich foreigners. Terrence and Tony hit it off right away over cocktails. They talked shop and eventually got around to discussing the house we were interested in. By the end of the evening, we had negotiated a price we thought was fair for the house and the furnishings and shook hands on it. There was a bit of red tape involved in buying property in Mexico, but Tony was experienced in the procedure, and it all was taken care of within a couple of months. We made another trip to Merida for the closing.

Merida became our vacation destination whenever I got time off between projects. We decided to hire the live-in caretaker to run the house in our absence. The house was comfortable, but Terrence found little things to improve upon. We spent time together buying our own pieces of art and furnishings, and before long, it felt like home. We met the who's who in town and joined the social activities of the city when we were there.

Many of our friends from New York came to visit and fell in love with the place. In fact, our friends Michel and Ross, who were originally from Spain, came for a visit and bought property on the outskirts of the town. Every visit brought me closer to the idea of early retirement and moving to Merida.

Sometimes I had to cut my visits short because of work in New York, and Terrence got to stay on. He kept himself busy redesigning and arranging the house, giving it his golden touch. I envied his freedom to stay and do what he loved.

As far as my retirement was concerned, I only had two and a half years before being able to consider retirement officially. But leaving my career at the top of my game was a huge decision for me. I wasn't quite ready yet. Over the years, I had received attention for my work. I was nominated for an Emmy for hairstyling on the *Kate and Allie* TV series. I received a Daytime Emmy nomination for my work on the educational show *The Magic School Bus* with Lily Tomlin. My first actual award was for an outstanding achievement in hair and makeup from the Westchester Film Festival in 2004. But despite my love of my career, I knew my life with Terrence was all I really cared about, and I started making long-term plans to ease out of the business.

Never content with a house for long, Terrence started planning a big renovation to our Merida home: extending the tile roof over the second-floor balconies and downstairs bedrooms. I agreed that it would make the house more comfortable, especially in the heat of the summer and during the rainy season. In the fall of 2006, he took some time off to begin the work. I was sorry to see him go to Merida without me but told him I'd join him after my current project was done.

I had started an independent film in New York called *Bernard and Doris*, a biographical picture about the life of Doris Duke starring Ralph Fiennes and Susan Sarandon, for which I received an Emmy nomination. The fee for my work on the production was the lowest I had received in a long time, but I accepted the pay cut for the chance to work with Ralph Fiennes as his personal stylist. Over the years, I came to the realization that in the film industry, big paychecks sometimes came with big headaches. Mr. Fiennes was extremely professional on set and very playful and humorous in the makeup room. He was a pleasure to work with. We worked so well together that I was given the opportunity to work with him again on Broadway for his role in *Faith Healer* not long afterward.

Terrence and I chatted almost daily while he was in Merida. He told me that he was making good progress on the roof. He also had made good contacts for some additional work projects in town. I really missed him, but I had the animals to keep me company, all three of them in bed with me. Of course, it wasn't the same as having his body next to mine with his arm around me. After a couple of weeks' work on the house, he returned to Yonkers, and our life continued as before.

Eighty

The Christmas holiday was approaching. I had just completed three weeks work on *Bernard and Doris.* I would have several more weeks of shooting after the Christmas break. Terrence informed me that he had invited six of our friends, a couple and their two children and two other guys, to spend the holiday with us in our house in Merida. They were good friends and I liked them, but not enough to have them visit over the entire holiday.

I told Terrence that I only had twelve days off from the film and I wanted to have some time just for us. I was rather pissed that he had done such a thing without discussing it with me. I was very fond of them, especially the two children, but I wondered why he had invited them for the entire time I was going to be there.

"Don't worry," he said. "Everything will work out." That was easy for him to say because when we had guests, I did most of the hosting. I knew from past experience that we would spend most of the time entertaining and less time together. Besides, he planned to stay on to work on the house and relax after the holiday, while I had to return to New York.

On December 23, we flew to Merida, taking our dog Coco with us for the first time. I was worried about her flying, but she fared quite well. As soon we entered the house, Terrence got a message inviting us that very evening to the social event of the year in the most prestigious house in Merida. Laurence, the host, was rather grand and flamboyant. I remembered meeting him when we first arrived in Merida, but I had never thought we would be invited to his famous Christmas party.

"How did we get on that list?" I asked.

"Laurence's architect. He and I are discussing some projects."

Like Tony, Laurence was a developer. He had a talent for buying a house in ruins, turning it into a palace, and selling it for a huge profit. He worked closely with his architect. I didn't give it a second thought, as I knew Terrence networked so well for his business.

The party was in full swing when we arrived. I was a bit tired after traveling all day, but I would not miss this party for anything. Terrence drifted off in search of the host. I was left to amuse myself by talking with people I did not know. Not something I enjoy doing. Forty-five minutes later, Terrence showed up with Laurence, the host, and his architect, Luis, a native of Merida in his early to midforties. He apologized for leaving me all alone for such a long time. He said he had been busy checking out the renovations that Laurence's architect had done since he had left and lost track of time. Terrence could be a little inconsiderate at times, and I decided to just let it drop.

As our guests weren't coming until the day after the holiday, Terrence and I celebrated Christmas alone, for which I was grateful. It was the first time we would be having six guests at the same time at the Merida house, and I was a bit worried about whether they would all get along. But Terrence was confident, since they all knew one another, that it would go smoothly.

Our guests arrived on time and settled into the house nicely. Terrence was the tour guide and planned the daily activities. We enjoyed showing them Merida and introducing them to the local cuisine. We even toured the Mayan ruins in Uxmal, on the outskirts of the city. Seeing the sights through the eyes of the couple's well-mannered children was refreshing. There were times the guys did a little exploring on their own and caught up with us in the evening. We usually ended our day on our roof with refreshments.

By January 2, everyone had gone. I was relieved to have the house to ourselves. While I enjoyed their company, I did not find entertaining relaxing. I was looking forward to spending that evening with Terrence before leaving the next day to get back to the film set. We had a quiet dinner and a stroll around the market area. When we returned home, I stopped at the front door, turned to Terrence, and said, "Do you hear that?"

"I don't hear anything."

"That's the point. It's quiet. No other voices."

"Yes," he said without any further comment. He didn't seem to share my relish in our being alone for the first time all week.

We started locking down the house and getting ready for bed. Terrence said he was going to take Coco for a walk and would be back soon. An hour later, Terrence was still out with Coco. I found that odd, but it was a lovely evening and guessed he just was enjoying the weather. A second hour passed, and still no sign of him. I got out of bed and looked out over the balcony, hoping to see him. I was beginning to worry something had happened.

Fifteen minutes later, I heard him come in. "Where the hell have you been?" I said, relieved but a bit angry. "I was worried that you were hit by a car, lying in the street, bleeding to death!"

He replied in his usual matter-of-fact manner, "I decided to stop at the café and have a glass of wine."

"With Coco?" He didn't answer. He was acting a bit strange. "In the town square café? I would have come with you if I had known."

"It was just a whim." His tone was a bit distant.

"Is anything wrong?"

"No. Just tired, I guess."

I was hoping for some lovemaking, but sadly, it did not happen. I tried falling asleep but couldn't. Something had happened that evening. I was sure of it.

I woke up the following morning concerned about Terrence's behavior last night. We chatted over breakfast as if nothing were wrong. I was hoping for an explanation, but he did not offer one. I knew him well enough to know not to press the subject. He helped me pack and drove me to the airport. On the ride to the airport, I told him I regretted having this job to finish in New York; otherwise, I could have stayed and helped with the work on the roof. He just said it was not a problem and told me he would be back in New York in three weeks. We embraced. He wished me a safe journey home and told me to call when I got in.

My flight home was long and lonelier than usual. I tried reading, but I could not concentrate. All I could think of was Terrence and his strange behavior the night before. I started to question myself. Had I said or done something to hurt him? Terrence was the kind of person who spoke his mind but not his feelings. I had no recourse but to wait this one out and hope he would talk about it when he got back.

Eighty-One

I resumed work on *Bernard and Doris* the following day. After working a grueling fourteen hours, my loneliness was replaced with fatigue. This project was particularly time consuming, despite the fact that it was shot locally. At least I could go home every night. But the house felt so lonely without Terrence.

Four weeks had passed, and Terrence was still in Merida working on our house. While we spoke frequently, he never gave me a concrete answer about when he was coming home. He said the work was taking longer than expected and asked me to send some extra money to buy the materials he needed. It was not the news I wanted to hear, because I missed him.

Knowing what a perfectionist Terrence was about his work, I was resigned to the delay but disappointed. Terrence said he would try to wrap it up in a couple of weeks after he received the money and return home. I told him I would send the money with Evelyn, a friend who was traveling to Merida and staying in our house for a week as our guest. I was grateful to her for this favor because it was chancy mailing money to Mexico.

My work on the film wrapped. Two weeks had come and gone, and he was still in Merida declaring the work was not completed. Evelyn returned with a glowing report on her visit. She could not stop raving about our house and how wonderful Terrence was. It had been six weeks since I had seen him. I was beginning to wonder what was going on. I never had any doubt about our relationship, but his behavior since that night with Coco seemed more than strange.

In the meantime, I was offered another film, *We Own the Night,* starring Joaquin Phoenix, Robert Duvall, and Mark Wahlberg. Principal shooting was scheduled to begin the first week of March in New York.

Terrence delayed his return again, telling me that some materials had arrived late and it would take two more weeks to finish. "Can't you just leave it as is and pick up on it the next time we are there?" I said. He said he was too close to finishing and wanted it done. I asked him if there was anything he wanted to talk about. His response was puzzling. He said, "No...not at this time." I was worried. Something serious was going on with him, but he wasn't ready to talk about it.

After eight weeks in Merida, Terrence finally returned home in March with our dog Coco. I was thrilled to see him—and, of course, Coco. He seemed happy to be home with me. But after twenty-five years together, I could sense something was still unresolved between us. I wanted to sit down right then and there and have a talk, but I decided to wait until he settled in.

A few days later, I decided to open up the discussion over dinner in one of our favorite restaurants. Our conversation during dinner was quite pleasant; he gave me no indication that anything was wrong. Toward the end, my curiosity got the better of me, and I asked if there was anything we needed to discuss about Merida. He said there was something on his mind, but he would rather wait until we got home. I respected his wish. I had no idea what he was going to say, but it sounded serious. We hardly spoke in the car on the way home.

We sat in the parlor facing each other, having a glass of wine. I broke the ice and said, "So what's going on?"

He looked at me, his eyes red and watery as if he was starting to cry, and said, "I met the love of my life. But I will always love you."

Those words were like a knife going into my heart. I had thought after all these years that *I* was the love of his life. I was not prepared to hear that. I had expected that he might confess that that he'd had an affair and was just guilty about it. I was in total shock and disbelief. After a few moments of silence, I asked if he wanted his freedom. As the words left my mouth, I regretted it. It was the last thing I wanted. I guess I was hoping he would say no.

He said he would.

We both started crying and couldn't stop for quite a while.

After another glass of wine, he told me it had happened last October when he was in Merida working on our house. He was surfing the web and met someone who wanted to get together for a little fun. It seemed harmless, and he was lonely. They spent a couple of days chatting over the Internet. They finally met.

"Met?" I asked. "Was he living in Merida?"

"Yes. He's an architect. We have a lot in common." Tears rolled down his cheeks "I did not mean for this to happen, and I am sorry to cause you so much pain."

"Is he the architect I met at Laurence's Christmas party?"

"Yes."

My mind was racing. It was the architect who had arranged for us to be invited to Laurence's Christmas party. That explained the two-hour walk with the dog the night before I left. Terrence had been with him that night. It also explained the many delays on his return home. He had been fucking this architect the entire time.

"Does anyone else know?" I asked, getting more upset by the minute.

"I told our friends at the house during the Christmas visit."

I felt like a fool, being the last to know. "When were you going to tell me? After I left my career and moved to Mexico with you?"

I tried to remain calm and rational, but my world as I knew it was falling apart. Terrence was the love of my life, my core, the person I had thought I would spend the rest of my life with. I knew our relationship had matured over the years, but I had hoped our love was only getting stronger for it. I thought we had the lifelong love my parents had shared. Despite all the challenges, they had remained devoted to each other until the end.

Maybe a lack of communication was our downfall. Terrence was as taciturn about his emotions as I was vocal. Maybe it was because I was away so much on film shoots. Maybe it was just we had been together for too long. Maybe he was in his midlife crisis and the young architect made him feel more youthful. A thousand thoughts went through my head as I tried to find an answer.

Terence stood up without another word and went to bed. I just sat there. I felt weak and in great need of support from my friends. I made several calls, desperate to speak to someone, to no avail. After all, it was the middle of the night. Terrence was asleep when I got into bed. I did not think of going into another bedroom. I guess I was in denial, hoping this was just a nightmare. Everything seemed surreal. I hoped I would wake up next to him and everything would be fine.

I didn't see Terrence the following morning, as I had an early call on the set of the new film. My tears were like a steady rain rolling down my cheeks as I drove to the studio. I was lucky I didn't have an accident. I walked into the makeup trailer, my eyes red from crying.

"Milton, what's wrong?" said Kelly, my friend who was doing makeup on the film.

Between sobs, I told her the whole sad story. She tried to console me by saying that I was lucky to have had the kind of love I had had with Terrence for so long. Most people only dreamed about having such a relationship. That was what made the pain so great, she said. To lose a love like that was devastating. Terrence was a jerk to throw it all away. Realizing the fragile state I was in, she put on a CD with one of our favorite songs, "I Will Survive," with the volume turned up all the way. When things got tough on the set, we always took strength from Gloria Gaynor's inspiring words. The mere sound helped me work through my pain and become the professional I had to be. With her support, I made it through the first week of the film.

Eighty-Two

Life at home became tense. Terrence and I barely spoke. One morning, as I got of bed, he made some rude remarks about my aging ass as I walked to the bathroom. I pretended I did not hear it, but it hurt. After all, he was no spring chicken himself after all these years. I knew Terrence could be bitchy, but he'd never directed it at me. After that, he decided to move out of our bedroom and into another on the other side of the house.

My film schedule was brutal, but I was grateful for the long hours and the responsibilities on the film as the diversion I needed to deal with the crisis in my private life. I saw very little of Terrence for the first few weeks after his confession. It was difficult for me, knowing he still lived in the house we'd built together. The bed I had shared with him for twenty-five years seemed so lonely. I could keep my mind busy during the day, but the nights were difficult. There were nights I'd lie in bed waiting to fall asleep, only to be kept awake with memories. The love of my life was only a few steps away, but it felt like miles.

We knew that it was too painful to share the Yonkers house under the present circumstances, so we agreed to put it up for sale.

Terrence and I continued living together until we sold the house. It took a year. We shared the household expenses, as we had for twenty-five years. Life seemed to continue as it had for so long, except we were living together as roommates, not lovers. He would call me on set to ask if I would be home for dinner. When I said yes, he would fix enough for the two of us. It was strange that we could sit together, share a meal, and chat about our day. Every now and then we argued, but we made it work, for the most part.

During this time, Terrence started throwing out all his clothes and buying new ones, as if he wanted to discard his past and start a new life. He was so anxious to rid himself of the past that he grabbed my tuxedo, thinking it was his, and threw it in the garbage. It was painful at times, but I was determined not to fight with him. It would make the already-difficult situation unbearable.

We led separate lives. He made several long trips to Merida, leaving me to run the Yonkers house. While his trips made me feel bitter, knowing he was spending time with his new "lover," his absence actually helped me deal with our breakup. My dear friends made sure I was not alone. My family, who had adored Terrence, were shocked when I told them the news and immediately cut off all communication with him. If they called the house and he answered, they just asked for me. Michele, our mutual friend, even left her home in Canada and stayed with me in Yonkers while he was gone and took care of the pets while I worked fourteen to sixteen hours a day on the film. She has become a very dear friend, someone who helped me through my darkest hours.

After the film wrapped, I started the dreaded task of looking for a new place to live. I looked at a two-bedroom apartment with a small balcony in Yonkers facing the Hudson River. As I stood on the balcony, I thought this would be a perfect place to sit, weather permitting, and enjoy the view. Then reality hit. I would be all alone, with no one to share it with, living in the burbs, isolated from my friends. The mere thought scared the hell out of me. I knew then and there that I had to move back to Manhattan. I needed the pulse of the big city and my friends around me.

My search for an apartment in Manhattan was long and tedious. Doing it alone for the first time in twenty-five years made it worse. Adjusting to my new single life of solo decision-making was not easy because over the years I had relied on Terrence so much. I realized that I had lost my own identity and self-confidence. I used to be so decisive, independent, but I had released the responsibility for so much of my life to Terrence that I had to rediscover those qualities in myself.

Our house had been on the market for eight months without an acceptable offer. Our hopes of selling it for what it was worth were looking rather bleak. Finally, a young couple arrived and fell in love with it. I knew immediately that they were the right people because they appreciated its beauty. Their offer was reasonable, and we accepted it. It was a bittersweet time for me because I realized that my life with Terrence was officially ending with the sale of that house, but I was comforted by the fact that this young couple would begin their life together there.

I had narrowed my apartment search two places in a building on the Upper West Side: a one-bedroom and a two-bedroom. Terrence was good at assessing space and design, so I decided to ask his opinion. He knew me and what I liked better than anyone. He recommended I consider two bedrooms for space and resale value, and he was right. He even offered to help renovate the apartment. I'm not sure whether he offered because he still cared for me or just felt guilty. Frankly, I felt it was a bit of both. I still admired his talent despite what had happened between us and was pleased that he would help me bring my living space together.

I made an arrangement with Terrence to hire his local crew to demolish and do all the heavy work in my new apartment. He acted as contractor and designer. He designed and built the entire kitchen and recommended the best appliances. The entire project took a couple of months.

Two months before the closing on the house, we started the monumental task of discarding furniture and collectables we had accumulated for over two decades. It's amazing how much one can accumulate in a twenty-five-year span. We arranged a tag sale and then a yard sale. What we did not sell was given away or put into a Dumpster. Seeing parts of our life together and all the happy memories they represented being sold or thrown away was heartbreaking.

I had to downsize big time because of the limited space in my new apartment. I packed my favorites and said good-bye to the rest. One of my biggest regrets was the loss of two boxes of photos of Terrence and me over the years. Vacations, holidays, our various new homes. So many wonderful moments captured on film, thrown out by mistake.

My new building didn't allow dogs. Terence felt that Mexico would be too hot for Coco to live in full time, so he didn't want to take her down there. Luckily, Michele had fallen in love with Coco during her time pet sitting in the Yonkers home, and she agreed to take her back to Canada with her when the house was sold. The cats could come with me.

We both attended the closing on the Yonkers home and shared the profits equally. As for the house in Merida, he agreed to buy my share, as I had no desire to see Merida or that house again. I did not attend the closing and sent my lawyer instead. We settled all other financial matters, the final links that legally bound us together. He seemed relieved that it was over and he was free. I was relieved to be free of the tension of the year-long disengagement but worried how I would face the future alone. My life with him had been so full. I had no tears left when we parted, just a broken heart and resentment for being left alone.

Eighty-Three

The first night in my apartment was about one of the loneliest nights I have ever had. Thank goodness for my two Abyssinian beauties, Pharaoh and Caesar. They had been in my life for many years and gave me unconditional love. I think they fared better than I did in our new home. They searched every nook and cranny when they arrived and were settled in by the next day. They needed me to care for them, and I was grateful that they were there to fill the void in my life.

My film work helped keep me sane. I had begun work on the film *Accidental Husband*, with Jeffery Dean Morgan, Colin Firth, Uma Thurman, and a host of other stars. The long workdays helped me get through the first few months in the new place. Werner, Stephen, Donna, my decorator friend, Evelyn, and other friends made sure to get me out of the house on weekends for dinner and shows. I developed a close relationship with my next-door neighbor Veronica. She became the kind of friend I could share my feelings with at a moment's notice. Michele and I spoke daily. She even came to New York and spent a week helping me paint one of my rooms. She introduced me to the world of computers and the Internet with saint-like patience.

I called Linda Ronstadt once I was settled in the new apartment and told her the news. She was in complete disbelief that we were split after so many years. She told me that she only knew two couples who were happy together. One was a straight couple, and the other was Terrence and I. I appreciated her friendship and support.

Eventually, my apartment became my sanctuary, a place of comfort and safety. I rarely went out socially on my own. The thought of meeting someone else never entered my mind. Love songs sent tears running down my cheeks. I would get all choked up watching a romantic scene in a movie or theater. I knew that in time, I would get used to my single life, but I wondered how long it would take to get over Terrence. I'd never find another man like him.

Terence and I had lived an almost idyllic life together. We had several homes. Loads of friends. Traveled extensively. He was a successful contractor. I had a busy and rather glamorous career as a professional hair stylist in the film industry. We had our ups and downs, as do most couples, but we always worked through them and came out stronger in our love.

A dark cloud hung over me for more than two years. I thought my romantic life was over and that I would never find someone to love again. Everyone noticed my depression. Social events did not interest me. Sex was out of the question. I started to accept my so-called new single life as all that was left for me.

Eighty-Four

I needed something to shake up my life and put it back on track. I had been in mourning too long. I simply could not see any way out of my funk. Then Frank, a friend and colleague of mine, told me about this gay cruise that he and his boyfriend had booked. It departed from Rome in mid-July and sailed around the Mediterranean for ten days. I'd never been on a luxury cruise, let alone a completely gay one. I couldn't see the allure. At sixty-six years old, single, with my peacock days behind me, how could I consider going on a cruise alone with twenty-eight hundred gay men in their prime?

"It's crazy," I said to Frank.

He looked at me with a skeptical expression. "Maybe you need something a little crazy right now."

Not being an impulsive person, it took me six weeks of gathering information about the cruise before making a decision. Atlantis, the cruise company, had been running gay cruises for years. From the testimonials, everyone seemed to have such a wonderful time that they went multiple times. Finally, after hearing me talk about it ad nauseam, my dear friend Evelyn stood over me while I made the reservation. There was no turning back now. I had to trust in my friends and my own instincts that I was doing the right thing. After all, I wouldn't be entirely alone. Frank and his lover would be on the cruise with me. I called them to say I'd join them, and they were thrilled at the news.

After I booked the trip, I started receiving the cruise itinerary, ports of arrival, suggestions for clothing, which was casual, and the onboard entertainment, including one of my favorites, Chita Rivera. Apparently, there would be themed costume parties during the cruise as well. That sounded like fun. Immediately, I thought what costume to wear, knowing very well that that crowd would probably be very critical. The first costume party theme was Mardi Gras, which was easy for me, but shopping for the right materials in New York was not. I managed to find a huge bag of doubloons, which are plastic souvenir coins the size of a silver dollar and thrown from the parade floats to the waving crowds during Mardi Gras. They came in three colors: gold, green, and purple, traditional colors of Mardi Gras.

I had an idea, and my friend Werner came to help me execute it. We took a flesh-colored T-shirt, one that fit me like skin, and covered it with doubloons, using rows of purple, green, and gold. When it was finished, it looked like a colorful shield of armor. I took a black knitted hat and covered it with Mardi Gras beads. Then I put a ton of beads around my neck and down my arms, put on a flesh-colored pink mask that covered my nose and eyes, and finished with dark leather pants. I looked at this costume, thought, "It's a winner!" and packed it.

The other themes were 1970s, Ancient Rome, and an All-White party. I started working on the other costumes. It certainly was fun to prepare. It reminded me of my days in the Quarter, playing for the drag balls and parties. I hoped I would have the guts to wear them on the cruise.

Eighty-Five

The departure date arrived, and off to Rome I flew with two full suitcases filled with all my pretty things. I was anxious but excited. It was my first time traveling alone in years. It would have been easier if I were traveling with Frank and his boyfriend, but they had left earlier and spent a couple of days in Rome before the cruise. The ship departed from Civitavecchia, the cruise ship port outside of Rome. I arrived at the ship only to find out that boarding was at least four to five hours away. The terminal was massive. Passengers for different ships were milling around, waiting to board. In about an hour, the men destined for my cruise started to arrive by the hundreds, and within an hour, all 2,800 passengers filled the area designated for our ship.

As I looked around, my fears escalated. As far as I could see, there were groups of good-looking younger men from all over the world looking quite buff, some in tank tops others in chick cruise wear, laughing and talking as if they had known one another forever. Most of them seemed half my age. I did not think I had a chance blending in. Even the couples seemed to know one another. But it was too late to turn around. I had to face my fear and not let myself down. In the midst of this sea of men, I was relieved to see Frank and his boyfriend, John. I embraced them warmly.

We started to board the ship. I found my cabin and got to meet my cabin mate for the first time. Ever thrifty, I had decided to share a cabin to save money. Given my emotional state, I didn't know how I would feel about sharing a cabin with a strange man, but we got along beautifully.

Andrew was about thirty-five and had rather boyish good looks. He was a composer of popular music. I think it helped that both of us were in the arts. We chatted as we unpacked. Andrew was finished first and was out of the room before me to join the party. I got the feeling that Andrew, although very friendly, preferred to hang around people his own age.

I made it to the main deck and started looking around the ship. Suddenly, I heard an announcement over the intercom from the captain. "We set sail at five p.m." I had heard that one must be on the top deck as this great vessel sailed out of the harbor, and I did not want to miss it. Everyone was on the top deck with a cocktail in hand, watching this huge vessel glide out to sea. Frank and John found me and put a drink in my hand, and we all waved as the ship slowly left port. They asked me if I would join them for dinner. I replied with a quick yes.

Dinner was delicious, and it was comforting to share it with friends. But the best part of the night was about to begin—the Mardi Gras costume party at eleven o'clock. I had had several glasses of wine at dinner to build up enough courage to put on that costume and take it out in the public. I went back to the room to get dressed. I called Frank to come over, see what I was wearing, take pictures, and push me out of the cabin. He was not going to the party but said my costume was fabulous.

My fears of going to the party alone mounted. The affair was on the top deck, on a large open-air dance floor with extremely loud disco music and strobe lights. The outskirts of the dance floor was so crowded that I could hardly make my way through. It reminded me of the Ice Palace on the island, which seemed like eons ago. The costumes were outrageous. Some men, mostly nude, were painted bright colors, and others were covered in feathers. Some guy walked around with a cape that lit up when he spread his arms out. Not in keeping with the actual Mardi Gras costumes, but fun nevertheless.

I stepped onto the dance floor. When the strobes hit my costumes, I looked like a disco ball, reflecting light off the dozens of coins on my shirt and strands of beads. As I passed through the crowd, I could hear the clicking of cameras. I was stopped several times for photos. I was a hit! The mask, which covered most of my face, gave me the courage to go out alone among a crowd of unknowns. I danced and enjoyed myself immensely. I returned to the cabin totally elated and ready for a well-deserved rest. I did not see Andrew the whole evening.

Every night, a program was sent to your cabin posting the next day's activities. There was something for everyone. Since I was traveling solo, I decided to join the singles' group, designed for passengers to meet other singles traveling alone. The plan was to gather at the martini bar to mingle and then go to dinner in the main dining room. It was a nice crowd of a hundred or more. We all sat in a special section of the dining room, eight to ten at a table. The host of the evening gave a number (one to ten) to each person at the table.

This started the evening off beautifully. I met new people from different parts of the country and the world. After the first course, a bell rang, and the host would ask the even numbers to change to an adjoining table, taking their napkins and wine glasses with them. Introductions would start again. And so it continued through the third course. At first, I thought this round-robin table-hopping would be awkward, but it turned out to be loads of fun.

I usually dread revealing that I work with celebrities to strangers. People tend to ask me for gossip about their favorite stars. During the introductions at the first-course table, I met a guy named Dean, who designed makeup and hair for celebrities, movies, and television, just as I did. That started an instant conversation between the two of us and made the rest of my night so much more enjoyable. As it turned out, we knew many of the same people. Dean and I have remained friends and get together often.

Another thing I hate about revealing my career is that people tend to ask for advice about their own appearance. On the second round, after I introduced myself and mentioned my career, one older man asked me for advice about his "look." I noticed his hair was dyed black, much too dark for his advanced age, and cut in a hairstyle of a twenty-year-old. At first, I demurred, trying to be polite. But he continued to ask for more specifics. I suggested that he might try a lighter hair color, more suited to his complexion, and a more conservative cut. He wasn't pleased with my suggestions but wouldn't let up. Finally, I just said, "A scarf would help." I think he got the hint. I did not see him the rest of the cruise.

Eighty-Six

The next day I checked out the pool area. That was where I felt most out of place. It was filled with stunning younger men strutting around their perfect bodies, looking fabulous in the most revealing bathing suits. I positioned my lounge chair far in the rear, a safe place to view the scenery without being viewed. All the hunks gathered together around the pool and hot tub, watching and no doubt commenting on everyone coming in and out. Later, I found another pool more suited for men of my age and demeanor.

I saw little of Frank and John after that first night. I suspected that John, who was younger than Frank, preferred being with younger people and that Frank tagged along. There were times, after seeing couples holding hands or playing in the pool together, when I felt a sharp pang over the loss of my longtime lover, but I snapped out of it, realizing where I was and what I was there to achieve.

I managed enough courage to dress and attend the 1970s party that evening. The music and the lighting were purely from the disco scene of the '70s. I had on the bellbottoms and shirt I had worn way back then. (Yes, they still fit.) There were some guys in a group wearing pale-blue satin bellbottom pants lined with rhinestones and huge blond afro wigs. It was a wild, colorful scene. I enjoyed seeing the parade of costumes, but I felt a little out of place. After all, unlike most of the men there, I had actually lived through that scene. The party was fun but a pale homage to the passion of that time.

Our first port of call was Naples. I was on a tour bus, sitting alone, when a friendly guy sat next to me. He introduced himself as one of the staff of the organization that chartered the cruise ship. We talked for a bit about the trip. Before I was aware, I opened up to him about my breakup of twenty-five years and how difficult it was for me to take this cruise alone. He was very understanding and gave me some comforting words. He also suggested I read *The Power of Now*, by Eckhart Tolle, which had helped him after his recent breakup after five years. He invited me to join him for dinner at the table he was hosting that night. Through him, I met several people who have remained friends. Slowly, I was coming out of my shell. It felt good.

I took advantage of all the activities offered, and the days passed quickly. There was only one thing missing—someone special to share it with.

Eighty-Seven

On the last evening of the cruise, there was a celebration party. After dinner, I found myself alone, standing on the deck, cocktail in hand, as we sailed west toward Rome at sundown. The air was warm with a gentle breeze as I watched the people dancing under the sky. Suddenly, I had a strange sensation. Something urged me to leave the party and walk toward the bow of the ship. I shrugged it off at first, thinking I had had too much to drink. But the feeling got stronger, and I decided to follow it. Wending my way through the enthusiastic crowd, I found a set of steps. I climbed the steps to the outside deck, guided by this mysterious force. Then I continued on higher and higher, finally arriving at the top deck of the ship's bow.

The structure of the bow was massive. It tapered to a point high above the water. It was empty except for a couple sitting toward the back. I passed them and walked to the very tip of the bow, stood alone, and looked down. It seemed as though I were floating above the sparkling water. Silence was all around me except for the wind and the rushing of waves as the ship moved forward. Over the horizon was an intense yellow, gold, and red sky, and just below it, a gray-blue sky. The beauty of it all was overwhelming.

I took this as a gift. I was alive to enjoy nature in all its glory and sheer wonderment. All at once I started to cry uncontrollably. Feeling embarrassed, I turned around to see if anyone was watching. No one was. I was completely alone. I turned back again, my tears trickling down my cheeks as I continued to glaze at the sunset. Suddenly, a gust of wind blew the tears off my cheeks. I felt as if it took my pain along with them. For the first time in years, I felt free, grateful to be myself and alive to the possibilities that the future might bring.

At that moment chills ran though my body. It was as if nature were filling me with a strength I thought I had lost. My eyes were dry, tears no more. I looked ahead and noticed the color in the sky was gone and night had fallen. As I turned around to walk away, a smile appeared on my face and a deep peace in my soul. Both have remained until this day. It was an unforgettable and transformative moment. A personal epiphany.

I have come to realize that it had been my destiny to be on that cruise. The entire experience helped me discover that there is still so much of life for me to enjoy. It took me out of my comfort zone. I met people from all over the world and learned to allow myself to have fun again. When I returned home, my friends and family thought I had connected with someone new. I had. Myself.

Just as I had many decades ago in New Orleans as a young boy searching for my identity, I listened to my heart, followed my instincts, and found my way.

Afterword

Several years have passed since I took that gay cruise and had a life-changing experience. I have reclaimed my identity and found comfort in my own company. I have found the strength to forgive Terrence for abandoning me and the beautiful life we had together. We have become friends, and I can speak with him without feeling pain, regret, or anger.

Since my first cruise ended on such a positive note, I have gone on five more gay cruises alone over the ensuing years. I was not looking for romance, nor did I find it. I just enjoyed the freedom to be myself and to visit parts of the world I had not seen. My travels brought me to places such as Tahiti, Asia, and the Baltic states.

I retired from full-time film work, but I do take on projects from time to time, usually early- to mid-twentieth-century period pieces. I continue to cut some of my private clients as well. Life has settled into a satisfying routine, and I am grateful for it.

For years, I was content with my single life. Then something extraordinary happened—in New Orleans, no less. It happened on the last night of one of my periodic visits to my family. I was standing at a gay bar in the Quarter when a young, attractive guy came alongside me and ordered two beers and a pen. He did not say a word to me. He wrote something on a napkin, slid one of the beers and the napkin in front of me, and then walked away to join his friends playing pool.

A bit surprised, I looked at the napkin. It had a phone number on it. I asked the bartender if he knew who that man was.

"His name is Stuart."

I smiled. Nice move, I thought, and drank the beer. Shortly after, Stuart passed again, and I leaned out and said, "Thank you."

He did not respond. Ten minutes later, he walked toward me, leaned in, and said, "You're welcome."

His charm matched his attractiveness. Stuart was six foot one, conservatively dressed for a gay bar, had light-brown hair, and spoke with a British accent. We engaged in conversation. All the while, I was thinking that this guy had to be half my age. He must prefer older men, or he was a classy hustler. Things got a bit more intimate, and he invited me to his place. I smiled and thanked him but said I had an early flight back to New York the next day and was just about to get going. I was frightened. I hadn't been with anyone for so long.

He smiled and said not to worry. It would be fun. I looked into his handsome face. Wasn't this what I had been missing in the years after Terrence? The only thing holding me back was fear. Why not? I said to myself, and I agreed.

Back at his place, he brought up feelings stored so deep inside me, I had thought I would never feel them again. Desire. Passion. Abandon. He was so attentive, so giving, he helped me rediscover my sexual self dormant for so long. That encounter lasted until the wee hours of the morning. I barely made my flight back to New York.

My encounter with Stuart made me realize that sexual attraction was not exclusive to the young, despite what our society said. My relationship with Stuart was living proof. We continue to see each other from time to time. He has since moved back to London, yet we maintain our long-distance relationship and look forward to our time together.

Acknowledgments

There are several friends I would like to thank for encouraging me to write my memoir. Without their guidance and trust, I could never have gotten it done. Before embarking on this book, I had never written anything longer than a letter. I had never dreamed that writing a book would be in my future.

My dear friend Ginny Altobello, who is an excellent writer, spent countless hours through the years reviewing page after page of my story. I do not know what I would have done without her.

Michael Shiffer, a friend whose opinion and knowledge I value, has been listening to me tell my stories for years. He suggested I write them down in book form. His encouragement gave me the strength and belief in myself to continue writing.

Michele Guindon, my confidant and dear friend who called every day from Canada after my breakup and gave me the support and love I so needed. She is also responsible for introducing me to world of computers. Before this project, I had never used one. Without her endless patience—and I do mean endless—I would still be writing my story longhand. I am truly indebted to her.

Linda Ronstadt, who heard most of my stories while I was working with her on tour, read chapter after chapter as I wrote them, and gave me helpful hints and the desire to continue.

My sisters, Carolyn and Bonnie, and brother Glenn for providing me with stories of our family I had forgotten. I love you all very much.

Paul Dinas, my editor, for taking on a first-time writer with stories and happenings going in every direction and arranging them in their proper order. Also, for giving me encouragement and direction on how to explain and expand on each character in my story. The knowledge I have gotten because of him has enriched my life.

Finally, I would like to thank all my devoted friends who were kind enough to read the earlier drafts and to give me feedback and support.

Made in the USA
Lexington, KY
21 January 2017